The Third World in Global Development

Ankie M. M. Hoogvelt

MACMILLAN

First published 1982
Reprinted 1983, 1984, 1985, 1987, 1989

Published by
MACMILLAN EDUCATION LTD
Houndmills, Basingstoke, Hampshire RG21 2XS
and London
Companies and representatives
throughout the world

Printed in Hong Kong

ISBN 0-333-27681-7 (hardcover)
ISBN 0-333-27682-5 (paperback)

(Part One)

Contents

Foreword and Acknowledgements   vii

List of Abbreviations   ix

List of Tables and Figures   xi

Introduction and Summary   1

PART ONE: FACTS

1   **The Changing World Economy**   15
    The Economic Differentiation of the Third World   15
    The Petro-dollar Lubrication of the World Economy   45
    The Internationalisation of Production   56

2   **Political Responses: The Rise and Fall of**
    Third World Solidarity   73
    The History of Third World Solidarity   74
    The New International Economic Order:
        Confrontation   80
    The New International Economic Order:
        Conciliation   87
    Equity in the South: from Global Keynesianism to
        Global Social Democracy — the Basic Needs
        Strategy   95

PART TWO: THEORIES

3   **Social Evolution and Development: The**
    Bourgeois Liberal Tradition   105
    Nineteenth-century Evolutionary Theories   106
    Twentieth-century Neo-evolutionary Theories   109
    The Modern Stage of Social Evolution   113
    Modernisation Theories   116

4   **From Modernisation to Global Growth: New
     Directions in the Bourgeois Liberal Tradition**   120
     World Futures Theories: Methodology   123
     World Futures Theories: Themes and Issues   128
     The Global Growth Debate   129
     International Keynesianism   137

5   **Theories of Social Evolution and Development:
     The Marxist Tradition**   149
     The Concept of Mode of Production and Historical
       Materialism   152
     The Capitalist Mode of Production   158
     Theories of Imperialism, Dependency and
       Underdevelopment   162

6   **From Dependency to Global Political Economy:
     New Directions in the Marxist Tradition**   171
     Re-examining the Concept of 'Exploitation': the
       Articulation of Modes of Production   174
     The 'Productionist' Argument: Dependency-
       associated Development, Historical Specificity
       and Class Reductionism   184
     The 'Circulationist' Argument: Deepening of the
       World System Perspective and Economic
       Reductionism   189
     The Global Political Economy of Samir Amin   198

Conclusions   208

Notes and References   215

Name Index   247

Subject Index   252

Foreword and Acknowledgements

Like any other textbook this one is, characteristically, a book about other books. At the present time, when financial resources are pulled out of higher education and stuffed into nuclear warheads, those few of us who (still) work in academic institutions are privileged to have access to the world of ideas. But even this privilege is a blessing increasingly mixed with frustration.

Gone are the days when new acquisitions were as common to a university library as newspapers to a breakfast table. With pin-money for a book grant our reading material has become strictly rationed: some eight books per course per year if we are lucky. New journals are no longer purchased, existing subscriptions are terminated. So how do we keep up with new developments in our respective academic fields? How did I, for example, manage to write a book about books? Somewhat unconventionally I should like to acknowledge two sources of help without which this book would never have been written. One is the documentation department of the Institute of Social Studies in The Hague, Netherlands. Although I ended my employment for that (richly financed) institute some twelve years ago, the department has continued to send me their valuable catalogues and abstracts, regularly and free of charge. The other source of assistance has come from the staff of the inter-library loan section of the library of my own university, at Sheffield. I especially wish to thank Ms Julia Dagg, who has always promptly and cheerfully processed my numerous requests for books, relentlessly chasing after works which I had often badly referenced and which sometimes did not even exist!

The thick crop of statistical evidence in Chapter 1 of the book is not the fruit of my labour only, though naturally I alone take responsibility for any errors. I thank Roger Richards of the university's computing department and Peter Jones, my one-time and temporary research assistant, for the good cheer with which they have processed a lot more material than I could in the end incorporate. When my own grand statistical ventures failed, it was, however, very nice to have available for reproduction the statistical tables produced by those very useful international number-crunchers: the World Bank and the OECD.

Sheffield   Ankie M. M. Hoogvelt
October 1981

The author and publishers wish to thank the following who have kindly given permission for the use of copyright material:

Bank for International Settlements for a table from the *50th Annual Report* (1980); Oxford University Press for a table from *Redistribution With Growth* by Hollis Chenery *et al.* (1974); the World Bank for tables from the *1980 Annual Report* and *Prospects for Developing Countries*.

List of Abbreviations

DAC	Development Assistance Committee (of the OECD)
DC	Developed Countries
ECLA	(UN) Economic Commission for Latin America
ECOSOC	(UN) Economic and Social Committee
ECSIM	European Centre for Study and Information on Multinational Corporations
EEC	European Economic Community
GATT	General Agreement on Tariffs and Trade
GDP	Gross Domestic Product
GNP	Gross National Product
GSP	General System of Preferences
IBRD	International Bank for Reconstruction and Development (the World Bank)
ICP	International Commodity Program
IDA	International Development Association (of the IBRD)
IFAD	International Fund for Agricultural Development
ILO	International Labour Organisation
IMF	International Monetary Fund
LDCs	Less Developed Countries

MNC	Multinational Company (Corporation) (*Note*: this abbreviation is also sometimes used to describe Most Needy Countries. The latter is a classificatory term used in UN documents to refer to those countries which are believed to be most in need of development assistance.)
MOP	Mode of Production
MSA	Most Seriously Affected (official UN classification of those countries most seriously affected by the oil price hikes)
NIC	Newly Industrialising Country
NIEO	New International Economic Order
ODA	Official Development Assistance (from OECD member countries)
OECD	Organisation for Economic Co-operation and Development
OPEC	Organisation of Petroleum Exporting Countries
SDR	Special Drawing Rights
UDC	Under-Developed Countries
UNCTAD	United Nations Conference on Trade and Development
UNDP	United Nations Development Program
UNIDO	United Nations Industrial Development Organisation

List of Tables and Figures

Tables

1.1 The countries of the world (GNP *per capita*, average annual rates of growth, and population)   18

1.2 Growth of gross national product and gross national product *per capita* 1960–80 (average annual percentage growth rates at 1977 prices)   25

1.3 Distribution of GDP (per cent)   27

1.4 Growth of production of manufacturing sector (average annual growth rates, per cent)   28

1.5 Composition of merchandise exports from developing countries (per cent)   29

1.6 Share of manufactures in exports from developing countries when excluding oil   29

1.7 Percentage share of manufactures in exports by country group   30

1.8 Average annual growth rates of imports and terms of trade of fuel and non-fuel mineral-exporting countries   32

1.9 Importance of developing countries as markets for industrial countries' exports of manufactures, 1973 and 1978 (percentage shares in total exports)   33

1.10 Cross-classification of countries by income level and equality   42

1.11 The location of absolute poverty by income groups, 1975   44

1.12 Oil-exporting countries: estimated deployment of investible surpluses, 1974–9 (billions of US dollars)   48

1.13 Global current account, 1973–6 (US billion dollars) 50
1.14 Debt outstanding and disbursed (eighty-one countries, at current prices, selected years, US billion dollars) 51
1.15 Total net resource receipts of developing countries from all sources (billions of US dollars) 52
1.16 Total external public debt outstanding (including undisbursed), 1972–8, of all developing countries (millions of US dollars) 53
1.17 Accumulated stock of direct investment in developing countries by major industrial sector (1966 and 1974) 61
1.18 Dependence on selected imported industrial raw materials (imports as a percentage of consumption) 61
1.19 LDC share in world trade for selected commodities (in percentages) 62
1.20 Stock of private overseas direct investments in developing countries, 1977 (principal hosts) 63
1.21 Share of multinational companies in the exports of manufactures from selected developing countries 64

Figures

1.1 Frequency distribution of GNP *per capita* by countries and population, 1967 37
1.2 Frequency distribution of GNP *per capita* by countries and population, 1978 38
3.1 The stages of social evolution 112
3.2 The structure of modern societies 114

Introduction and Summary

This book is a sequel to the introductory text published in 1976, *The Sociology of Developing Societies*. I decided to write a wholly new text rather than a revised edition of that book because of the qualitative changes that have taken place both in the facts and in the theories of 'development'.

The Sociology of Developing Societies, though not published until 1976, was a review of theories of development which had emerged in the 1950s and 1960s. At that time it was fashionable and indeed appropriate to *generalise* the plight of the so-called 'developing' countries of Asia, Latin America and Africa. Both the right-wing 'modernisation theories' and the left-wing 'theories of imperialism' shared one conception, namely that of the ubiquity of the development experience throughout these three continents. It was thought that whatever forces, economic, social or political, impinged on the countries in these three backward regions affected all of them more or less equally. These theories differed of course in their identification and in their interpretation of such forces, and this contrast was what I tried to capture in the previous book. But even if the sociology in the theories was different, the unitary category 'developing societies' was acceptable to both sides. For the same reasons the concept of the 'Third World' became part of a common vocabulary.

A principal economic fact of the Second United Nations Development Decade (1970–80) has been the *differentiation of the Third World*. In the late 1960s and in the early 1970s substantial variations were recorded in the development experience of different developing countries, regions and continents. Some countries showed impressive rates of economic growth, others stagnated or declined. Some developing countries, for instance in the Middle East, are now richer than the developed countries as measured by their 'income *per capita*', and some, the so-called 'newly industrialising countries', have a structure of production equally or even more industrialised than those of some countries conventionally classed as 'developed'. Other developing countries, by contrast, are still exclusively dependent on agriculture and two decades of development have left them poorer than they were before.

This diversity of the development experience is slowly inching its way into the development literature. Both liberal and Marxist analysts are now beginning to acknowledge that the world is a rather more finely graded hierarchy of nations than was at first portrayed, and even the official UN and World Bank classifications of world development data into three categories (developed market, developing market and centrally planned economies) are giving way to finer classifications: industrialised, middle income, low income, centrally planned, and capital-surplus oil economies; or developed market, developing market, least developed, centrally planned and OPEC countries. In UN documents the least developed countries are variously referred to as 'most needy countries' (MNCs) or 'most seriously affected nations' (MSANs), and the poorest of the poor countries are now commonly referred to as belonging to the Fourth World. For its part, Marxist literature is now ready to speak of super-imperialist, junior imperialist, sub-imperialist and underdeveloped states.

A second key economic fact of the past decade has been the acquisition of vast financial surpluses by a handful of Arab OPEC countries, themselves previously classed as 'developing' countries. Since the trebling of oil prices in 1973, against the backdrop of an incipient world recession, these Arab countries have been receiving incomes far in excess of the development needs of their own small populations. Their accumulated reserves, which now account for a major proportion of total world reserves, were mostly absorbed by the international capital markets, which in turn lent these 'petrodollars' at prevailing market interest rates to a number of rapidly developing countries whose economic performance or potential were seen to qualify them for such credits. In this way the oil price increases spurred on the process of economic differentiation of the Third World. While some Third World countries could benefit either directly from increased oil revenues, or indirectly from easier access to world capital markets, others who were too poor to borrow found that the increase in price they had to pay for oil plunged them into even greater poverty and economic decline.

This differentiation of the Third World and the changes in the world's financial markets together have interacted with yet a third key economic fact of the last decade, namely the changing organisation of world production. It had already become widely recognised at the beginning of the 1970s that as a consequence of the growth and the changing scope of activities of multinational corporations, *international production* had surpassed international trade as a vehicle for international economic exchanges. That is to say, the combined production of all multinational corporations abroad (e.g. outside their countries of origin) is now greater than the total value of goods and services that enter the trade between countries (outside the so-called Socialist bloc). World production has become more important than world trade. This process of internationalisation of production has not only continued throughout the decade; it has also blended in with the other two key economic phenomena. First, the internationalisation of production has tended to run parallel with the process of economic differentiation of the Third World. For the rapidly developing countries of the Third World are precisely those which have become more closely involved with the process of world production organised by the multinational corporations. While *they* have become important links in the widening chain of international production, the poorer countries of the Third World are characteristically excluded from this widening chain. Second, the petro-dollar-fuelled expansion of the international capital markets has contributed to an increased involvement by international finance capital with multinational-controlled (if not owned) productive enterprises inside the Third World. Today there is a return to colonial practices, when so-called 'portfolio' investments were the advanced countries' preferred method of investment in their colonial countries, as opposed to direct investments by individual enterprises. The mediating link between lending and production now — as indeed it was then — is the (colonial) state. Paradoxically the very demands for national economic liberation which had led to practices of expropriation of foreign-owned enterprises inside Third World countries resulted *not* in a greater national control over such enterprises, which continue to be managed and directed by multinational corporations, but in a need on the part of the nationalising state to find alternative sources of international capital funding for their nationalised enterprises. In order to offset the loss of foreign equity, governments had to borrow from foreign banks. In this way foreign loans replaced foreign equity, and risk capital became loan capital.

The new tripartite collaboration between international finance capital, multinational corporations and the state in Third World countries articulates international relations of production which are wholly consistent with the escalating costs and risks, political as well as financial and technological, characteristic of present-day raw-material explorations and industrial ventures. It also permits a degree of exploitation of labour and resources reminiscent of the colonial days when the state could be fully relied upon to intervene directly on behalf of capital, in the suppression of wages, in the granting of lands, and in the safeguarding of monopolistic trading rights in defiance of competitive market arrangements.

Chapter 1 discusses the major changes in the Third World's participation in the world economy. The object of the chapter is to give the bare-bone *facts* of the economic background to which recent departures in *theories* of development (which will be discussed in later chapters) can be referred. Economic events, however, are not only recorded and reflected in academic theories. In between economic base and theoretical superstructure stand concrete political ideologies, alignments and party programmes. The new facts of world economic development, and the oil crisis of the early 1970s in particular, have prompted the creation of *new political alignments, novel political institutions, and fresh political ideologies.*

Political developments, it must be said, do not always follow economic realities step by step. There is always a time lag between what is happening at the economic base and what is happening at the political level, namely the formation of appropriate organisation and action. Some of the political responses in the earlier part of the decade were in many respects belated responses to world economic arrangements prevailing in the 1950s and 1960s. The achievement of Third World *solidarity*, as we shall argue in Chapter 2, is a case in point. For the Third World countries, OPEC's successful cartelisation became at once a manifestation of the idea of self-assertion, an encouraging example of what Third World solidarity might achieve, and (paradoxically) an immediate motive behind a broad political unity which would place the wealthy Arabs firmly in the Third World camp. Only by continuously recreating the myth of Third World solidarity could the poor Third World countries hope to obtain relief from the financial burdens inflicted upon them by their richer brothers. And so it has happened that, in contrast to the diverging facts of their respective economic positions, the Third World countries have, in the earlier part of the decade, managed to forge a greater political unity and solidarity than ever before. Increasingly, through the various institutional venues, in the Group of 77 (now consisting of 120 nations), or in the Group of Non-aligned Nations, or as caucus groups within various sub-organisations of the United Nations, as indeed in the General Assembly of the United Nations itself, Third World Leaders have succeeded in presenting a united front. In 1974 this political unity culminated in the formulation of a coherent set of 'Third World demands' for a New International Economic Order. The demands for NIEO, as it became known, were accepted by a Resolution of the UN Special Assembly in May 1974 and confirmed in the *Charter of Economic Rights and Duties of States* (1974), itself a paradox of facts and fancy, as it prescribes the economic sovereignty of nation-states in a world where the economic power of states is actually declining. The NIEO demands, which we shall discuss in detail in Chapter 2, all involve deliberate *intervention* in world economic exchange: NIEO seeks to replace the 'invisible hand' which has ruled world markets since the rise of capitalism with a set of international agreements stabilising export earnings of Third World countries, guaranteeing the transfer of capital resources to them, reorganising the international division of labour and legislating the economic behaviour of multinational enterprises.

The newly found political unity amongst Third World leaders, which — it should be noted — addressed itself primarily to the developed capitalist world, inevitably also forged a certain diplomatic alliance amongst the capitalist advanced nations (Japan included) in their relations with the Third World. The establishment of the Conference on International Economic Co-operation and Development in 1976, where nineteen representatives of the Third World sat facing eight representatives of the developed capitalist world, marked a novel institutional arrangement in international affairs. The *North–South dialogue* became an important institutional feature of the Second Development Decade, and one moreover which seemed much in contrast to the reality of increasing economic differentiation.

After 1975 the economic and political forces that had wrought the solidarity of the Third World gradually began to erode. The emerging facts of economic divergence between Third World countries made it difficult to translate the general NIEO demands into specific policies, and to maintain unity at other than the level of rhetoric. For their part, the advanced countries smartly seized upon these real economic differences by encouraging a process of 'embourgeoisement' of the most advanced Third World countries. They propagated a new perspective of 'global management' of an 'interdependent' world. This perspective, while essentially leaving the old world economic order intact, would forge and legitimate closer links between international big business and global institutions on the one hand, and the repressive states of the fast-growing developing countries on the other. In this perspective the twin problems of global inequality and poverty are being redefined as problems issuing *not* primarily from international economic relations, but from domestic social injustice and lack of internal reform.

Despite its uneasy diplomatic alliance in confronting the South, the North itself displays ideological differences between those who hold an orthodox marginalist position and those who adopt a Keynesian view of international economic relations. The marginalists continue to believe in the efficiency of world markets in allocating resources and they are suspicious of what they refer to as 'unwieldy' bureaucratic machineries necessary to fix and regulate supply, demand and prices in international economic exchange. They tend to take a strictly nationalist view of economic growth and this leads them to a protectionist stance *vis-à-vis* international trade. The Keynesians, on the other hand, take a more global view of economic growth which leads them to a more interventionist and redistributive position, seemingly closer to that of the Third World itself. Although the USA, West Germany and Japan have consistently declared positions closer to the marginalist view, while the EEC (minus West Germany) has tended to opt for interventionist approaches, I yet believe these ideological preferences to have less to do with the contrasting attitudes of these nations than with differences between concerns for national capitalist interests on the one hand and global capitalist interests on the other, or — what amounts to the same thing — concerns *for* short-term economic interests versus concerns *with* long-term economic interests. The latter are formulated particularly by the essential international institutions of world capitalism, namely the World Bank, the IMF, the OECD secretariat and various affiliated agencies of the United Nations such as the International Labour Organisation (ILO) and the UN Economic and Social Committee (ECOSOC), as well as many semi-affiliated academic institutions of the North. Unlike the national governments of the North who can rarely afford to look beyond the next election, these international organisations and institutions are dedicated to long-term global capitalist development. Because of their concern with the 'world economic system' these think-tanks of Northern capitalism are appreciative of the need for balanced economic development of *all* regions of the world, and consequently they advocate structural changes in international economic relations superficially much along the lines demanded by the Third World. There is even energetic cross-fertilisation of ideas between these two groups as some of their expert personnel overlap. The World Bank and the UN organisations employ many experts from the Third World, and several of these, *ex officio* and as Third World citizens, have been very instrumental in generating the ideas contained in NIEO, just as they have, as staff members of the various international institutions, been influential in shaping the international organisations' philosophies. Last, but not least, we should remember that the *Charter of Economic Rights and Duties of States*, and the accompanying programme for a New International Economic Order, were accepted by the General Assembly of the United Nations (where, to be sure, Third World countries now have a majority membership) and that this, if nothing else, means that the vast intellectual machinery of the United Nations and its affiliated organisations has thrown its weight behind these Third World demands.

Beneath the surface alignment of contemporary Third World ideology and 'globalist' capitalist ideology, however, there gapes one deep gulf that separates the two. Whereas the Third World demands for a New International Economic Order arise out of a determined quest for national economic independence, the globalist concept of a world economic system aims at supra-nationalism. While Third World countries see nation-building, national identity and national economic liberation as necessary prerequisites for their economic development, the globalists speak of a world community and a world consciousness overriding narrow nationalism. Admittedly, fanciful ideas about a world community comprising world citizens have been with us for a long time, but until recently they were just that: fanciful ideas. What is new about the Second Development Decade is that they have started to blend successfully, if somewhat indiscreetly, with international assistance of Third World development programmes. Since the turn of this decade, the Northern think-tanks have evolved a new and, according to their own testimony, radical development approach which is widely referred to as the *basic needs approach*.

As a development strategy the basic needs approach indeed involves a fundamental reorientation: a shift away from concerns with over-all national economic growth of Third World countries, to concerns with the standards of living of the poorest 40 per cent of the people in these countries. The basic needs approach, which we shall discuss at length in Chapter 2, attempts to define minimum, internationally accepted, requirements for the satisfaction of human, physical and social needs; it urges internal redistribution of income to the poorest sections of the population as a top priority in development strategy, and last, but not least, it proposes to make measures of international redistribution of wealth (i.e. foreign assistance) conditional upon implementation of redistributive policies within Third World countries. It is this latter aspect of the basic needs approach which strikes at the heart of the economic sovereignty of Third World nations, international recognition of the right to which they, ironically, have only just obtained with the *Charter of Economic Rights and Duties of States*. It marks a first step towards an international social policy designed to complement the global management of an increasingly internationalised system of world production.

Having surveyed the economic and political *facts* of the Second UN Development Decade in Chapters 1 and 2, we shall examine the new departures in *theories* of development which have graced the past decade. While political ideologies are primarily normative, theories of development are *interpretative*. That is to say, they 'objectively' aim to locate and explain contemporary events on some very abstract and general path of human social evolution. Political ideologies, by contrast, simply assert what should be the next step on this path.

As before, and in contrast to more common classifications, conservative, reformist and radical, I believe that to date there are still only two opposing theoretical frameworks, two competing paradigms that are utilised to make economic realities intelligible. These are the *liberal theories of growth* and the *Marxist theories of imperialism*. Both types of theories have their antecedents in very general theories of evolution which were first formulated in the nineteenth century. These antecedents are fundamentally important, for the new directions in the theories since 1970 do not only take their cues from economic and political events today, but they interpret these events in a mould that was cast over one hundred years ago. Therefore, in each case we shall have to go back to their roots (Chapters 3 and 5). Examining these roots will also make it clear just how fundamental the difference between the two perspectives is, and how relevant the difference continues to be as a principle for classifying all contemporary contributions to the development dialogue.

Both the theories of growth and the theories of imperialism have in recent years been remodelled to accommodate the latest transformations of the world economy, the shifting patterns of wealth and poverty of nations and the increasing interdependence of world economic activity. Indeed, theories of growth and theories of imperialism today seem to share a common academic concern with the nature and the boundaries of what both like to refer to as a 'world system' and with the developmental chances of the Third World within this system. Depending on their characterisation of the nature of this system (as one of increasing functional interdependence or as one of sharpening exploitation) the theories write different scenarios for 'co-operation' or 'confrontation'. To the growth theorists the boundaries of the world system are environmental and physical (e.g. depletion of mineral resources, population explosion, environmental pollution) and therefore urgently demand political recognition of the 'one-world' concept by all nations, global administration of resources, increased international co-operation and the shedding of narrow nationalisms. Conditional upon certain necessary reforms of the world system, particularly world-wide redistribution of capital resources, international redivision of labour and expansion of world trade, the growth theorists see a chance for most (though not all) Third World countries to develop within the system. To the imperialist theorists, on the other hand, the boundaries of the system are political and man-made: they arise out of the nature of its dominant mode of production, namely capitalism. Capitalism has, and always will, generate richness and poverty, development and underdevelopment as joint aspects of the same process. The global capitalist system is seen as a hierarchy of concentric circles of centre and periphery spheres of production with lines of authority and subordination connecting the capital-accumulating centres with the exploited periphery. As in any dynamic system, the integrated elements (e.g. nations, or classes or people) may shift positions in the hierarchy over time. But the dynamic of the system adds up to a zero-sum game: the gains of some nations cause the losses of others, the benefits of some classes represent the costs to others. And although some relative shifting in positions does occur within the hierarchy, its over-all directional tendencies remain loaded in favour of the already advanced countries because of their historical advantage and their consolidation of this advantage in political and military terms. Therefore, the imperialist school sees the best chances for development of the Third World either in a radical transformation of the capitalist world system, or in a relative alienation from the system, in collective self-reliance and in national liberation. These are the contrasting perspectives of the theories of growth and the theories of imperialism. Variations within each of these contrasting perspectives will be discussed in Chapters 4 and 6 respectively.

This book has been written as a guiding text for students of the Third World. It makes no claim to offer an original thesis, nor does it expressly and consistently favour one point of view as against another. Of course, from the selection of facts as well as in the presentation of the theories, the writer's preference for a Marxist perspective of world development will be made clear. However, no attempt is made to develop any one particular angle of vision within the Marxist tradition. The aim of the book is primarily to assist students in their intellectual voyage through an ever-expanding field of world development studies.

PART ONE
FACTS

1

The Changing World Economy

The Economic Differentiation of the Third World

All told there are now 182 countries in the world, and membership of the United Nations stands at 150, but only 125 countries which have a minimum of 1 million population are regularly included in 'official' (that is, World Bank, OECD and UN sponsored) world development statistics. And when it comes to statistical comparisons involving more detailed social and economic data, the number of countries included is usually smaller still, between sixty and eighty.

Despite its many weaknesses, GNP (Gross National Product) *per capita* remains the most important single measure of a country's ranking in the hierarchy of economies, just as the equally dubious 'average annual growth rate' remains the most important single indicator of a country's economic performance through time.[1] However, over the years, painstaking academic research, scholarly methodological debates and even bitter ideological controversies have helped to produce, perhaps not a deeper understanding of what development is, but certainly a more complex range of indices of comparative socio-economic performance and more ingenious techniques for measuring them. And if we pause to reflect on the role of the international institutions as not unimportant definers of the world situation we might even be optimistic that their increasingly refined list of development indicators will sometimes be matched by governments eager to produce the facts to be measured (for real and not on paper) lest they be singled out as 'poor performers'.

In the course of the first two UN Development Decades the concept and measurement of economic development has been broadened to include the level of industrialisation, food production, value of manufactures in exports, size and distribution of the labour force and, more recently, patterns of income distribution. Each time the addition of a new variable has reflected novel trends in economic development theory, and new problems occurring in the cycle and development of world capitalism. However, this is a subject for Chapter 2. Here we shall first examine how the various *countries* of the Third World have fared in terms of conventional measures of economic performance, and next we shall see how that performance has affected the well-being of their *peoples*.

The data used in this chapter are drawn from various World Bank documents, the UN report *Economic and Social Progress in the Second Development Decade*, and various ILO, OECD and GATT reports. These international organisations continue to distinguish sharply between market economies and centrally planned economies, a practice which I have followed here. I have departed, however, from this standard practice in one quite important respect. I have included China amongst the 'market economies'. There are several reasons for this. First, there is China's recent reorientation in economic organisation, its emphasis on modernisation and rapid economic growth in preference to the socialisation of production relations, its progressive widening of market relations, and most significantly its re-linking via trade and capital relations with the developed market economies. Second, it has always seemed to me misleading when talking about international distribution of income and comparative levels of poverty to exclude the single largest country of the poor world where nearly one billion people live. Finally, and most importantly, China has recently joined various international organisations such as the World Bank, as well as various sub-organisations of the United Nations, and she has made it clear that she wishes to be considered by the World Bank and other donor institutions as a low-income country — a status which qualifies a country for special aid treatment. To this end the Chinese government has shrewdly insisted upon a much lower estimate of its GNP *per capita* than had been previously recorded. This highly dubious practice of course may be interpreted as a posthumous stab at Chairman Mao's policies. The World Bank reports in

1978 and 1979 had recorded China as having a GNP *per capita* of 400 and 490 dollars respectively. In the 1980 edition of this report this GNP *per capita* has been adjusted downwards to a mere 230 dollars — a footnote explains that this was done on the basis of recent data released by the Chinese government involving 'a different method of calculation of GNP than used previously', and that the World Bank has not had the time to evaluate the results in relation to their own, conventional estimates.[2] As a result of this revision the outgoing President of the World Bank had to announce in his address to the Bank of Governors in 1980 that the 'number of people who now have a claim on the Bank's resources has increased by nearly one billion'.[3] It is for these reasons that I have added China to the low-income countries. In every other respect Table 1.1 overleaf presents the *per capita* incomes for 1978 and the populations of the world's nations according to the World Bank's classification.

A classification of countries

Today there are over 4 billion people in the world, and, including China, some 2,200 million of these live in thirty-nine countries whose *per capita* income in 1978 was recorded to be less than 360 dollars per annum; this is the level at which the World Bank to date draws the dividing-line between low-income and middle-income countries. Apart from this low GNP per head, the countries in this group appear to have in common a small manufacturing base typically contributing a mere 10 per cent of GNP (India (17 per cent) and Sri Lanka (23 per cent) are the exceptions), annual *per capita* growth rates which have averaged over the last twenty years below 2 per cent per annum, and finally stagnant or even declining levels of food production (the latter problem is shared by some of the middle-income countries). To this low-income group belong mostly the countries in Sub-Saharan Africa and some of the more populated countries of Asia (namely India, Pakistan, Bangladesh, Sri Lanka). Even within this fairly homogeneous group of poor nations it is impossible to generalise the causes of poverty. While the fundamental problem for

TABLE 1.1
The countries of the world (GNP per capita, average annual rates of growth, and population)

	Population (millions, mid-1978)	GNP per capita	
		Dollars 1978	Average annual growth (per cent 1960—78)
Low-income countries			
1. Kampuchea, Dem.	8.4	—	—
2. Bangladesh	84.7	90	−0.4
3. People's Dem. Rep. of Laos	3.3	90	—
4. Bhutan	1.2	100	−0.3
5. Ethiopia	31.0	120	1.5
6. Mali	6.3	120	1.0
7. Nepal	13.6	120	0.8
8. Somalia	3.7	130	−0.5
9. Burundi	4.5	140	2.2
10. Chad	4.3	140	−1.0
11. Mozambique	9.9	140	0.4
12. Burma	32.2	150	1.0
13. Upper Volta	5.6	160	1.3
14. Vietnam	51.7	170	—
15. India	643.9	180	1.4
16. Malawi	5.7	180	2.9
17. Rwanda	4.5	180	1.4
18. Sri Lanka	14.3	190	2.0
19. Guinea	5.1	210	0.6
20. Sierra Leone	3.3	210	0.5
21. Zaïre	26.8	210	1.1
22. Niger	5.0	220	−1.4
23. Benin	3.3	230	0.4
24. Pakistan	77.3	230	2.8
25. Tanzania	16.9	230	2.7
26. China (mainland)	952.2	230	3.7*
27. Afghanistan	14.6	240	0.4
28. Central African Republic	1.9	250	0.7
29. Madagascar	8.3	250	−0.3
30. Haiti	4.8	260	0.2
31. Mauritania	1.5	270	3.6
32. Lesotho	1.3	280	5.9
33. Uganda	12.4	280	0.7

TABLE 1.1 (*continued*)

	Population (millions, mid-1978)	GNP *per capita*	
		Dollars 1978	Average annual growth (per cent 1960—78)
34. Angola	6.7	300	1.2
35. Sudan	17.4	320	0.1
36. Togo	2.4	320	5.0
37. Kenya	14.7	330	2.2
38. Senegal	5.4	340	−0.4
39. Indonesia	136.0	360	4.1
Middle-income countries			
40. Egypt	39.9	390	3.3
41. Ghana	11.0	390	−0.5
42. Yemen PDR	1.8	420	−
43. Cameroon	8.1	460	2.9
44. Liberia	1.7	460	2.0
45. Honduras	3.4	480	1.1
46. Zimbabwe	6.9	480	1.2
47. Zambia	5.3	480	1.2
48. Thailand	44.5	490	4.6
49. Bolivia	5.3	510	2.2
50. Philippines	45.6	510	2.6
51. Yemen Arab Rep.	5.6	520	−
52. Congo, People's Republic	1.5	540	1.0
53. Nigeria	80.6	560	3.6
54. Papua New Guinea	2.9	560	3.6
55. El Salvador	4.3	660	1.8
56. Morocco	18.9	670	2.5
57. Peru	16.8	740	2.0
58. Ivory Coast	7.8	840	2.5
59. Nicaragua	2.5	840	2.3
60. Colombia	25.6	850	3.0
61. Paraguay	2.9	850	2.6
62. Ecuador	7.8	880	4.3
63. Dominican Rep.	5.1	910	3.5
64. Guatemala	6.6	910	2.9
65. Syrian Arab Rep.	8.1	930	3.8
66. Tunisia	6.0	950	4.8
67. Jordan	3.0	1,050	−

TABLE 1.1 (*continued*)

	Population (millions, (mid-1978)	GNP *per capita* Dollars 1978	Average annual growth (per cent 1960—78)
68. Malaysia	13.3	1,090	3.9
69. Jamaica	2.1	1,110	2.0
70. Lebanon	3.0	—	—
71. Korea, Republic of	36.6	1,160	6.9
72. Turkey	43.1	1,200	4.0
73. Algeria	17.6	1,260	2.3
74. Mexico	65.4	1,290	2.7
75. Panama	1.8	1,290	2.9
76. Taiwan	17.1	1,400	6.6
77. Chile	10.7	1,410	1.0
78. South Africa	27.7	1,480	2.5
79. Costa Rica	2.1	1,540	3.3
80. Brazil	119.5	1,570	4.9
81. Uruguay	2.9	1,610	0.7
82. Argentina	26.4	1,910	2.6
83. Portugal	9.8	1,990	5.9
84. Yugoslavia	22.0	2,380	5.4
85. Trinidad and Tobago	1.1	2,910	2.2
86. Venezuela	14.0	2,910	2.7
87. Hong Kong	4.6	3,040	6.5
88. Greece	9.4	3,250	6.0
89. Singapore	2.3	3,290	7.4
90. Spain	37.1	3,470	5.0
91. Israel	3.7	3,500	4.2
Industrialised countries			
92. Ireland	3.2	3,470	3.3
93. Italy	56.7	3,850	3.6
94. New Zealand	3.2	4,790	1.7
95. United Kingdom	55.8	5,030	2.1
96. Finland	4.8	6,820	4.1
97. Austria	7.5	7,030	4.2
98. Japan	114.9	7,280	7.6
99. Australia	14.2	7,990	2.9
100. France	53.3	8,260	4.0

TABLE 1.1 (*continued*)

	Population (millions, mid-1978)	GNP *per capita* Dollars 1978	GNP *per capita* Average annual growth (per cent 1960—78)
101. Netherlands	13.9	8,410	3.4
102. Belgium	9.8	9,090	4.1
103. Canada	23.5	9,180	3.5
104. Norway	4.1	9,510	4.0
105. Germany, Fed. Rep.	61.3	9,580	3.3
106. USA	221.9	9,590	2.4
107. Denmark	5.1	9,920	3.2
108. Sweden	8.3	10,210	2.5
109. Switzerland	6.3	12,100	2.2
Capital-surplus oil exporters			
110. Iraq	12.2	1,860	4.1
111. Iran	35.8	2,160†	7.9†
112. Libya	2.7	6,910	6.2
113. Saudi Arabia	8.2	7,690	9.7
114. Kuwait	1.2	14,890	(15.8)‡
Centrally planned economies			
115. Korea, Dem. Rep.	17.1	730	4.5
116. Albania	2.6	740	4.1
117. Cuba	9.7	810	−1.2
118. Mongolia	1.6	940	1.5
119. Romania	21.9	1,750	8.6
120. Bulgaria	8.8	3,230	5.7
121. Hungary	10.7	3,450	5.0
122. Poland	35.0	3,670	5.9
123. USSR	261.0	3,700	4.3
124. Czechoslovakia	15.1	4,720	4.3
125. German Dem. Rep.	16.7	5,710	4.8

* Note the figure for China is a preliminary estimate (cf. p. 17).

† The GNP for Iran is based on calculations for 1977.

‡ The growth rate for Kuwait is a personal estimate, since the World Bank *Development Report*, here quoting −2.3, is likely to be a misprint.

Source: World Bank, *World Development Report, 1980*, annexe table 1.

the Sub-Saharan countries is their dependence on declining export earnings from non-fuel primary commodities, as yet uncompensated for by their small and unsophisticated manufacturing sector, the problem of the Asian low-income group lies primarily with the growth of their population in relation to their stagnant food production.

Towards the end of the First Development Decade it had not escaped the attention of the professional observers that there was some variation in economic performance amongst the 'developing' countries as they were all then optimistically called. A comprehensive and authoritative UN-sponsored report on the experiences of the First Development Decade, for example, observed that in 1969 (their time of writing):

> Of the population of the less developed world 22 per cent live in countries where per capita income has grown at less than 1 per cent per year, 48 per cent live in countries where it grew between 1 and 2 per cent and 30 per cent in countries where per capita income grew by more than 2 per cent per year.[4]

These differences, however, did not yet direct attention to the essential variability of the economic basis of these countries. The report dismissed these economic differences as due largely to differences in economic management and administration.[5]

An *ad hoc* group of experts reporting to the UN Committee for Development Planning in 1970 was the first to alert the world to the growing disparities in economic performance amongst the developing countries.[6] Acting upon this Committee's recommendations, the UN General Assembly on 24 October 1970 adopted Resolution No. 2626(XXV) in which it created a category of Least Developed Countries for whom the international development strategy of the Second UN Development Decade was to provide special measures 'to enhance their capacity to benefit fully and equitably from the policy measures of the Decade'. On the basis of three criteria, namely (i) *per capita* income of 100 dollars or less, (ii) share of manufacturing in total gross domestic product of 10 per cent or less, and (iii) literacy rates of 20 per cent or less,[7] twenty-five countries were allocated to this category: Niger, Uganda, Chad, Central African Republic, Laos, Upper Volta, Gambia, Mali, Benin, Rwanda, Burundi, Nepal, Bangladesh, Somalia, Afghanistan, Ethiopia, Guinea, Haiti, Lesotho, Tanzania, Sudan, Malawi, Botswana, Yemen (Democratic), Mauritania – all of course appearing in the World Bank's list of low-income countries.

However, it is really only since the quadrupling of oil prices in 1974 that the differences have become very noticeable and have started to reveal the root cause of the economic differentiation: *the great divide between the Third World countries is between, on the one hand, those countries which have either the resources (oil, or non-fuel, scarce, minerals) or the industrialising markets that permit continued participation in contemporary world economic exchanges and, on the other hand, those countries which have not.*

This reappraisal and the subsequent new language of development came soon after 1974, when it became clear that many countries simply did not and would perhaps *never* have the resources to pay for their increased oil import bill, as well as the increased food import bill (food price rises, in part, being themselves a result of the oil price rises). Indeed, starting from their pitiful economic position any attempt to increase production and earnings to pay for oil would boomerang back in its requirement for more oil as a source of energy. The UN General Assembly was quick to label these countries 'most seriously affected nations' (MSA nations) in its Resolution No. 3203(S–VI) and to set up a special programme as part of its programme of action to establish a New International Economic Order, so as to assist the MSA countries in meeting the increased oil import bill. The number of countries originally designated as 'most seriously affected' was thirty-two, later expanded to forty-three, and now encompasses all the World Bank's low-income countries (Table 1.1) *minus* Indonesia (itself an oil-exporting country) and *plus* a few Latin American middle-income countries such as Honduras, El Salvador and Guatemala.

At the other end of the spectrum, the oil price hikes of course radically changed the economic fortunes of the oil-exporting countries, and five of these obtained incomes far in excess of the development needs of their relatively small populations. The time came therefore for the world economy watchers to isolate these Arab fortunes from the aggregate statistics of developing countries, and to set them apart in a class all by themselves. The World Bank now calls these capital-surplus oil exporters. (The World Bank classifies in this category Iran, Iraq, Saudi Arabia, Libya and Kuwait.)

This leaves some fifty-five countries with a total population of 900 million in the World Bank's middle-income category. This middle-income category is far more heterogeneous than the low-income group. Average GNP *per capita* here ranges from 390 to 3,500 dollars, and sustained economic growth (as recorded over the last twenty years) varies greatly between the countries from 1 to 7.4 per cent (see Table 1.1). But most importantly there are profound differences in their respective production structures, generating different sources of future earnings and growth potential. Although in most, though not all, middle-income countries the rate of industrialisation has been noticeably faster than in the low-income countries, it has been the *pattern of industrialisation*, particularly in the last decade, that has been responsible for the greatest dispersion of economic performance within this group. This variation in the pattern of industrialisation has been largely a function of level of industrialisation already obtained. Although *most* of the middle-income countries have *only started* their industrialisation process in the last fifteen years or so, concentrating on import substitution and the initial processing of agricultural produce, *others* (notably some Central and Latin American countries) had already completed that first stage of the industrialisation process and could now deepen their industrial structure (making producer goods) as well as diversify into export markets. A small number of countries in South-East Asia concentrated more or less at once on export-orientated manufacturing, predominantly under the wings of the multinational corporations (see pp. 64–5).

These two groups, the Latin American diversifying economies and the export-led South-East Asian economies are now called 'newly industrialising countries' (NICs) — a label they share with the rapidly growing economies of Southern

TABLE 1.2

*Growth of gross national product and gross national product per capita
1960—80 (average annual percentage growth rates at 1977 prices)*

	GNP		GNP *per capita*	
	1960—70	1970—80	1960—70	1970—80
All developing countries	5.6	5.3	3.1	2.9
Low-income countries	4.2	4.0	1.8	1.7
Middle-income countries	6.0	5.6	3.5	3.1
Industrialised countries	5.0	3.1	3.9	2.4
Capital-surplus oil exporters	10.5	8.4	7.3	5.0
Centrally planned economies	—	5.2	—	3.8

Source: World Bank, *Annual Report 1980*, p. 16.

Europe. Official lists vary as to the number of countries to be
included in this list. The OECD's list of NICs, for example,
includes ten countries: Singapore, South Korea, Hong Kong,
Taiwan, Brazil, Mexico, Spain, Portugal, Yugoslavia and
Greece.[8] Its definition of the common characteristics of this
group refers to: (i) rapid penetration of world market of
manufactures, (ii) a rising share of industrial employment,
and (iii) an increase in real GDP *per capita* relative to the
more advanced industrial countries.[9] The World Bank, on the
other hand, restricting itself to a characterisation of countries
where manufacturing now accounts for 20 per cent of total
GDP, comes up with an expanded list which includes, besides
the above-mentioned countries, Malaysia, Argentina, Turkey,
the Philippines, Columbia and South Africa.[10]
   Because it was the convention in the First Development
Decade to group together *all* countries in Asia, Latin America

and Africa as the 'Third World' or as 'the developing world', there was a tendency to gloss over the already existing differences in industrial base (see Table 1.3). *All* the developing world was seen as poor, helpless and oppressed (the radical variant) or as poor, helpless and backward (the conservative variant) — and deserving of charity. As a consequence the public in the advanced countries was not prepared for it when apparently quite suddenly their objects of charity turned into threats: competitors for jobs and markets.

Between 1960 and 1978 production of manufactures in the middle-income countries, seen as a group, grew by over 7 per cent per annum. This was more than was the case in the low-income countries (5 per cent) and also more than in the industrialised countries (4.8 per cent). But in the newly industrialising countries manufacturing grew faster still, in some cases by over 15 per cent per annum (see Table 1.4). More important for an understanding of the changed world economic structure, exports of manufactures from the Third World grew faster than either total world production or total world trade in manufactures. Although the developing countries as a whole managed to increase their share of world trade in manufactures from 6 per cent in 1960 to over 10 per cent in 1979,[11] this was largely due to the penetration of the world market by manufacturing exports from the NICs. Some 80 per cent of all manufacturing exports from the developing countries originate in twelve newly industrialising countries plus India (which, note, is in the low-income group) and no less than 45 per cent of all manufacturing exports comes from four countries only, South Korea, Taiwan, Spain and Hong Kong, which together have just 3 per cent of the population of all developing countries.[12] These really spectacular advances by just a few countries do not, however, detract from the impressive progress made by many more developing countries in the participation in world industrial trade. Thirty-eight out of fifty middle-income developing countries have increased the percentage share of manufactures in their total exports; the total number of developing countries that export manufactures is growing; and finally, amongst the newly industrialising group of countries there are now some who are moving away from exports of light manufactures, traditionally

TABLE 1.3

*Distribution of GDP (per cent)**

	Agriculture		Industry		(Manufacturing)		Services	
	1960	1978	1960	1978	1960	1978	1960	1978
Low-income countries	50	38	17	24	11	13	33	38
Middle-income countries	22	16	31	34	22	25	47	50
Industrial	6	4	40	37	30	27	54	59
Capital-surplus oil exporters	—	5	—	65	—	8	—	30
Centrally planned economies	—	—	—	—	—	—	—	—
In selected newly industrialising countries								
South Korea	40	24	19	36	12	24	41	40
Hong Kong	4	2	34	31	25	25	62	67
Brazil	16	11	35	37	26	28	49	52
Argentina†	17	13	38	45	31	37	45	42
Spain†	21	9	39	38	27	30	40	53
Portugal	25	13	36	46	29	36	39	41
Turkey	41	27	21	28	13	18	38	45

* These group percentages are weighted by country GDP.
† The figure in the 1978 column is for 1977, not 1978.
Source: World Bank, *World Development Report, 1980.*

TABLE 1.4

Growth of production of manufacturing sector
*(average annual growth rates, per cent)**

	1960–70	1970–8
Low-income countries	6.6	4.2
Middle-income countries	7.6	6.8
Industrialised countries	6.2	3.3
Capital-surplus exporters	–	–
Centrally planned	–	–

In newly industrialising countries

	1960–70	1970–8
Singapore	13.0	9.2
South Korea	17.2	18.3
Hong Kong†	–	5.6
Taiwan	17.3	13.2
Malaysia	–	12.3
Brazil	–	9.5
Mexico	9.4	6.2
Argentina	5.7	2.0
Spain	9.7	7.8
Portugal	8.9	4.6
Yugoslavia†	5.7	9.3
Turkey	10.9	8.7

* These growth rates are weighted by country GDP in 1970 in dollars.
† Figure in 1970–8 column is for 1970–7.
Source: World Bank, *World Development Report, 1980.*

the preserve of developing countries (e.g. textiles, footwear
and clothing), and are now competing with the advanced
countries in the export of electronics, steel, machinery and
transport equipment. In 1977 for the first time engineering

TABLE 1.5

*Composition of merchandise exports from developing countries
(per cent)*

	1960	1976
Fuels and energy	38	38
Other primary	51	35
Manufacturing	11	27

Source: World Bank, *World Development Report, 1979*, p. 5.

products replaced textiles and clothing as the principal broad
category of manufactures exported by developing countries
(see Tables 1.5, 1.6 and 1.7).[13] This increased participation
in world industrial production and trade on the part of the
middle-income countries testifies to their increased participation in the *capitalist* world economy rather than in the world
economy as a whole. The direction of their trade remains
significantly loaded in favour of the industrialised market
economies which absorb just over three-fifths of their manufactures, as opposed to the centrally planned economies
(6 per cent). Moreover, their *growth* of exports of manufactures has been largely absorbed by the industrialised market
economies, notwithstanding an encouraging increase in trade
amongst the developing countries themselves.

TABLE 1.6

*Share of manufactures in exports from developing countries
when excluding oil*

1955	10%
1965	20%
1975	40%

Source: Brandt Report, *North—South, a Programme for
Survival*, 1980, p. 174.

TABLE 1.7

Percentage share of manufactures in exports by country group*

	Textiles and clothing		Machinery and transport equipment		Others		Percentage of total exports	
	1960	1977	1960	1977	1960	1977	1960	1977
Low income	12	7	–	2	5	10	–	19
Middle income	4	10	2	9	8	18	14	37
Industrialised	7	5	30	39	29	32	66	76
Capital-surplus oil exporters	0	–	0	10	1	1	1	–
Centrally planned	–	4	–	31	–	25	–	60

Percentage share of manufactures in exports from individual NICs

Singapore	5	5	7	24	14	15	26	44
South Korea	8	32	–	17	6	36	–	85
Hong Kong	45	46	4	16	31	34	80	96
Brazil	0	4	–	11	3	11	–	26
Mexico	4	4	1	6	7	19	12	29
Spain	7	6	2	26	13	39	22	71
Turkey	0	18	0	1	3	6	3	25

* In current dollars and weighted by country GDP.

Source: World Bank, *World Development Report, 1980.*

The changed composition and growth of *manufacturing exports* of (some) middle-income countries is not the only hallmark of a change in world economic relationships. A second is the much improved earnings of the *mineral export economies*, especially, of course, the oil-exporting economies. The dazzling fortunes of the Arab oil exporters (the capital-surplus oil exporters) have tended to overshadow the improved export performance of the other oil-exporting developing countries (e.g. Nigeria, Algeria, Venezuela, Mexico, Gabon, Indonesia) and of a few mineral-exporting countries with scarce, non-fuel minerals (e.g. Congo, Bolivia, Tunisia). Between 1960 and 1976 these mineral (fuel and non-fuel) economies grew at an average annual rate of 6.5 per cent, a slightly better performance than the middle-income countries group to which most of them belong. Their possession of a resource that is readily converted into a large financial flow has permitted these countries to increase greatly their participation in world economic exchanges (see Table 1.8), and it is this feature, rather than the success of their over-all development performance, which distinguishes them from the low-income group.[14]

Finally, a third hallmark of the changing structure of world economic relations is that *the structure of Third World imports* has also changed substantially during the post-1945 period. In consequence of vigorous import-substitution programmes in many countries the share of imports which is typically accounted for by manufactured consumer goods has fallen and those made up by intermediate inputs (including energy) and capital goods have increased.[15]

Pulling these various facts together it should come as no surprise that the developing world as a whole has increased its importance as markets for the industrial countries' exports of manufactures and especially of engineering products for which traditional outlets in the industrial countries are declining (see Table 1.9). This truth was brought home with particular force during the economic recession of the past decade. As a GATT report comments:

> A remarkable feature of the world economy since 1973 has been the steadier economic growth in developing countries as compared with the industrial areas. As a result, the

TABLE 1.8

Average annual growth rates of imports and terms of trade of fuel and non-fuel mineral-exporting countries

	Growth rates (per cent)		Terms of trade (1970 = 100)	
	1960–70	1970–80	1960	1978
Indonesia	1.9	15.8	138	225
Bolivia	8.1	12.2	69	130
Nigeria	1.7	25.0	97	290
Congo	−1.0	6.7	98	114
Ecuador	11.6	12.7	110	129
Syrian Arab Republic	4.2	15.5	94	139
Tunisia	2.2	30.3	104	133
Algeria	1.0	16.6	115	281
Venezuela	4.3	14.9	112	292
Capital-surplus oil exporters				
Iraq	1.3	21.1	112	403
Iran	11.3	22.9	108	373
Libya	15.4	18.7	98	280
Saudi Arabia	11.1	41.5	107	396
Kuwait	10.4	19.2	105	393
Low income	5.0	3.2	98	98
Middle income	6.8	5.8	93	90
Industrialised	9.4	5.1	99	95

Source: World Bank, *World Development Report, 1980.*

markets of developing countries have become relatively more important as outlets for manufactures produced in industrial countries.[16]

It would thus seem that, judging by measures of economic production and trade performance, (i) there has been an economic differentiation of the Third World into developing and stagnant, or even declining economies, and that (ii) this

TABLE 1.9

Importance of developing countries as markets for industrial countries' exports of manufactures, 1973 and 1978

(percentage shares in total exports)

	All manufactures		Engineering products		Textiles	
	1973	1978	1973	1978	1973	1978
North America						
to Western Europe and Japan	29	26	27	23	36	35
Developing countries	24	32	23	32	26	32
Japan						
to North America and Western Europe	47	44	53	49	19	20
Developing countries	42	46	39	43	63	65
Western Europe						
to North America and Japan	11	9	11	9	8	6
Developing countries	15	20	17	25	10	12

Source: GATT, *International Trade 1978–9,* 1979.

economic differentiation is associated with the degree of integration of such countries with the capitalist world economy.[17]

The widening-gap debate

The fact that there are now some developing *economies* in the Third World which have increased and improved their participation in world economic exchanges has led some observers to argue that there is no longer a 'widening gap' between rich and poor countries.[18] This is a politically highly divisive conclusion which is based on both an economic and a statistical error.

First, the *economic* error. Widening-gap debates conventionally refer to a 'widening gap' in *incomes* between rich and poor countries. Now, there is no *necessary* relationship between a country's improved production and trade structure (e.g. manufacturing output, increased export performance and improved terms of trade) on the one hand, and its GNP *per capita* on the other, for GNP measures the total final output of goods and services within a country's territory by residents and non-residents *plus* the factor incomes accruing to a country's residents from abroad, but *minus* the income earned in the domestic economy accruing to persons abroad. To the extent that productive activities, in developing countries especially, may be owned by foreigners and the income arising therefrom is remitted abroad, any improved performance of and gains from such productive activities will not be reflected in an increase of GNP *per capita*. Improved terms of trade and export earnings of resource-based economies, therefore, are not necessarily reflected *pro rata* in increased levels of incomes of the nationals of a country. The same holds true for increased value of manufacturing output and exports.

Second, the *statistical* error. As it happens, both arguments *for* and *against* the widening-gap theory usually nestle upon a heap of improperly used statistics. The widening-gap theory (which was the orthodoxy until a few years ago) referred to a widening gap in the 'average' income of the advanced countries of the First World (the Socialist bloc always being excluded

from such considerations) and the 'average' income of the
Third World. The non-widening-gap theory (which is now the
new orthodoxy) is based on a statistical aggregation of the
remarkable growth rates and high *per capita* income levels of
some Third World countries, namely the capital-surplus oil
exporters and the newly industrialising countries, four of
which are located in Southern Europe and were never really
part of the Third World anyway, with those of a general group
of middle-income countries, and on a comparison of this
'average' income of the middle-income countries with that of
the low-income group and the advanced industrialised group
respectively. The trouble with such arguments is that one groups
together that which should not be grouped together. The
GNP *per capita* and the growth rate *per capita* of each individual country is itself already a dubious statistical average,
for it ignores the wide dispersion of incomes within a nation.
What is next done is to lump together these domestic 'average'
incomes and growth rates into aggregates of countries on the
basis of some preconceived notion of groups, i.e. First World,
Third World, middle-income country, etc. Here again, ignoring
the wide dispersion of average incomes between countries
within each group, one then compares these meaningless
means over a certain period of time and concludes that the
'gap' between these means is or is not widening.

There is an additional problem of relative versus absolute
gaps. Consider two countries *A* and *B* which have an average
income of 100 and 1,000 dollars respectively. Initially,
country *B* has ten times the income of country *A*. This is
the *relative* gap. The absolute gap is 900 dollars. If country *A*
has a *per capita* growth rate of 10 per cent per annum, and
country *B* has a mere 5 per cent, then after ten years country
A has a *per capita* income of 259 dollars, while country *B* has
a *per capita* income of 1,634 dollars. Their differential growth
rates have resulted in a narrowing of the relative gap, while
the absolute gap between them has still widened.

Bearing these considerations in mind, let us for the moment
set aside the problem of a country's *internal* distribution of
income and take its *per capita* income as an 'average' measure
of income. Let us next forget any preconceived notions about
First or Third World countries, and, instead of aggregating

the *per capita* income of countries in each of these preconceived groups, simply treat the distribution of the *per capita*
incomes as one would any ordinary statistical frequency
distribution. I have done this in Figures 1.1 and 1.2.[19] In
1967 the *per capita* incomes of all the countries in the world
ranged from 50 dollars in Upper Volta to 3,670 dollars in the
USA. As with any other frequency distribution we next divide
the distribution into a nominal range of equidistanced intervals, i.e. 50–140, 150–240, etc. The point is that while the
decision to divide the range into thirty-seven blocks or 'intervals' of 100 dollars each is, initially, an arbitrary decision –
one must when comparing this range with the data series of
the next time period (1978) present *that* new frequency
distribution in the *same* number of intervals. Since in 1978
the *per capita* income in the world varied from 50 dollars to
14,890 dollars (Kuwait) we now obtain thirty-seven blocks of
400 dollars each.[20] This allows for a historical comparison of
international income distribution which is not only statistically correct but also makes economic sense. For, when allow-
ing for the growth of the world product and world inflation,
the size of the units or intervals in the respective distributions
is indeed comparable. That is to say, within the international
hierarchy of incomes, a country with an income of below
400 dollars in 1978 is in the same relative position on the
international income ladder as it was when it had an income
of below 150 dollars in 1967, and so on. It is only when
countries shift from one comparable interval to another that
we may speak of a relative improvement or deterioration in
their position within the international hierarchy.

Now what can we learn from the diagrams about widening
or non-widening gaps?

(1) First of all, the dispersion of income levels within the
'group of advanced countries' was greater both in 1967 and
1978 than within the group of the so-called 'Third World'.
There was not, at any time, a discontinuity or 'gap' in income
levels between the lower-placed advanced countries and those
of the higher-placed Third World countries.

(2) The 'gap' in incomes between the countries of the
advanced world has narrowed considerably in the past decade;
this is mainly due to the considerable decline of the USA,
which is the most populous state in the region.

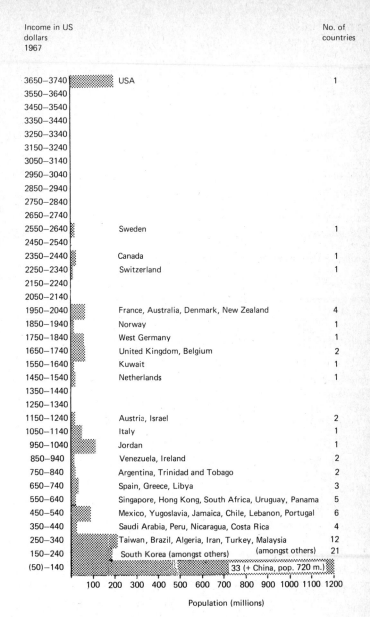

Income in US dollars 1967		No. of countries
3650–3740	USA	1
3550–3640		
3450–3540		
3350–3440		
3250–3340		
3150–3240		
3050–3140		
2950–3040		
2850–2940		
2750–2840		
2650–2740		
2550–2640	Sweden	1
2450–2540		
2350–2440	Canada	1
2250–2340	Switzerland	1
2150–2240		
2050–2140		
1950–2040	France, Australia, Denmark, New Zealand	4
1850–1940	Norway	1
1750–1840	West Germany	1
1650–1740	United Kingdom, Belgium	2
1550–1640	Kuwait	1
1450–1540	Netherlands	1
1350–1440		
1250–1340		
1150–1240	Austria, Israel	2
1050–1140	Italy	1
950–1040	Jordan	1
850–940	Venezuela, Ireland	2
750–840	Argentina, Trinidad and Tobago	2
650–740	Spain, Greece, Libya	3
550–640	Singapore, Hong Kong, South Africa, Uruguay, Panama	5
450–540	Mexico, Yugoslavia, Jamaica, Chile, Lebanon, Portugal	6
350–440	Saudi Arabia, Peru, Nicaragua, Costa Rica	4
250–340	Taiwan, Brazil, Algeria, Iran, Turkey, Malaysia	12
150–240	South Korea (amongst others) (amongst others)	21
(50)–140	33 (+ China, pop. 720 m.)	

100 200 300 400 500 600 700 800 900 1000 1100 1200

Population (millions)

FIGURE 1.1   *Frequency distribution of GNP per capita by countries and population, 1967*

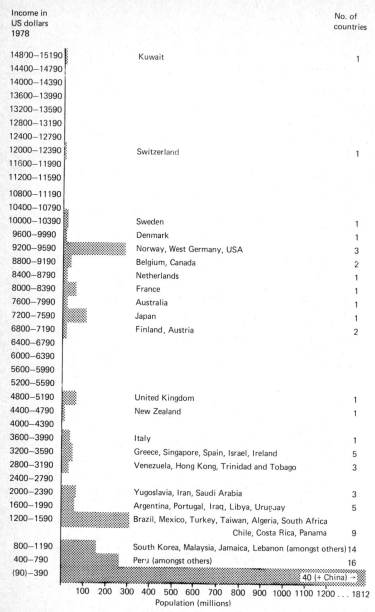

Income in US dollars 1978		No. of countries
14800–15190	Kuwait	1
14400–14790		
14000–14390		
13600–13990		
13200–13590		
12800–13190		
12400–12790		
12000–12390	Switzerland	1
11600–11990		
11200–11590		
10800–11190		
10400–10790		
10000–10390	Sweden	1
9600–9990	Denmark	1
9200–9590	Norway, West Germany, USA	3
8800–9190	Belgium, Canada	2
8400–8790	Netherlands	1
8000–8390	France	1
7600–7990	Australia	1
7200–7590	Japan	1
6800–7190	Finland, Austria	2
6400–6790		
6000–6390		
5600–5990		
5200–5590		
4800–5190	United Kingdom	1
4400–4790	New Zealand	1
4000–4390		
3600–3990	Italy	1
3200–3590	Greece, Singapore, Spain, Israel, Ireland	5
2800–3190	Venezuela, Hong Kong, Trinidad and Tobago	3
2400–2790		
2000–2390	Yugoslavia, Iran, Saudi Arabia	3
1600–1990	Argentina, Portugal, Iraq, Libya, Uruguay	5
1200–1590	Brazil, Mexico, Turkey, Taiwan, Algeria, South Africa Chile, Costa Rica, Panama	9
800–1190	South Korea, Malaysia, Jamaica, Lebanon (amongst others)	14
400–790	Peru (amongst others)	16
(90)–390		40 (+ China) →

Population (millions): 100 200 300 400 500 600 700 800 900 1000 1100 1200 ... 1812

FIGURE 1.2   *Frequency distribution of GNP per capita by countries and population, 1978*

(3) Several more 'advanced' countries, namely the United Kingdom, New Zealand and Italy, have lost status in the international hierarchy. Their downward mobility has brought them into close range of two of the upwardly mobile Southern European NICs, namely Greece and Spain, and two South-East Asian NICs, namely Hong Kong and Singapore. It is this fact, coupled with the meteoric rise of Saudi Arabia, Libya and Kuwait (capital-surplus oil exporters) that has led some observers to proclaim the new orthodoxy:

> The growing gap — which plays such a central role in the debate about the developing countries — does not run between industrialised countries and developing countries. It runs between the billion people in the poorest countries on earth and the rest of the world.[21]

My answer to that is 'One swallow does not make a summer', especially when one considers the very small size of populations of these upwardly mobile countries. When one looks at the progress of other rising NICs such as Brazil, Taiwan, South Korea and Turkey which do have sizeable populations, it is worth noticing that they have improved their position by one step only, and starting from the near lowest rung of the ladder. Mexico, for all its much praised virtues as a 'rapidly' industrialising (and oil-exporting) country, has actually declined in position, as have Argentina and Venezuela.

(4) Comparing the 'group' of advanced countries from Finland to Switzerland (a statistical aggregation that is permissible because of the limited dispersion of incomes here) with the Brazil, Taiwan group of NICs, it is true that the relative gap between their respective income levels has narrowed, though the *absolute gap* has continued to *widen*.

(5) As for the rest of the Third World, namely the Fourth World or low-income group (see bottom interval) *and the bottom of the middle-income countries* (between which two there is no 'gap', note), *their* average income level, when compared with that of the group of advanced countries, has deteriorated in both relative and absolute terms. Although it was always statistically dubious to aggregate the *per capita* incomes of advanced industrialised countries and compare

their 'average' with the equally dubious aggregates of Third
World incomes, such classification made good *political* sense.
It provided a rallying ground for Third World solidarity and —
as we shall see in the next chapter — this brought some positive results. But the reclassification of Third World countries
into low-income (Fourth World) and middle-income countries
on the basis of the rapid advance of just a few countries with
small populations (some of them not even in the Third World)
is used to create the illusion of a 'bridgehead across the
"gap" '. This is both statistically false and politically divisive.

A classification of people

When examining the world's development record, it is one
thing to observe a relative change in the economic production
and trade performance of *countries*, it is another to look at
the relative distribution of income between countries, and it
is yet a third task to assess the relevance of the changing
performance of economy and income levels for *people*.

A central concern in development studies in the last decade
has been the extent to which rapid economic growth is associated with deepening social inequalities. The latter phenomenon is, of course, not expressed in GNP *per capita*. Some
writers have suggested that the pattern of economic development frequently and successfully followed typically involves
a heavy reliance on imported capital-intensive techniques and
a neglect of food production. This is said to result in the
phenomenon of *marginalisation*, i.e. an exclusion, and even
an expulsion, of large sections of rural and urban poor from
economic life and development.[22] The favourite example
here is that of Brazil, whose economic miracle effectively lost
more industrial jobs than gained them,[23] increased the percentage share of total income accruing to the top 10 per cent
of the population,[24] and led to swelling numbers of people
living at or below the poverty line (estimates vary from
between 50 and 80 per cent of the population).[25] There are
other studies, however, that suggest that there is no firm
empirical basis for the view that higher rates of growth *inevitably* generate greater inequality, though there is some evidence

that income inequality first increases and then decreases with development.[26] This is now referred to as the Kuznets curve.[27] Table 1.10, based on one such study, shows the diversity of inequality levels amongst high-growth developing countries.

Since the beginning of the 1970s the global institutions concerned with the world economy have developed an increasingly obsessive interest with the 'forgotten poor', namely the poorest 40 per cent of the population of Third World countries, who — in the words of McNamara, ex-president of the World Bank — 'collectively receive only 10 or 15 per cent of the total national income'.[28] In the course of the decade the attack on poverty has gathered much ideological strength and a lot of official research effort has gone into the estimation of both poverty levels and income distributions. It has become a routine obligation for any text on development or on the world situation to keep a running count of the numbers of people living in relative poverty, and of those living in absolute poverty.[29] The *absolute* poor comprise those people living 'below "minimally" acceptable life-sustaining and life-enhancing support systems'.[30] What is meant here in plain English is a level of income below which, under prevailing local conditions, one cannot survive physically. *Relative* poverty, on the other hand, refers to those segments of the Third World population, including that in rapidly growing countries such as Brazil, Mexico, Taiwan, etc., who receive less than one-third of their national *per capita* income.[31]

In the mid-1970s, on the basis of a 50 dollar annual income (which was then the official global cut-off point for defining absolute poverty), some 650 million people were believed to live in absolute poverty, while another 300 million lived in relative poverty, at incomes of around 75 dollars.[32] Recent texts refer to an updated figure for the absolute poor of 800 million, or even 1,000 million.[33] Such indeed is the indictment of two decades of considerable national economic progress that while the proportion of people in absolute poverty in the developing countries as a group (except in Sub-Saharan Africa) is estimated to have fallen, the number of people in absolute poverty has increased because of population growth.[34] Table 1.11 gives the location of absolute

TABLE 1.10

Cross-classification of countries by income level and equality

High inequality
Share of lowest 40% less than 12%

Country (year)	Per capita GNP US$	Lowest 40%	Middle 40%	Top 20%
Income up to US $300				
Kenya (1969)	136	10.0	22.0	68.0
Sierra Leone (1968)	159	9.6	22.4	68.0
Philippines (1971)	239	11.6	34.6	53.8
Iraq (1956)	200	6.8	25.2	68.0
Senegal (1960)	245	10.0	26.0	64.0
Ivory Coast (1970)	247	10.8	32.1	57.1
Rhodesia (1968)	252	8.2	22.8	69.0
Tunisia (1970)	255	11.4	53.6	55.0
Honduras (1968)	265	6.5	28.5	65.0
Ecuador (1970)	277	6.5	20.0	73.5

Moderate inequality
Share of lowest 40% between 12% and 17%

Country (year)	Per capita GNP US$	Lowest 40%	Middle 40%	Top 20%
El Salvador (1969)	295	11.2	36.4	52.4
Turkey (1968)	282	9.3	29.9	60.8
Burma (1958)	82	16.5	38.7	44.8
Dahomey (1959)	87	15.5	34.5	50.0
Tanzania (1967)	89	13.0	26.0	61.0
India (1964)	99	16.0	32.0	52.0
Madagascar (1960)	120	13.5	25.5	61.0
Zambia (1959)	230	14.5	28.5	57.0

Low inequality
Share of lowest 40%, 17% and above

Country (year)	Per capita GNP US$	Lowest 40%	Middle 40%	Top 20%
Chad (1958)	78	18.0	39.0	43.0
Sri Lanka (1969)	95	17.0	37.0	46.0
Niger (1960)	97	18.0	40.0	42.0
Pakistan (1964)	100	17.5	37.5	30.0
Uganda (1970)	126	17.1	35.8	47.1
Thailand (1970)	180	17.0	37.5	45.5
Korea (1970)	235	18.0	37.0	45.0
Taiwan (1964)	241	20.4	39.5	40.1

Income US $300—$750

Country (year)	GNP					
Malaysia (1970)	330	11.6	32.4	56.0		
Colombia (1970)	358	9.0	30.0	61.0		
Brazil (1970)	390	10.0	28.4	61.5		
Peru (1971)	480	6.5	33.5	60.0		
Gabon (1968)	497	8.8	23.7	67.5		
Jamaica (1958)	510	8.2	30.3	61.5		
Costa Rica (1971)	521	11.5	30.0	58.5		
Mexico (1969)	645	10.5	25.5	64.0		
South Africa (1965)	669	6.2	35.8	58.0		
Panama (1969)	692	9.4	31.2	59.4		
Dominican Republic (1969)	323	12.2	30.3	57.5		
Iran (1968)	332	12.5	33.0	54.5		
Guyana (1956)	550	14.0	40.3	45.7		
Lebanon (1960)	508	13.0	26.0	61.0		
Uruguay (1968)	618	16.5	35.5	48.0		
Chile (1968)	744	13.0	30.2	56.8		
Surinam (1962)	394	21.7	35.7	42.6		
Greece (1957)	500	21.0	29.5	49.5		
Yugoslavia (1968)	529	18.5	40.0	41.5		
Bulgaria (1962)	530	26.8	40.0	33.2		
Spain (1965)	750	17.6	36.7	45.7		

Income above US $750

Country (year)	GNP			
Venezuela (1970)	1004	7.9	27.1	65.0
Finland (1962)	1599	11.1	39.6	49.3
France (1962)	1913	9.5	36.8	53.7
Argentina (1970)	1079	16.5	36.1	47.4
Puerto Rico (1968)	1100	13.7	35.7	50.6
Netherlands (1967)	1990	13.6	37.9	48.5
Norway (1968)	2010	16.6	42.9	40.5
Germany, Fed. Rep. (1964)	2144	15.4	31.7	52.9
Denmark (1968)	2563	13.6	38.8	47.6
New Zealand (1969)	2859	15.5	42.5	42.0
Sweden (1963)	2949	14.0	42.0	44.0
Poland (1964)	850	23.4	40.6	36.0
Japan (1963)	950	20.7	39.3	40.0
United Kingdom (1968)	2015	18.8	42.2	39.0
Hungary (1969)	1140	24.0	42.5	33.5
Czechoslovakia (1964)	1150	27.6	41.4	31.0
Australia (1968)	2509	20.0	41.2	38.8
Canada (1965)	2920	20.0	39.8	40.2
USA (1970)	4850	19.7	41.5	38.8

Note: The income shares of each percentile group were read off a free-hand Lorenz curve fitted to observed points in the cumulative distribution. The distributions are for pre-tax income. Per capita GNP figures are taken from World Bank data files and refer to GNP at factor cost for the year indicated in constant 1971 US dollars.

Source: M. Ahluwalia, 'Income Inequality', in Hollis Chenery et al., Redistribution With Growth (Oxford University Press, 1974) table 1.1 Ahluwalia's own sources are listed in his appendix.

TABLE 1.11

The location of absolute poverty by income groups, 1975

	Number of absolute poor (million)	Percentage of total population
Low-income countries	571	43.9
Middle-income countries	147	16.3
of which in NICs and		
mineral-exporting countries	(48)	6.2
Capital-surplus oil		
exporters	5	8.3
	723	

Note: Data have been recalculated to fit the classification.

Source: World Bank, *Prospects for Developing Countries 1978–85* (Washington, 1977) p. 8.

poverty by country income groups. There is no doubt that while the great majority of the absolute poor do live in the poorest countries, there are still sizeable pockets of absolute poverty in the middle-income countries.

Distressing though these figures are, there is one comforting aspect in them, namely that they overstate their case. It has recently come to light that there is a downward bias in the GNP *per capita* calculations of the less advanced countries, because domestic price levels in the non-traded sectors are not directly related to exchange rates (upon which the GNP calculations are based). The lower the level of income and trade dependence of a country — which by corollary means the poorer the country — the *larger* this downward bias.[35] What this means is that the absolute poor are still living in domestic subsistence sectors on something that is not actually reflected in GNP *per capita*. This is just as well, for by the very logic of the definition of absolute poverty the 650 million people who were recorded in 1975 to be living below the absolute poverty levels should now all be dead.

This is not to mock attempts to record international distribution of incomes. To the contrary, international distributions of income reflect international distribution of *purchasing power*, and through it the power to allocate world resources, to determine methods of production, and to define human wants and needs. The greater the disparity in incomes between rich world and poor world, the more the rich world violates the rights of the poor, prejudices their chances for better standards of life, forces them to live in abject misery. Wealth causes poverty, more wealth causes more poverty. But this is also why international comparisons of income levels between countries are not as relevant as international comparisons of income levels between *rich and poor people*.

When we compare the evolution of incomes of the richest and the poorest *people* of the free-market world, we do at last come upon the real widening gap. Basing ourselves upon, first, the *per capita* incomes of countries (Table 1.1), next the estimates of domestic distributions of income (Table 1.10), and finally on McNamara's statement that the bottom 40 per cent of people in poor countries receive typically only 15 per cent of GNP, we may — albeit roughly — calculate the percentage share of the free market world's income which accrues to the poorest 40 per cent of all the people in all the free-market world.[36] In 1967 this group of people received, collectively, 2.9 per cent of the total of the free market world's income, while the 20 per cent of the free market world's people who live in the advanced countries received 66 per cent of that income. In 1978 this gap had widened, with the poorest people's share falling to 2.1 per cent, while that of those living in the advanced countries had increased to 70 per cent.

The Petro-dollar Lubrication of the World Economy

A second key economic fact of the Second Development Decade has been the unprecedented and continuing transfer of financial resources from the advanced industrialised countries to the Third World, or more accurately to the oil-exporting and the rapidly growing middle-income countries of the Third World.

The massive expansion of this transfer has taken chiefly two forms:

(1) *Direct payments* from the oil-importing rich countries to the OPEC countries. After the first round of OPEC price rises in 1973–4 these payments increased from 35 billion US dollars per year to around 140 billion dollars per year in 1978.[37] And while a subsequent increase in OPEC's import prices eroded some of the gain, its terms of trade in 1978 were still about 110 per cent above their 1973 level,[38] suggesting a net transfer of financial resources from the rich countries to the tune of 40 billion dollars per annum. This is 1½ times as much as the total net capital flows (public and private) from the rich countries to the poor countries in 1973. A second series of price increases put into effect after 1978 brought the annual oil bill of the OECD countries to 290 billion dollars by the spring of 1980.[39] It is as yet too early to calculate the net transfer effect of these latest increases.

(2) The rapid expansion of *international credit*. The main source of this expanding credit are the current-account surpluses of those in OPEC[40] with a limited import capacity who took the *political* decision to act 'economically responsibly', as they were urged to do by every spokesman from the advanced Western world. Theoretically, after the oil price explosion of 1973 the oil-rich Arab countries had five options. four of which — when acted upon — would have endangered the survival of the global capitalist system and especially of the advanced industrial countries in this system. These options were:

(a)   to reduce their oil exports to match their import capacity;
(b)   to burn their dollars and sterling earnings in the desert;[41]
(c)   to set up a 'cartelisation' fund for the benefit of those Third World non-fuel mineral-exporting countries who would have liked to follow the example of their oil-exporting brethren and hold the rich countries over a barrel, but who lacked the resources to withdraw even temporarily from world markets; and
(d)   to buy up the equity of Western economic enterprises on a truly massive scale.[42]

But they did none of these things. Instead they chose to

behave 'responsibly' and – having increased the volume of their imports by some 180 per cent – to place their surplus income predominantly at the disposal of the *international financial markets* (see Table 1.12). There it functioned as the world's monetary lubricant, permitting the matching up of the globally dispersed trade deficits and surpluses in a manner and on a scale that has begun to belittle the role of the International Monetary Fund which had originally been set up for precisely this purpose.

Compared with the advanced industrialised countries, the oil-importing developing countries, as a group, were hit harder by the oil price hikes of 1973 (see Table 1.13). Their collective deficit rose from some 8 billion dollars in 1973 to over 39 billion dollars in 1975, when it presented a peak of 5.1 per cent of GNP (in contrast to the modest 1.5 to 2 per cent of GNP that the OECD countries 'lost' to OPEC). Paradoxically, both the richest and the poorest countries of the world adjusted to the oil price rises in similar ways: they decided to cut their cloth to their size and to reduce their other imports drastically in order to shift their deficits. In so doing, the low-income countries slowed down or halted their development programmes, while the OECD countries 'deepened the recession that followed the 1972–73 boom'.[43] By contrast, the adjustment response of the middle-income developing countries was to *expand vastly* their borrowing abroad. In this way they not only averted a current and future decline in growth in their economies but they contributed to the recovery of the international economy. As the World Bank stated:

> In retrospect it is clear that by pursuing expansionary policies in response to the recession, the developing countries contributed to the recovery of the international economy. Thus, the developing countries' share of OECD total exports which had declined from 21% in 1966 to 19% in 1973 began to increase in 1974 and reached a peak of 25% in 1975 in the depth of the recession.[44]

Already, since just before the OPEC price rises of 1973, these middle-income countries had increasingly taken to borrowing development finance from the international capital

TABLE 1.12

Oil-exporting countries:

estimated deployment of investible surpluses, 1974—9 (billions of US dollars)

Items	1974	1975	1976	1977	1978	1979	1974–8
Bank deposits and money-market placements:							
Dollar deposits in the USA	1.9	1.1	1.8	0.4	0.8	4.9	6.0
Sterling deposits in the United Kingdom	1.7	0.2	-1.4	0.3	0.2	1.4	1.0
Deposits in foreign currency markets	22.8	9.1	12.1	10.6	3.0	31.2	57.6
Treasury bills in the USA and the United Kingdom	4.8	0.6	-1.0	-1.1	-0.8	3.4	2.5
Total	31.2	11.0	11.5	10.2	3.2	40.9	67.1

Long-term investments							
Special bilateral arrangements and other investments	11.8	12.4	12.2	12.7	8.7	11.8	57.8
Loans to international agencies	3.5	4.0	2.0	0.3	0.1	-0.4	9.9
Government securities in the USA and the United Kingdom	1.1	2.2	4.1	4.5	-1.8	-0.9	10.1
Other*	8.7	6.1	8.5	5.8	3.3	2.4	32.4
Total	25.1	24.7	26.8	23.3	10.3	12.9	110.2
Total new investments	56.3	35.7	38.3	33.5	13.5	53.8	177.3

* Including equity and property investments in the USA and the United Kingdom, and foreign currency lending.

Source: Bank for International Settlements, *50th Annual Report*, 1980, p. 161.

TABLE 1.13

Global current account, 1973–6 (US billion dollars)

	1973	1974	1975	1976
Non-oil developing countries	−8.6	−29.7	−38.3	−28.1
Major oil exporters	6.2	67.2	35.3	44.0
OECD*	11.6	20.1	8.8	6.9
Other†	−4.3	−10.1	−17.7	−16.1
Memorandum item‡	4.9	7.3	−11.9	−7.1

* Excluding Turkey.
† South Africa, Israel, Malta and centrally planned economies.
‡ Total of the four above specified regions, i.e. world total; this item thus reflects inconsistencies in balance-of-payments recordings.

Source: World Bank, *Prospects for the Developing Countries 1978–85*, 1977, p. 97.

markets, where since 1970 as a result of the phenomenal growth of the so-called 'euro-dollar' market money had become easy and bank lending rules lax.[45] From 1974 onwards the avalanche of petro-dollars which flooded the international banking system (mostly short- and medium-term deposits) made international lending even less subject to traditional bankers' caution.[46] I shall return shortly to this question of the banking community's behaviour and the alleged 'exposure' of major international banks.

I now discuss the size of this expanding credit and the type and the characteristics of borrowers and lenders respectively. Studying recent reports from the World Bank, the International Monetary Fund and the Bank of International Settlements, one can begin to trace several novel trends in developing countries' borrowing during the past decade.

First, there has been a pronounced shift in borrowing away from official sources to private sources (see Table 1.14). While *official* lending to developing countries, at current prices, little more than doubled between 1970 and 1976, an increase only just ahead of the world inflation rate, borrowing from private sources increased more than four times. In the

TABLE 1.14

Debt outstanding and disbursed (eighty-one countries, at current prices, selected years, US billion dollars)

	From official creditors	From private creditors officially guaranteed	Other private	All sources
1967	23.8	9.2	2.7	35.7
1970	34.6	14.5	6.4	55.5
1973	52.1	27.1	16.2	95.4
	(17.7)	(1.7)	(0.3)	
1976	80.8	61.0	27.0	168.8
	(26.2)	(2.7)	(0.5)	

Note: Figures in brackets are for low-income countries.

Source: World Bank, *Prospects for the Developing Countries 1978–85*, 1977, pp. 110, 111.

so-called 'euro-currency markets' developing countries in 1979 dominated borrowing with an annual total of around 40 billion dollars (around 60 per cent of all euro-currency borrowing).[47] This figure is up from a mere 300 million dollars in 1970.[48]

Second, within this private-sector borrowing there has been a relative shift away from private direct foreign investment (not normally included in debt figures) and private supplier credits (which are included) towards borrowing from private financial markets (banks and bonds) (see Table 1.15). This development is the combined outcome of the generous recycling of petro-dollars via international financial markets, and the changed attitude of host countries towards foreign investment (about which more in the next section). Between 1975 and 1977, for example, net private direct foreign investment in developing countries was equivalent to only about 15 per cent of the net inflows of medium- and long-term loans in that period.[49]

Third, increasingly there has been a divergence in borrowing behaviour between middle-income countries and low-income

TABLE 1.15

Total net resource receipts of developing countries from all sources
(billions of US dollars)

Net disbursements	1970	1974	1978
ODA	7.89	15.24	22.47
(a) DAC bilateral	5.66	8.26	13.12
(b) Multilateral agencies	1.10	2.85	5.91
(c) OPEC bilateral	0.35	3.02	2.52
(d) Centrally planned economies	0.78	1.11	0.82
(e) Other donors, bilateral	–	–	0.10
Non-concessional flows	10.97	17.73	55.92
(a) Multilateral	0.69	1.80	3.41
(b) Direct investment	3.89	1.12	11.44
(c) Bank sector*	3.00	10.00	22.20
(d) Bond lending	0.30	0.40	3.30
(e) Private export credits	2.14	2.49	9.69
(f) Official export credits	0.55	0.70	3.50
(g) OPEC bilateral	0.20	0.92	1.02
(h) Other†	0.20	0.30	1.36
of which centrally planned economies	0.11	0.09	0.10
Total receipts	18.86	32.97	78.39

* Excluding bond lending and export credits extended by banks, but including offshore lending.

† Apart from centrally planned economies and 'other donors' (Ireland, Luxemburg), includes DAC miscellaneous non-concessional.

Note: Figures concerning non-DAC member countries are based as far as possible on information released by donor countries and international organisations, and completed by OECD Secretariat estimates based on other published and unpublished sources. It has therefore not been possible fully to verify that they comply in all respects with the norms and criteria used by DAC members in their statistical reports made directly to the OECD Secretariat.

Source: *OECD 1979 DAC Review* (Paris, 1979) table A.1, p. 199.

countries. While the former have opted for private-source borrowing, the latter have had to rely more and more exclusively on official lending. Table 1.14, where the figures in brackets give the low-income countries' total borrowings, describes this trend. At the end of 1977, 94 per cent of the debt owed to private sources was held by middle-income countries.[50]

Fourth, within the group of middle-income countries themselves, there has been a concentration of borrowing. Ten leading developing countries (all but one belonging to either the group of newly industrialising countries or to successful mineral exporters)[51] accounted for 68.5 per cent of the total external debt outstanding and disbursed to all private creditors, and eighteen countries, predominantly, too, from the same two successful economic groupings, accounted for 80 per cent of the total external debt.[52]

Fifth, while the nominal size of the developing countries' total debt grew to alarming proportions (nearly 350 billion dollars in 1978; see Table 1.16), causing many commentators to speak of a debt explosion, several factors combined to contain the *real* growth of the developing countries' indebtedness. The galloping world-wide inflation rate, which itself was in no small measure the consequence of the oil price rises, has had a substantial impact on the real debt burden, as has the depreciation of the US dollar which inflates the dollar

TABLE 1.16

Total external public debt outstanding (including undisbursed), 1972–8, of all developing countries (millions of US dollars)

1972	96,812.9
1973	118,657.8
1974	153,348.1
1975	184,370.3
1976	228,868.7
1977	281,912.0
1978	348,485.3

Source: World Bank, *Annual Report 1980*, table on p. 132.

figure of debt incurred in other currencies. According to the World Bank, 'In real terms, total debt actually grew more slowly from the late mid-1960s than before. Even during the peiod of rapid accumulation of debt from private sources between 1973 and 1976, the rate of growth of indebtedness from private sources was lower in constant prices than before.'[53] The obverse side of this story, of course, is that real interest rates throughout the period have been low. It is estimated that between 1973 and 1975 real interest rates on debt to private creditors could not have exceeded 1 per cent.[54] This being the case, it is not surprising that some of the high-growth developing countries have started to borrow money in the capital markets, not to finance current-account deficits, or for the purpose of capital investments, but in order to shore up their international reserves. Between 1970 and 1977 the reserves of all developing countries increased by more than 80 billion US dollars, which was the equivalent to over 40 per cent of the increase in their medium- and long-term debt outstanding.[55]

To the extent that the high-growth middle-income countries have aggressively snapped up the recycled petro-dollars in the international financial markets, the low-income countries have found it even more difficult and sometimes impossible to obtain general-purpose loans from these private capital markets. This is the reason why it is increasingly being urged that *official* lending, whether bilateral or multilateral, should discriminate in favour of the low-income countries.[56] And to some extent the OECD donors, the World Bank and its soft-loan subsidiary IDA have tried in recent years to redirect their lending to these countries. But the successes of these policies so far are limited, for there are very powerful forces and interests that keep the bulk of official lending directed to the successful middle-income countries.

These forces and interests are those of the international banking community and the international financial bourgeoisie who have become deeply involved with countries of the Third World. Under the pressure of sharpened competition in a highly liquid market and of their own speculative greed, banks and banking consortia have recycled petro-dollars to those developing countries which previously they would have ignored as a bad risk. Further and further they have gone down the slippery slope of aggressive and adventurous lending practices, e.g. massively employing short-term deposits to finance long-term loans, expanding the total volume of credit relative to their funds, concentrating lending amongst clients and extending 'unsecured' loans.[57]

The ensuing fear in financial centres about potential defaults by economically unstable and politically unreliable borrowing countries, and the consequence of such defaults for the entire, highly concentrated and interactive fabric of the financial markets, has driven these nerve-centres of world capitalism straight into the arms of the aid lobby, with whom they have been strange bedfellows ever since. Reminding their governments and their public of the dire domestic economic consequences of bankruptcies and collapse of the integrated and exposed banking world, they suggest that the governments of the creditor countries, as well as official international financial institutions such as the IMF and the World Bank, should come to the aid of their Third World clients and their own capitalists by

(a) massively increasing their official aid programmes, bilateral and multilateral (preferably to the countries in which the banks are 'exposed'); and/or
(b) underwriting and guaranteeing the bankers' adventurist loans.[58]

Many of the bourgeois theorists whom we shall be reviewing in Chapter 4 also advocate a reorganisation of the international monetary order along these lines.[59] One of the attractions of this position is that it is in keeping with some of the radical demands for a New International Economic Order formulated by the Third World itself.[60]

Finally, turning to the characteristics of the sources of credit in the private capital markets, there are novel developments here too. Apart from the sheer expansion in liquidity in these markets, not least because of the placement of some 100 billion 'petro-dollars' between 1973 and 1979 which immediately made the Arab OPEC members the largest *net* contributors to the international banking system,[61] we also discover a relative decline in the presence of the almighty dollar and a gradual diversification of overseas dollar holdings into other currencies. This diversification had started in 1971 with the suspension of the convertibility of the dollar, but the phenomenon has been accelerating more recently. The euro-currency markets (previously called euro-dollar markets) now hold 40 per cent of the recycled petro-currencies instead of 20 per cent as was the case in the post-1973 period.[62]

Since the plan for this present chapter is to display the facts as bare to the bone as possible, and since the reader may feel that I have already gone beyond my brief in the previous paragraph, I refer him to Chapter 6, where the implications of the decline in hegemony of the American dollar and economy for the global political economy are discussed. Let me therefore just summarise this section by listing the most important features of the new world monetary order, as these have emerged in the 1970s:

1. The effective recyling of petro-dollars points to an emerging role of oil surpluses in financing the continued expansion of world trade.
2. There has been a shift in the ultimate source of development capital from the OECD to OPEC.
3. There are diverging patterns of participation in the world monetary order on the part of (some) middle-income countries and low-income countries respectively. While the middle-income countries have become active borrowers in the world's capital markets, the low-income countries have become virtually exclusively reliant on concessionary forms of aid.
4. There has been a significant decline in the position of the dollar *vis-à-vis* the euro-currencies.

The Internationalisation of Production

A new international division of labour

A third prime economic fact of the Second Development Decade has been the development of global enterprises to such a degree that they are now effectuating a qualitative change in the existing world economic order.

Multinational corporations (i.e. economic enterprises with production facilities in more than one country)[63] have existed for a very long time. But what has made them a dominant feature of the recently evolved world economic order is certain cumulative changes in their size, in their number, and in the scope and nature of their activities. These cumulative changes together have added up to a qualitative change in the organisation of the world economy itself, namely one involving a shift away from international trade and towards international production. What we are witnessing is a change from 'world market' to 'world factory'.[64]

Thus far in this presentation of the facts of the Second Development Decade I have stuck fairly closely to the conventional selection and presentation of these facts. The world economy is conventionally seen as consisting of a number of independently producing countries. These countries meet in the world market where they exchange their goods and services at prices determined 'neutrally' by the market forces of supply and demand. The proceeds of these sales are distributed amongst the producing individuals of each country concerned. The success of a nation's performance in the international hierarchy, and hence the *per capita* income of its people, is seen largely as a function of a nation's industriousness at home and its competitiveness abroad. Governments are thought able to affect the national economic performance by adopting and implementing policies designed to encourage industriousness at home and improving the competitive position abroad.

Things, however, are never as they seem. Today, for instance, the four largest *transnational* corporations together have an annual turnover greater than the total GNP of the whole continent of Africa. The top thirty-four companies, with turnovers over 10 billion dollars per year, outdistance the GNPs of some seventy countries normally ranked in the 'world economic hierarchy'. Together these companies have a global production in excess of the total product of some eighty poor countries in which over half of the world population live.[65] All MNCs together employ some 13—14 million people, of which an estimated 3–4 million are in the developing countries.[66] Some of the larger ones with up to 400,000 employees effectively affect[67] the lives of at least as many people as a one-million population nation.

Yet, when reporting on the world economic situation, the World Bank, the IMF, the Bank for International Settlements, the OECD and the UN Economic and Social Council will ignore these global economic enterprises with grim determination. The latter, apparently, are to be considered as 'epiphenomena', best examined and reported on by separate, *ad hoc*, groups of experts, by a specially set up Commission of the United Nations. Despite an abundance of information available on the subject, collected moreover by these same eminent groups of experts (from which I shall quote below), the official annual recording of the world economic situation will simply not mention it.

This is really a most intriguing phenomenon. We have seen how the *World Bank Development Report* (glowingly described by *The Guardian* as the nearest thing to having an annual report on the present state of the planet and the people who live on it)[68] puts a premium on a country's participation in world trade. Indeed, in its view, the rise and fall of nations in the world economic hierarchy is ultimately attested by their participation in international trade. And much of the World Bank's current optimism regarding the middle-income countries' future stems from the observation that they have increased their percentage share of world exports of manufactures from 6 to 10 per cent. Yet as early as 1973 an *ad hoc* group of experts from the United Nations concluded that 'international production defined as production subject to foreign control or decision and measured by the sales of foreign affiliates of multinational corporations has surpassed trade as the main vehicle of international economic exchange'.[69] In that year there were some 10,000 enterprises identifiable as 'multinational' (i.e. firms with at least one foreign affiliate link, even though the link itself can include more than one outlet per host country). It was estimated by UN experts that in 1971 international production reached approximately 330 billion dollars, somewhat larger than the total exports of all market economies. Using the same measures of estimation a second group of experts some five years later put the figure for 1976 at 830 billion dollars.[70]

This is what is meant by 'international production surpassing international trade'. We can appreciate the metaphor of international production being a *vehicle* for international exchanges even better if we consider that national and world trade figures always include, and hence conceal, so-called intra-firm sales, that is, sales between various affiliates of the same multinational group and between these and the parent company. It is estimated that in 1974 nearly half of all imports to the USA and just half of all exports from the USA consisted of such intra-firm transactions. Comparable figures for other OECD countries were, however, lower, putting the figure at one-third of the trade of these countries.[71]

The discrepancy between international production data and international trade data bears out with special penalty for precisely those countries which are most deeply involved in international production, both as 'home' countries and as 'host' countries.

The USA, for example, remains the most important domicile for the headquarters of multinational corporations, particularly if measured by size of firms. In 1976 the foreign affiliates of US companies sold 212 billion dollars worth of goods. This is the equivalent of about one-quarter of total US domestic industrial production.[72] Of the total of affiliate sales 161 billion dollars worth was sold in the foreign countries hosting the affiliates, while 14.1 billion dollars, or 6.6 per cent, was exported to the USA, and 37.7 billion dollars, or 17.7 per cent, was exported to third countries.[73] The latter figure represents, as it were, US 'foreign' exports as opposed to US domestic exports. It is no wonder that when we look at the list of the fifty leading US 'domestic' exporters, we find the real giants of the US business world poorly represented (thirteen out of fifty).[74] After all they are doing their 'exporting' from foreign lands. What this points to, of course, is that there are two American economies in the world: one domestic, one foreign; one the largest, the other about the fifth largest; one officially recorded and statistically represented, the other invisible and statistically absent. The divergence between the USA's domestic economy and its 'foreign' economy has consequences for its position as a 'super power' as well as for the general organisation of the world capitalist economy. This is a central focus of debate amongst Marxist writers on imperialism (see Chapter 6, p. 187).

As for the hosts of international production, here — contrary to popular myth — the Third World *as a group* is not of very great importance. In fact, the role of the Third World (again, as a group) as receiver of foreign direct investment has been steadily declining. In 1960 the Third World accounted for one-half of total direct overseas investments. This percentage had declined to one-third in 1966 and to one-quarter in 1974.[75] Instead, international production has been more and more concentrated in the already advanced market economies, and much of the growth of this international production has been due to the rapid expansion of cross-Atlantic penetration, particularly since the creation of the EEC. This geographical redirection of direct foreign investment has accompanied a reorientation of investments by branch of economic activity. As the investing countries became more industrially developed, so they switched their investments away from raw-material production (and cost-reducing profit strategies) into manufacturing industries (and market-orientated strategies). (See Table 1.17.) This, note, is a *relative* change in investment pattern and not an absolute one, just as the implied decline of the advanced world's dependence on the Third World is also relative and not absolute.

While it is true that the advanced countries have become less dependent on the procurement of agricultural commodities from the Third World, and while technological development has helped them also to reduce their dependence on a variety of raw materials traditionally supplied by the Third World, their vulnerability in respect of a limited range of 'critical' minerals of which certain Third World countries are significant suppliers has increased.[76] In descending order of import dependence, these critical minerals are chromium, tin, cobalt, nickel, petroleum, manganese and bauxite. Of these, the developing countries can be said to control only four major commodity markets at present: again in descending order, tin, bauxite, petroleum and copper (Tables 1.18 and 1.19).[77] Precisely because the number of Third

TABLE 1.17

Accumulated stock of direct investment in developing countries by major industrial sector (1966 and 1974)

	1966	1974
Mining and petroleum	49%	18.6%
Manufacturing	27%	44.0%
Utilities plus services	24%	37.3%

Sources: for the 1966 data see Lester B. Pearson, *Partners in Development* (London: Pall Mall Press, 1970) p. 100;) for the 1974 data see *Transnational Corporations in World Development* (New York: United Nations, 1978) table III, 38 (this table excludes data on Japanese overseas investment).

TABLE 1.18

Dependence on selected imported industrial raw materials, 1975 (imports as a percentage of consumption)

	USA	European Community	Japan
Aluminium (ore and metal)	84	75	100
Chromium	91	98	98
Cobalt	98	98	98
Copper	*	98	90
Iron (ore and metal)	29	55	99
Lead	11	85	73
Manganese	98	99	88
Nickel	72	100	100
Petroleum	37	93	100
Tin	84	93	97
Tungsten	55	100	100
Zinc	61	70	53

* Net exporter.
Source: Council on International Economic Policy, *International Economic Report of the President*, Washington, D.C., January 1977, quoted in W. Arad and Uzi B. Arad, *Sharing Global Resources* (New York: McGraw-Hill, 1979) p. 43.

TABLE 1.19

LDC share in world trade for selected commodities (in percentages)

Tin	86
Bauxite	79
Petroleum	73
Manganese	56
Copper	54
Iron ore	39

Source: Ronald J. Redker (ed.), *Changing Resource Problems of the Fourth World* (Johns Hopkins University Press for Resources for the Future, 1976).

World countries that possess these resources is limited, direct foreign investment in extractive industries generally is concentrated in a limited number of countries. On the other hand, and simultaneously, the relative shift away from investments in extractive industries into manufacturing industries has meant that private capital, when penetrating into developing countries, has become selective in respect of the host countries' potential either as market or as supplier of cheap labour.

Along with the scarce mineral exporters, we find the newly industrialising countries the most favoured recipients of direct foreign investment. Table 1.20 lists those developing countries that at the end of 1977 played host to the largest stock of accumulated private foreign investment. Besides the Bermudas and the Bahamas (which are tax havens) all the countries in the list are either mineral exporters or newly industrialising countries, including India. Between them they accounted for 77 per cent of all outstanding direct foreign investment in 1977. This marks a degree of concentration of direct foreign investment greater than in the preceding decade.[78]

It was observed before that the success of the development performance of the rapidly developing countries was associated with their success in participation in world trade, either as producers of vital resources or as industrialising markets (see

TABLE 1.20

Stock of private overseas direct investments in developing countries,
1977 (principal hosts)

Total of all developing countries = **$84,996 m.**

	$ m.	% of total	Classification
Antibes (Neth.)	2,000	2.3	Mineral exporter
Argentina	2,850	3.3	NIC/mineral exporter
Bahamas	1,470	1.7	Tax haven
Bermuda	4,068	4.7	Tax haven
Brazil	10,700	12.5	NIC/mineral exporter
Chile	1,215	1.4	Mineral exporter
Colombia	1,410	1.6	Mineral exporter
Hong Kong	1,730	2.0	NIC
India	2,450	2.8	Low-income/ industrialising
Indonesia	5,160	6.0	Low-income/mineral exporter
Iran	1,000	1.2	Capital surplus oil exporter
South Korea	1,280	1.5	NIC
Liberia	1,035	1.2	Mineral exporter
Malaysia	2,700	3.1	Mineral exporter/NIC
Mexico	5,070	5.9	Mineral exporter/NIC
Nigeria	1,040	1.2	Mineral exporter
Panama	2,750	3.2	Mineral exporter
Peru	1,930	2.3	Mineral exporter
Philippines	1,620	1.9	NIC
Singapore	1,500	1.7	NIC
Spain	5,114	6.0	NIC
Taiwan	1,720	2.0	NIC
Trinidad and Tobago	1,260	1.5	Mineral exporter
Venezuela	3.300	3.8	Mineral exporter
Zaire	1,110	1.3	Mineral exporter
Sub-total	$65,482 m.	77%	

Source: *OECD 1979 DAC Review* (Paris, 1979) table E.1, pp. 255–6.

pp. 28–9).[79] It is now becoming obvious that to a not insignificant extent this participation in world trade in its turn is a matter of being 'co-opted' into an expanding system of international production. For example, recalling the data on manufacturing exports from developing countries, four NIC countries (South Korea, Taiwan, Spain and Hong Kong) are known to contribute 45 per cent of all manufacturing exports from developing countries, while the NIC as a group plus India are responsible for no less than 80 per cent. Looking at these same countries (in so far as data are available) we discover that the percentage share of multinational companies in the exports of manufactures of these same countries varies from 20 per cent in Taiwan in 1971 to 90 per cent in Singapore in 1976 (see Table 1.21). This leads one to estimate that probably the larger part of Third World export-orientated

TABLE 1.21

Share of multinational companies in the exports of manufactures from selected developing countries

Country	Year	MNC share in the exports of manufactures (%)
South Korea	1974	27.8
Taiwan	1971	20.0
Singapore	1976	90.0
Colombia	1970	35.0
Argentina	1969	30.0
Mexico	1969	25.0
Brazil	1969	43.0

Source: P. K. M. Tharakan, *The International Division of Labour and Multinational Companies* (European Centre for Study and Information on Multinational Corporations, in co-operation with Saxon House, 1979) table 3.3. Tharakan's own sources are as follows: B. I. Cohen, *Multinational Firms and Asian Exports* (Yale University Press, 1975); data on Mexico and Brazil were supplied by G. K. Helleiner; the 1976 figures for Singapore are from the *Singapore Bulletin*, vol. 5, no. 9, May 1977, p. 5.

industrialisation is controlled by multinational corporations with headquarters in the West.[80]

When one transposes such facts of international production on to the picture of Third World differentiation and development described earlier, one may well conclude that what we are witnessing is not so much the rapid industrialisation of certain successfully developing countries, but rather the selection of certain *sites* in the Third World for the purpose of relocation of industrial activity from the advanced countries. What appears from one point of view to be the rapid development of independent countries appears from another angle to be but a new phase in the development of one single world economy. This, for example, is the view taken by Fröbel *et al.* in what is to date the most comprehensive and detailed survey of multinational manufacturing operations in developing countries. One of the more marked aspects of multinational corporate development over the past fifteen years, they argue, has been the setting up of so-called 'world market factories' in certain selected Third World countries. The locations designated for such factories are variously referred to as 'export-processing zones', or 'free producing zones', or 'industrial parks'. On these sites the MNCs have relocated the more labour-intensive parts of their globally fragmented production process in order to benefit from the availability of free and unorganised labour. Fröbel *et al.*, in their extensive investigation into the origins, the pattern of development and the consequences of such industrial relocation, observe that 'whereas scarcely any industrial production for the world market existed in Asia, Africa and Latin America in the mid-1960s, by the middle of the 1970s world market factories were in operation in seventy-nine free production zones in thirty-nine countries and in many sites outside the zones, employing in all 725,000 workers'.[81] To the extent that production in these world market factories is integrated into the MNCs' global production and distribution flows, they accuse it of being next to useless from the point of view of the establishment of an integrated industrial complex in the host countries themselves.[82] Indeed, as if to underscore the disarticulation from the domestic economy, the majority of such export-processing zones are physically separated and fenced off from their surrounding environment.

Not only do industrial relocation plants not contribute to a country's economic development, their initial selection as preferred sites seems also unconnected to the level of economic development already obtained or even the availability of skills and/or other natural endowments. All that matters is whether a country has a cheap and abundant labour force and a government willing to suppress it as well as offer generous tax allowances and profit-remittance legislation.[83]

The changing organisation of international production

It is risky to say anything definitive about trends in international production, because quite apart from the run of the mill problems of reliability inherent in all statistical data collection, we encounter additional problems when studying multinational corporations. For multinational corporations are 'invisible empires' because they are not by convention, or by law, subject to the kind of detailed systematic information-gathering that national account data are. Furthermore, multinational enterprises are like chameleons, adapting their outward appearance and organisational form remarkably swiftly to changes in their respective environments. A good example of this is the way in which multinational corporations in recent years have acquiesced to demands for nationalisation by their Third World hosts. Already, long before the *Charter of Economic Rights and Duties of States* was adopted by the UN General Asssembly in 1974, and gave the practice of nationalisation of foreign enterprises legal status in international law, the mad rush of nationalisations had receded and MNCs were rapidly diversifying into a great many different non-equity or part-equity 'cross-border' arrangements. These novel arrangements included: joint ventures, management agreements and service contracts, licensing and franchise agreements, production-sharing agreements, and sub-contracting. While in 1951 only about one-fifth of 1,276 manufacturing affiliates of 391 MNCs had been established as co-owned or minority-owned affiliates, by 1970 this proportion had risen to over one-half.[84] And in the extractive industries (especially petroleum) the phenomenon of wholly owned or majority-owned subsidiaries has by now become, if not entirely extinct, distinctly rare.

The relative decline of the wholly owned and majority-owned subsidiaries and the emergence of many novel forms of cross-border arrangements between independently owned economic enterprises of course greatly distorts our perception of the size and development of international production. For, when measured by the conventional criterion of 'direct overseas investments' and of 'sales of wholly owned or majority-owned affiliates', it does appear, first, that the rate of growth of international production has stabilised since its meteoric expansion in the 1960s,[85] and that, second, intra-firm trade constitutes a declining phenomenon in trade between rich and poor countries. Since it is the Third World countries and not the advanced countries who are sensitive about the degree of foreign ownership of their domestic economic activities, and demand novel arrangements, we should not be surprised if the statistics tell us that developing countries are increasingly being left out of the process of 'multinational corporatisation' of world trade. Helleiner reckons that between 1967 and 1975 the share of total US imports which originated with US majority-owned affiliates had risen markedly in Europe and Canada, yet had actually fallen in Latin America, Asia and Africa. He, too, puts the blame for this distortion almost entirely on the diversification of the organisational forms of international production.[86]

The crucial issue when contrasting international production data with national development and trade figures is the extent to which nationally owned economic enterprises are *subject to control and decision* by (foreign) multinational enterprises. The question is ultimately who decides what is to be produced, how much of it is to be produced, how it is to be produced, where it shall be sold, at what price, and what shall be done with the proceeds. Earlier estimates of international production had correctly linked this concept of control to ownership of *capital*, as indeed there used to be a close correspondence between the two. But in the course of the last twenty years two developments — one political, the other technological — have interacted upon one another in such a manner as to permit a far greater separation of owner-ship and control. In a bid for national economic liberation and acting upon the belief, correct at the time, that owner-ship of capital conveys control, host governments of Third World countries demanded an *equity* stake in the foreign companies operating on their soil. Multinational corporations, for their part, responded by developing novel forms of organisation that did not require formal ownership of the capital of the subsidiary operations but instead hinged upon the parent company's *formal ownership of the product* as this is protected by international patent law. This product could be either an end-product or a technological operation, a piece of 'know-how' or a producer good. Contractual agreements (licence and franchise agreements as well as management and service contracts) between the parent com-pany and the ex-affiliate would specify in minute detail all manner of plant operations, production and sales. The agree-ments would cover anything ranging from production volume and product range to tied purchase clauses, transfer prices, sale and export markets, use of personnel, etc.[87]

It did not take long before host governments realised that economic control over their enterprises remained as elusive as ever, and soon the corridors of the international organisa-tions and conferences were chanting the calls for inter-national codes of conduct for MNCs and even for radical changes in the Paris Convention on International Patent Rights.[88] To date several such draft Codes have been pre-pared by international groups of experts for UNCTAD, for the ILO, for the OECD and for the UN Department of Economic and Social Affairs (see p. 85). Although the chances for international ratification remain slim, that is not really important. The drafting exercise itself has been very enlightening and educational for host governments. Equipped with a growing arsenal of documents on the nature and scope of 'restrictive' practices, many Third World hosts are now operating a sophisticated screening process of all contracts with MNCs.[89]

However, what is enlightening to some is, of course, equally enlightening to others. As host governments scrutinised con-tractual agreements, so MNCs began to prepare to abandon them. There is now some evidence of yet a new practice by parent companies involving the *relocation* of control over their foreign operations away from their 'legal' ownership of the product, and towards the *technological properties* of that product. By making the physical characteristics of their plant and machinery, of their technical operations, and of their end-product, critically different from other similar machinery, processes and products that are available in the world markets, MNCs can establish and preserve future supply, servicing and maintenance links quite independently of any written agreement or any form of legal ownership. In other words, contractual restrictions are being replaced by 'technology-embodied' restrictions, as (for example) when the MNC plans the technological indivisibility of the 'package' it sells to its subsidiaries.[90]

In this way technological dependence has begun to take over where first political dependence, and then economic dependence, have left off. Ironically it is the very ownership of the equity capital of foreign operations that make Third World hosts (be they governments or individual entrepreneurs) unable and unwilling to resist this technological dependence. It would indeed be the height of financial folly if they were to buy up a foreign establishment and next strip it of all its physical apparatus and equipment so as to shop around for 'alternative' technology on a world-wide basis.

For the MNCs the ultimate purpose of effective control is the ability to appropriate the surplus produced by the subsidiaries. Whether this is for purposes of enhancing the growth and viability of the corporation or in order to pay handsome dividends to the parent firms' stockholders is beside the point here.

With the shifting location of control just described have come different methods of appropriation of surplus by the parent firm from its subsidiaries. In the days when control was firmly rooted in the parent company's ownership of the affiliate's capital, surplus appropriation took the familiar route of payments of dividends to the shareholders (e.g. the parent firm) requiring the remittance of profits overseas to wherever the MNC's headquarters were located. With the divestment of equity to bodies or persons outside the MNC's corporate circuit came new methods of surplus appropriation. The traditional profit and loss account lost its status as a financial record of the affiliate's performance and the concept of 'profit' became meaningless. Profits could be arbitrarily adjusted downwards depending on the degree to which cost items consisting of a variety of financial payments to the parent (e.g. royalties, interests on loans from the parent, loans *to* the parent, 'transfer prices' for tied purchases from the parent or any of its other subsidiaries, management costs, service and maintenance payments, etc.) were increased. The discovery of these 'hidden' transfers occasioned vigorous research activity, especially on the part of scholars from Latin America, where 54 per cent of all Third World foreign investments are located. An epoch-making study by Vaitsos in 1970 set the scene.[91] He discovered that, for example, in the pharmaceutical industry in Colombia as little as 3.4 per cent of the effective returns to the parent company consisted of 'declared profits'. Another 14 per cent was accounted for by royalty payments and 82.6 per cent was contributed by the parent company's 'over-pricing' of its sales to the affiliates. Clearly, then, an important conclusion from this is that *trade earnings are rapidly replacing traditional 'invisible' earnings* such as declared profits and royalty payments as method of surplus appropriation by parent companies of their affiliates. To the extent, furthermore, that defensive legislation on the part of host governments in order to counter the abuses of 'over-pricing' in intra-company trade and in order generally to dismantle the contractual purchasing links between affiliates and parents have been successful, it is now encouraging a degree of 'technological overspecification' of products and producer goods that completes the process of replacement of invisible earnings by trade earnings.[92]

Considerations of a similar kind apply to primary production. International extractive industries are typically small in number and consist of vertically integrated firms. They direct their output according to the global requirements of the parent firm or of major customers linked by long-term contract. Because they control market outlets, it has proved often hard for a country which has nationalised its raw-material production to sell large quantities of the material, even disregarding the question of a collective boycott by potential purchasers.[93]

In conclusion, it is useful to compare the recent developments in international production, notably the apparent decline of overseas investments in Third World countries, its concentration in the rapidly growing Third World countries, the separation of ownership and control and the new methods of surplus appropriation, with the facts on international borrowing presented earlier in this chapter. For, as the 1977 World Bank report notes in a remarkably perceptive passage, there is a connection between declining direct overseas investments in the Third World on the one hand, and the phenomenal expansion of *bank lending* to the Third World (or rather, the rapidly growing countries of the Third World) on the other:

With the steady growth of direct foreign investment in developing countries, the larger banks also became active in developing countries, firstly on behalf of their corporate clients who were investing in these countries and then directly on their own account. For large projects *syndicated loans became increasingly common, replacing, at least in part, equity investment.* The principal transformation came in lending for mineral exploitation. There were at least two reasons. Firstly, mineral and associated processing projects were becoming larger. But more importantly, investors wanted to reduce their equity exposure. As developing countries began to increase the share of resource rents they wished to appropriate, returns to equity were regarded as profits and were therefore taxable, whereas interest on loans was a cost and therefore deductible from taxable income. Countries which nationalized their mineral resources were only interested in loans, not in equity participation. Mineral-rich countries thus became heavy borrowers in private markets, where previously they had accepted equity capital. But whereas returns to equity capital fluctuated with changes in mineral prices, service obligations on loans were fixed, creating liquidity problems in price downswings [my emphasis].[94]

Instead of viewing Third World governments' nationalisation programmes with dismay, the MNCs were smart enough to realise that local participation in their overseas affiliates opened up still greater opportunities for making super-profits, and (what is more) without carrying any additional risk. When viewed in this context there are two more developments in the 1970s worth noting: (i) the phenomenal increase in direct overseas investments in developing countries by the *banking* sector (see Table 1.17, under 'utilities and services', 50 per cent of which represents banking),[95] and (ii) the intensification of the process of integration of bank capital with industrial capital, again more particularly noteworthy inside the Third World.[96] As one observer put it, 'the dyke which separates the land of banking from the sea of commerce has sprung a leak'.[97] Swollen with recycled petrodollars, banks have increasingly ventured into non-banking activities overseas, while conversely multinational industrial companies have acquired banking interests.

2

Political Responses: The Rise and Fall of Third World Solidarity

In the introduction I said that I would be reviewing what has been happening to the Third World in world development:

(a) at the level of economic realities;
(b) at the level of international political responses; and
(c) at the level of theoretical appraisals.

The period under study is the 1970s, that is, the Second United Nations Development Decade.

One problem that this form of presentation brings into focus is that there is always a time lag between what is happening at the economic base on the one hand and at the level of the institutionalisation of political purposes on the other. Economic realities tend always to move faster than political responses and theoretical interpretations. We are forever running behind the facts and this time lag becomes even more pronounced when we deal with global affairs. The sheer magnitude of the economic phenomena, the material diffi-culties in processing global information, in reporting and dis-seminating this information, and the inertia of political organisations, parties and communities in redirecting their attention and energies, and — even more time-consuming — in building new alliances in order to address the new economic realities, all this is bound to lead to a time lag of at least five to ten years.

It is one of the main themes of this chapter that the politi-cal solidarity amongst Third World countries which found its climax and its clearest expressions yet in the formal demands for a New International Economic Order in 1974 (and these demands themselves) has been largely overtaken by the turn of economic events in the last decade. What is more, in so far as these demands are still on the negotiating tables in the 'North—South dialogue', they are being gradually appropriated by a new political alignment, namely that of global institutions and corporations on the one hand, and the states of the fast-growing developing countries inside the Third World on the other. This appropriation of the NIEO demands also involves a reformulation of these demands to reflect more accurately the present-day needs of the global capitalist system.

The History of Third World Solidarity

We can trace two lines of development in the history of Third World solidarity. At first running independently of each other, they later begin to converge, and finally merged at the special session of the UN General Assembly 1974 in the *Declaration of the Establishment of a New International Economic Order*. One line of development is that of the 'non-aligned movement', which really began in 1955, at the Bandung Conference of African and Asian countries. There, the recently decolonised nations of the world met for the first time *as a group*, and recognised their communality of interests as both ex-colonial and as underdeveloped countries. They proclaimed a common identity distinct from the two advanced industrial worlds, namely the capitalist world on the one hand, and the socialist world on the other: they were a *third* world. Although they decided on collective action to be taken *vis-à-vis* certain economic issues such as the stabilisation of international prices and demand for their primary export commodities, the principal concern and the significance of the Bandung Conference was *political*. Its energies were devoted to political issues of anti-colonialism, the setting up of a non-aligned movement, the solidarity of the Third World, and on getting a political say for the non-aligned countries in international fora. This preoccupation with political issues was also a distinctive characteristic of the non-aligned conferences in Belgrade in 1961, Cairo in 1964, and Lusaka in 1970. Latin American countries did not partake in the non-aligned movement until 1973, when Peru and Argentina became members.[1]

The second historical line springs from Latin America, where the countries had had a longer experience with the frustrating combine of political independence and economic underdevelopment. Under the inspiring intellectual leadership of Raoul Prebisch,[2] who wrote the founding script for what was eventually to grow into a programme for a New International Economic Order, they concentrated from the start on the *economic* relationship existing between the advanced world and the underdeveloped world. Prebisch's work *Towards a New Trade Policy for Development*[3] (a seminal version of which had been published as early as 1950) dismissed the leading orthodoxy of the day, namely the *theory of comparative advantage*. This theory of international trade says that it is in the best interest of each country to maximise production of those commodities which it produces most efficiently or most cheaply and to import what it cannot produce efficiently. Prebisch argued that this theory was not applicable in the context of the existing international division of labour in which poor countries traded unprocessed primary commodities for manufactures from the West. Instead of bringing universal prosperity, as most economists maintained, it only led to persistent and ever-growing inequality between the rich and poor countries.[4] (For a lengthier discussion of his analysis, see Chapter 5.)

Throughout the 1950s the scholars of the Economic Commission for Latin America (ECLA), of which Prebisch was the director, elaborated this theme of trade-generated inequality and its consequence, structural underdevelopment.[5] The ground was being prepared for a demand for *economic concessions* from the advanced countries, in the form of a bureaucratic *intervention* in the sacred cow of the free world market. In 1962, at the behest of the non-aligned nations, the UN General Assembly approved a resolution calling for a world-wide conference on trade and development. The first UN Conference on Trade and Development, held at Geneva in 1964, was a landmark in the history of Third World solidarity precisely because it was here for the first time that Third World countries confronted the rich countries *as a group*, demanding certain economic reforms in the world economic order (i.e. price stabilisation and improvement for primary products, market access for manufactures from developing countries and greater financial flows from the rich to the poor countries).[6] At that conference a caucus group was formed of seventy-seven underdeveloped countries (the Group of 77). Throughout the decade the Group of 77 (eventually enlarged to 120 countries) played a key role in formulating a 'Third World' perspective on the world economic situation, and in defining a unified response from the Third World on matters of economic development and trade. In this they were greatly assisted by a network of very prolific Third World scholars who themselves worked on the staff of specialised agencies such as the World Bank, the ILO and UN special bodies (UNDP, UNIDO, UNCTAD). (The network became an officially established association only in 1975.)[7] In the years that followed these intellectuals would play a considerable role in forging a convergence between the global institutions' perspectives on world *development* and Third World perspectives on the world *economy*. For, in the course of the late 1960s and the 1970s, the 'Third Worldist' analysis of the inbuilt structural inequalities of the world *economy* began to make sense to those institutions, be they administrative or academic, whose main concern was closely bound up with long-term world economic *development*. As a result, even the World Bank turned into a global social democrat once it had fully understood that the poor of the world would present a serious bottleneck to future world economic growth (see also Chapter 5, pp. 137ff, on global Keynesianism).

Owing to the unity of the Group of 77, and despite opposition from the advanced countries, UNCTAD graduated from a one-off conference to a special body of the United Nations. The significance of this was that the disadvantaged position of the developing countries in world economic relations had now become an ongoing concern of the United Nations. Moreover, the decision to make UNCTAD directly responsible to the General Assembly (which implies the opportunity to bring resolutions and recommendations directly to the General Assembly rather than to ECOSOC, in which the developing countries did not yet have a voting majority) proved to be advantageous. The developing countries could view UNCTAD as a means of circumventing developed country control of the various international financial institutions, a control which was ensured through weighted voting. UNCTAD thus became the institutional forum of the LDCs: it was *their* agency.

The themes of UNCTAD II, held in New Delhi in 1968, echoed those of UNCTAD I and did not add any new ones. Rather, UNCTAD II tried to formulate concrete proposals for the implementation of the recommendations of UNCTAD I. The success of UNCTAD in effecting changes in world economic relations was strictly limited, and arguably, inasmuch as there was a success, this may well be put down to the changing needs of the world capitalist economy itself. Concretely, the generalised system of preferences (GSPs) which provided for a lowering of tariffs on imports by developed countries of bilaterally agreed semi-manufactures and manufactures from developing countries, was indeed eventually implemented by the advanced countries, but the lists of goods covered by these GSPs were suspect for their inclusion of those products which originated in MNC-controlled branches of industry in the Third World, and for their exclusion of those products more likely to come from domestically owned industries as well as processed agricultural products.[8]

As for the much-discussed price-stabilisation measures, such as financing of 'buffer stocks' in commodities like tin, cocoa and sugar (which were already governed by individual commodity agreements), the developed countries refused to contribute to the financial base needed to make them a reality.

UNCTAD III, held at Santiago in 1972, included, alongside the old demands, two new themes as well as a taste of new tactics to come.[9] One new theme was that of the *international monetary order*. The immediate cause for its inclusion in UNCTAD's concerns had been the monetary crisis of 1971 precipitated by President Nixon's declaration of the inconvertibility of the dollar, the effective devaluation of the dollar that followed, and the ensuing intense discussions by the Group of 10 (advanced nations only) on the reform of the international monetary system. Having thus once again had their noses rubbed into their own impotence and insignificance in respect of how the world economy was run, the Group of 77 (now consisting of ninety-eight nations) at UNCTAD III demanded full and equal participation in discussions and decisions concerning international monetary reforms. The second theme was that of the *power of the multinational corporations*. Against the local backdrop of Chile's very recent nationalisation of its two US-based copper companies, the multinational corporations too were singled out for attention. The exceptionally rapid growth of MNCs in the previous decade at last blasted into the consciousness of everyone studying international economic relations, and the first calls for some global supervision of MNCs were made.[10]

But much more important, UNCTAD III decided to adopt new tactics in its confrontation between rich and poor countries. The Group of 77 realised that UNCTAD would always remain a 'talk shop'[11] and that it lacked the bargaining power to force change on the economically more powerful nations of the world. It would be better if the Third World placed the issues before them *directly* on the agenda of the United Nations, where meanwhile they had grown into a comfortable two-thirds majority. President Luis Echeverria of Mexico masterminded a plan to *codify* the aspirations of the Third World in international law and — by analogy with the *Declaration of Human Rights* — have it accepted by the General Assembly of the United Nations as a *Charter of Economic Rights and Duties of States*. UNCTAD III took up this suggestion of translating the principles governing international economic relationships into a legal instrument.[12] It instructed a working party to prepare such a Charter for submission to the UN General Assembly and to incorporate in it nearly all the demands that the developing countries had made so far in previous international fora.

While UNCTAD was becoming politicised, the non-aligned movement (now counting seventy-five member states compared with twenty-five in Belgrade in 1961) for its part was shifting the parameters of discussion too, but in the opposite direction: from political to economic grounds, from 'colonial' oppression to confrontation between 'rich' and 'poor' countries. The resolutions adopted at Algiers in 1973 represented formal recognition by the non-aligned countries that their problems were not only a function of their political status but also of their economic status. Having elaborated the concept of 'self-reliance' at Lusaka (1970), they now recognised that self-reliance unless embedded in a framework of altered world economic relations was just so much pie in the sky.[13]

The Algiers resolutions entitled 'Economic Declaration' and 'Action Program for Economic Co-operation' graduated to become, often line by line, the *Declaration on the Establishment of a New International Economic Order*. This, and the accompanying *Program of Action*,[14] were adopted without a vote at the Sixth Special Session of the UN General Assembly in May 1974,[15] and were confirmed in November 1974 in the *Charter of Economic Rights and Duties of States*, which was accepted by a majority vote at the 29th annual session of the UN General Assembly.[16] (One hundred and twenty countries voted for, six voted against and ten abstained — the latter sixteen being all free-market developed countries minus Sweden, New Zealand and Australia, which joined the Third World vote along with the socialist countries.) Although the *Declaration* and the *Program of Action* on the one hand, and the *Charter* on the other, address the same issues in much the same way, their respective status is different. While the former two are declarations of intent to work for a New International Economic Order, the latter is a codification of agreed principles on which such a new order should be based.

The preparations for the Sixth Special Session (the first ever Special Session in the history of the United Nations convened to address *economic* problems) and again for the 29th annual General Assembly saw the *de facto* merger of UNCTAD's Group of 77 and the non-aligned movement, if not in membership, at least in programme and objectives.[17] But what completed the Third World's solidarity and what gave it the confidence to proceed from an informal caucus position to the central stage of international negotiations was undoubtedly the success with which OPEC (whose members were themselves members of the Group of 77) in late 1973 had unilaterally raised the prices of their export commodity, oil. The Algerian Minister of Foreign Affairs, Bouteflika, whose President Boumedienne, acting as President in office of the group of non-aligned countries, had formally requested the UN Secretary-General to convene the Sixth Special Session, summed up the mood:

> We know now that they[the developing countries] do not need to depend on the charity of others but have the means to take their destinies and their resources into their own hands.[18]

The Third World's demands for a New International Economic Order stretched over a wide range of issues (e.g. trade, industrialisation, international finance, food and agriculture, science and technology) but were all too weakly supported by the following two bargaining assumptions: first, the alleged extent of the dependence of industrial nations on the Third World's raw materials; and second, the continued willingness of capital-surplus oil exporters to throw their weight and their money behind Third World demands. In the years that followed much of the negotiating tactics on the part of the industrialised countries would be directed towards undermining precisely these two assumptions.

The New International Economic Order: Confrontation

Many texts have been written on the NIEO, including some excellent ones, so it suffices here to describe the NIEO demands in broad outline only. In this section I concentrate on the demands as they were originally formulated by the Group of 77. But I first consider the *Charter*. Besides affirming certain *fundamental* principles of international relations which did not cause insurmountable friction between rich and poor countries, e.g. sovereignty, non-agression, non-intervention, peaceful coexistence, equality of all states, and access to seaports for land-locked countries, the *Charter* stipulates *two new sets of general principles*:

(1) *Those revolving around the economic rights of states.* These include national sovereignty over natural resources, over foreign properties and transnational companies, the right to nationalisation and the right to regulate the compensation to be given for the nationalised goods and properties. These principles present a departure from existing international law, which so far had recognised only nationalisation with the duty to pay 'appropriate' compensation in accordance with international law.[19] It is this particular article that generated the most dissension.

(2) *Those revolving around the economic duties of states, more especially of the developed states.* The *Charter* clearly aims to achieve equality in international economic relations. It expresses this aim (i) by giving one-sided advantages to developing countries, e.g. interventionism and discrimination in the market in favour of the developing countries, and (ii) by placing on the developed countries the obligation to redress the existing unequal economic power structure, e.g. reorganising the decision structure of international financial organisations such as the IMF and the World Bank, increasing *net* transfers of resources to the developing countries, and ensuring the access of developing countries to science and technology in a manner that is in accordance with their development objectives and needs.

If the *Charter*, as it were, captures the 'spirit' of the NIEO, and the *Program of Action* outlines the directions in which the NIEO should be developed, we must look for the *concretisation* and *detailing* of the proposals to a number of important other international fora and conventions that took place in the middle of the decade. I shall highlight the principal ones in each of the main areas of NIEO demands.

International trade reforms

Given that the developing countries as a whole still derive some 80 per cent of their export earnings from the exports of primary commodities, and that, furthermore, the majority of these commodities have experienced a secular (i.e. long-term) deterioration in value in relation to the value of manufactures, it is small wonder that international trade relations are the priority item on the NIEO agenda.

At a Dakar meeting of 'Developing Countries on Raw Materials' in 1975 very radical resolutions were adopted. It was proposed that developing countries should set up producers' associations modelled after OPEC, and that they should establish a *solidarity fund* to finance buffer stocks.

The UNCTAD IV Conference in Nairobi in 1976 modified and enlarged these proposals in its plan for an *integrated commodity programme*. The details for this programme were:

(a)   the establishment of internationally owned stocks covering eighteen commodities;
(b)   the establishment of a common financing fund (a solidarity fund) that would make resources available for the acquisition of stocks;
(c)   the institution, in circumstances which justify it, of a system of medium- to long-term commitments to purchase and sell commodities at agreed prices;
(d)   the institution of more adequate measures (than existing at present) to provide compensatory financing to producers to cover shortfalls in export earnings; and
(e)   the initiation of an extensive programme of measures to further the processing of commodities by the producer countries themselves.

The strength of this programme lay in its *integrated* nature. Only when taken together would these various mechanisms stabilise the earnings of developing countries from their commodity exports at adequate levels and in real terms.[20]

At a UNIDO conference in 1974 in Lima the Group of 77 adopted proposals for a *global redistribution of world industry*. It called on the developed world to assist the developing countries to increase their percentage share of world industrial production from the present 7 per cent to 25 per cent by the end of the century. This target was soon to become widely known as the 'Lima target'. Developed countries should assist by *liberalising the general system of preferences* (giving preferential access to their markets to manufactures from developing countries without demanding a similar preferential treatment in return) and by adopting *industrial readjustment* policies. These are policies designed to compensate domestic manufacturers for loss of earnings due to competition from Third World countries, and to encourage these domestic manufacturers to enter into new product lines and/or branches of industry.[21]

International monetary reform

Until 1971 the world's monetary affairs were governed by the Bretton Woods agreement of 1945, so named after the village of Bretton Woods in the USA where the agreement was reached. The Bretton Woods agreement provided for fixed currency values expressed in terms of dollars and gold. When the system broke down in 1971 after the dollar had been declared no longer convertible into gold, it was replaced by a system of floating exchange rates. Since the currencies of most developing countries were pegged to a reserve currency (i.e. a currency of one of the major rich countries) they thus found themselves unhappily floating upwards or downwards due to forces outside their control.

The International Monetary Fund was set up at Bretton Woods to manage the world monetary system; its priority was to assist the ironing out of global balance-of-payments surpluses and deficits that inevitably arise in a world where one country's trade gains are another country's trade losses. The unit of account used by the IMF, more especially since 1971, is the Special Drawing Right (SDR). SDRs are determined by reference to a 'basket' of currencies.

The IMF's Articles of Agreement reflect beautifully the truism that wealth begets power, and power begets wealth. For member countries can — as of right — only borrow from the IMF an amount that is in direct ratio to their subscription (quota) to it, and their voting power, too, is related to this subscription. If they wish to borrow more than they are entitled to, they have to submit themselves to conditions set by the IMF. Of the 141 member countries, the 114 Third

World countries have together about 36 per cent of the vote. Decisions affecting most of the IMF's rules require three-fifths of the members and 85 per cent of the voting power. The obverse of this is that the USA alone, with over 15 per cent of the vote, can block any major proposal for change.[22]

At the IMF Conference in Kingston, Jamaica, in 1976, the developing countries pressed for the following reforms: a change, in their favour, of the IMF's imbalanced voting structure; increased allocation of Special Drawing Rights to them so they could peg their currencies to SDRs; and the linking of these SDRs to development financing.[23]

Transfer of resources and debt relief

The disappointing aid performance of the developed countries during the 1960s and early 1970s, when aid flows fell well short of the official UN target of 0.7 per cent of GNP of donor countries, has led to repeated claims by Third World countries — in every meeting and every forum — to again fix *a minimum target of official transfers at 0.7 per cent by 1980.* The developing countries have also called for *minimum targets of food aid* and for the establishment of an International Fund for Agricultural Development (IFAD). Developing countries have suggested, furthermore, the need for *substantial increases in the capital of the World Bank*, in particular of its soft-loan agency, IDA, so as to increase the flows of concessional lending to the poorest countries. They have also pleaded for *debt-service payments on official loans* to the 'most seriously affected' countries (MSAs) *to be waived* for the remainder of the decade.[24]

Interestingly the negotiations for transfers or resources are the only NIEO negotiations where the developing countries have been willing to differentiate between different groups of developing countries. The consensus is that the poorest countries should be 'official aid targets', while the middle-income countries should be given easier access to the world's private capital markets. The international recession, which affected their export earnings, the absence of a satisfactory system of compensatory finance to help them offset the loss in foreign exchange earnings, and the dismal level of aid, have all resulted in many developing countries seeking commercial loans on competitive terms and conditions (e.g. high interest rates, and short- to medium-term maturities). These middle-income countries are now asking the developed countries to help them *refinance their debt payments* by the setting up of an international fund that will have the function of refinancing for a certain period of time the service payments on their commercial debts which carry original maturities from one to ten years.

Regulating the transfer of technology

With less than 5 per cent of modern technology originating in the developing countries, and an estimated annual bill for 1.5 billion dollars for patents, licences, know-how and trade-marks to pay for technology coming from the advanced countries,[25] it is not surprising that the concern with technological dependency has featured prominently on the NIEO agenda. The fact that some 75 per cent of technology transfers to the Third World are channelled through multinational corporations, whose operations are recognised to be frequently in conflict with domestic development needs and priorities, explains why the technology debate has revolved around the drafting of codes of conduct for multinationals. At the behest of UNCTAD, an intergovernmental group of experts set out to prepare a draft 'Code of Conduct on Transfer of Technology', to be submitted to UNCTAD IV in Nairobi, and, when no conclusions could be reached there, to be revised and resubmitted to a plenipotentiary conference under UNCTAD's auspices held in Geneva in 1977. Meanwhile the group of 77, meeting at Manila in 1976 to prepare for the Nairobi conference, had drafted its proposals for a 'compulsory' code which it submitted to the intergovernmental group.[26] Besides demanding a *legally binding code for regulating the conduct of MNCs*, the Group of 77 also called for a *review and a revision of the international patent system* in such a manner that developing countries would be able to use patented processes relevant to their needs, and at nominal charges.[27] It also called for assistance from the developed countries for *special 'technology treatment'* to help strengthen the indigenous technological base of the developing countries.

Economic co-operation amongst developing countries: collective self-reliance

The failure of the existing international economic order to solve the problems of poverty and economic backwardness of the Third World has imparted a sense of urgency to the need for developing countries to reduce their dependence on the developed centres and to reorientate their development strategy on the basis of their collective self-reliance. To this end the NIEO plan of action and various UNCTAD conferences have discussed, be it minimally, measures of trade and economic co-operation between developing countries,[28] while the *Charter* asserts the right of developing countries to 'grant trade preferences to other developing countries without being obliged to extend such preferences to developed states'.[29] The theme of economic co-operation has two aspects: first the notion of co-operation for the purpose of enhancing the developing countries' 'collective bargaining' power *vis-à-vis* the outside world; and second, the notion of intensifying trade and other linkages.[30] Although some progress has been made in respect of the latter objective (trade among developing countries in the 1970s grew faster than the trade between the developing countries and the advanced world) and although recently some special conferences have addressed the problem of economic co-operation and collective self-reliance,[31] it is still the case that this item of the NIEO agenda is the least elaborated of the NIEO demands in all relevant fora and discussions. In my opinion the reason for this is that the need for collective self-reliance reveals the Achilles heel of the NIEO ideology. It is an ideology uneasily balanced upon contradictory principles: greater *inter*dependence between rich and poor world, and *in*dependence from the rich world; better links with the rich world, and de-linking from it.[32] And for the time being the balance is in favour of the former. The NIEO demands do not call for a radical transformation of the world-wide system of economic production and exchange, which – so they none the less claim – has led to their exploitation and poverty. All that the developing countries want is better opportunities for participating in it. They are like beginner-golf players who want the better golf players to accept a handicap. They do not wish to stop playing golf.

Marxist analyses have neither informed nor inspired the NIEO demands. Far from it. The NIEO inherently accepts the mutuality of benefits from trade and foreign investment and rejects Marxist contentions of inevitable exploitation.[33] It is indeed the view of both right-wing and left-wing critics of the NIEO that whatever NIEO is, it is neither radical nor Marxist.[34] There is no questioning of a system that produces for profit in the market irrespective of whether the things produced meet human needs or wants. There is no questioning of a system that by its own logic is driven to allocate nearly half of its R & D budget and half of its scientists to produce arms instead of bread, jobs, schools and hospitals. There is no questioning of a system of production that is based upon (i) the exploitation of labour and (ii) the competition between exploiters of labour with the result (iii) that it is forced to replace labour by capital, ultimately leading to (iv) contradictions of over-production and under-consumption, etc. etc. The NIEO demands concentrate exclusively on the *exchange* relations of the world capitalist system and ignore totally the *production* relations of that system. It is for this reason not possible to classify it as a Marxist approach. But this is precisely also the reason why the advanced capitalist countries, once they had overcome their initial reaction of shock and hostility, were soon to realise that the NIEO demands, or at any rate a moderated version of them, could actually strengthen the existing world capitalist system.

The New International Economic Order: Conciliation

The Sixth Special Session of the United Nations and the 29th Annual Session, both held in 1974, had been exclusively Third World Affairs. The reaction of the Western industrialised

countries to the NIEO demands was at first cool and negative, as in the case of the European countries and Japan,
or openly hostile, as in the case of the USA. Their tactic
immediately following the adoption of the *Charter* was to
try and drive a wedge between OPEC and the rest of the
developing countries by calling for an energy conference to
be held in late 1975 in Paris, with delegates from oil-producing
countries, oil-consuming developed countries and oil-consuming developing countries. But at the preparatory session
for this conference it became clear that the OPEC's solidarity
with the rest of the Third World was holding: they refused to
talk about oil except in the context of a wider NIEO agenda
that included other raw materials, reform of the international
monetary system and international co-operation in favour of
development. Within a month after the failing of the preparatory session, the USA, with the rest of the industrialised
nations in tow, moderated its position, and under the diplomatic genius of the US Secretary of State, Henry Kissinger,
adopted a more intelligent long-term strategy while deploying
successful time-buying tactics in the medium term.

These *tactics* included:

(a)   A *watering down of resolutions* to vaguer and more abstract terminology. And next:

(b)   The suggestion that the *hard details be worked out elsewhere*, in technical committees, newly set up organisations, etc. As Hveem points out, the objective of the
tactics of changing a political issue into a technical
matter is 'to get the hot burning issues out of the fire'.[35]
For the industrialised nations this has the additional
advantage that, being so few in number, there is a great
overlap of membership on various technical sub-com-
mittees studying and negotiating different aspects of the
NIEO. In this way the industrialised nations can maintain and monitor a cohesive over-all approach more
easily than the developing world, which — numbering so
many countries — finds itself scattered and dispersed,
and hence has greater difficulty in achieving inter-issue
co-ordination. Connected with this tactic is:

(c)   *The fragmentation of the integated NIEO programme.*
This has been a constant feature of the industrialised

countries' approach, most notably in their opposition to the integrated commodity programme. The industrialised countries prefer to negotiate on a commodity-by-commodity basis, just as they prefer to separate the issues of industrialisation from technology transfer, financial transfers from monetary reform, and so on. Separating the issues for 'technical' reasons has the political effect of eroding the cohesion of the Third World, as issues will affect different countries in different ways.

(d) *The institutionalisation of the dialogue.* This is the time-buying tactic. The longer the negotiations continue, the greater the chances that potential economic differences between the Third World countries (notably the effects of oil price increases on the oil-importing developing countries) will take their toll, and erode the communality of interests on which their solidarity is based.

The Kissinger *strategy* (as distinct from the tactics), inasmuch as it can be reconstructed as a coherent strategy from public statements and relevant documents in the NIEO period, seems to have had two key components: *global efficiency* and *embourgeoisement*.[36] The principal concept of global efficiency surfaced within US administrative circles soon after the demise of the Paris preparatory talks and the failure of the confrontation tactics. 'There was a growing appreciation that parts of the new international economic order were not necessarily inimical to the interests of the industrial nations',[37] says one analyst of the relevant US discussion documents at the time. In particular, it was appreciated that the strengthening of the *existing* world economic order was conditional upon sustained Third World economic growth and raw-material production.[38] The latter would be especially threatened in a climate of hostility and confrontation. And, while the consensus amongst policy-makers in the industrial countries held that 'OPEC's experience should be regarded as unique rather than as a situation that can be generalised',[39] it was yet admitted that other raw-material-producing Third World countries also had some potentially disruptive power in commodity markets. More importantly, the escalating costs and risks (political as well as financial and technological) involved in present and future raw-material explorations undermined the capability of private enterprises to control and manage international raw-material markets, and pressed for some form of 'intergovernmental management of world markets'.[40] As one writer sums it up:

> From a global efficiency perspective there has risen, in other words, a moderate concern over optimizing world raw material resources by doing more in those developing states where there are rich and accessible deposits of natural resources, an interest in stabilizing Third World export earnings through a liberalization of compensatory financing schemes, a willingness to discuss international assistance to public and private raw material investors, a new willingness to consider means of improving access to existing credit facilities to defray balance of payments crises and interest in expanding foreign assistance burden sharing responsibilities with a restructuring of roles in international organizations.[41]

In other words, the perspective of global efficiency has in turn given rise to a perspective of global Keynesianism (e.g. the idea that some marginal resource transfers to the Third World are necessary in the interests of the advanced world, because the latter needs the Third World as a source of raw materials and as a market for industrial products).

Let me hasten to add that we do not owe this global efficiency and Keynesianism to the genius of Kissinger alone. Very interestingly, the year 1973 saw — besides the triumph of OPEC and Third World solidarity — the formation of another, less obtrusive, political alliance, namely the Trilateral Commission.[42] This brainchild of the American oil magnate and financier David Rockefeller which was delivered to the world by midwife Brezinski (later to become Secretary of State under President Carter) embodies simply an alliance between international big business, enlightened national political elites, and leading lights of international organisations. As one commentator puts it, 'The Trilateral Commission is the executive Committee of Transnational Finance Capital.'[43] The name 'Trilateral' was chosen to express the desire to overcome inter-imperialist rivalries between the USA (at the time a declining imperialist power) and the EEC and Japan (both rising stars).

The Commission, consisting of some 200 members and a host of eminent advisers, meets about once a year. Its work is made up of *Task Force Reports* on topics of current interest, monetary policy, energy, relations with the developing countries, trade, etc., all held together by one single theme: how to make the world safe for 'interdependence', interdependence being the new euphemism for 'transnational investment'. The *trilateral process* in the production of each report involves an exhaustive collection and exchange of views from leading academic, political and business people on each of the three continents, interspersed with 'brainstorming sessions', interim report meetings, and so on.[44] The objective is clearly to uncover some existing 'trilateral' consensus opinion – or if it is absent, to create one.

The recommendations contained in the reports which the Trilateral Commission published during the height of the NIEO season in the middle of the decade closely resemble – indeed may well have ideologically informed – the conciliatory 'community of interests' speech made by Kissinger to the Seventh Special Session of the United Nations in 1975 in which he bombarded the Third World with constructive US initiatives. His proposals included:[45]

(1) Stabilisation of Third World export earnings to be achieved by (i) the setting up of a *development security facility* within the IMF (to strengthen the already existing *compensatory finance facility*); and (ii) by setting up consumer–producer forums (rather than producer associations) for every key commodity separately (instead of an integrated commodity programme).
(2) The adaptation of non-tariff barriers to provide 'special consideration' for developing countries (instead of making the generalised system of preferences a permanent feature of world trade).
(3) The use of public, multilateral, finance facilities to support and encourage private risk capital in developing raw-material resources (to this end the capital base of the World Bank and the International Finance Corpora-

tion would be enlarged and a new international investment fund set up).

(4)   Various measures to increase concessionary aid flows to the poorest countries.

(5)   The setting up of a world food reserve system, of which the USA would hold the major share.

(6)   The setting up of several organisations to help Third World countries collect and digest information relevant to their interests: an international industrialisation institute, an international centre for exchange of technological information, and an expansion of the capacity of the International Agricultural Research centres.

(7)   Last but not least, Kissinger set in motion the 'institutionalisation' of the North—South dialogue by suggesting that an intergovernmental committee (the previously aborted Paris Committee on International Economic Cooperation, CIEC) should begin more talks immediately. He announced the year 1976 as the year of review and reform.

To be fair, Kissinger's speech was a tactical masterpiece. The closing words of the speech were calculated to warm everybody's heart: 'We have heard your voices. We embrace your hopes. We will join your efforts.'[46] Overwhelmed by such affection and dizzied by the sheer number of 'US initiatives', the Group of 77 too began to shift its position towards 'the need for compromise'. Already in the preparatory meetings to the Seventh Session, the moderates' view had begun to prevail, namely that no major economic reform could take place without the active support of the USA, and that it was better to go for the possible rather than reach for the unattainable.

Thus the resolution adopted at the Seventh Special Session, and entitled *Development and International Economic Co-operation*, was a compromise, a consensus resolution: 'The compromise was struck by having the final document follow the format of the Third World position paper but depart little in general principle from the substance of the US position.'[47]

The Kissinger initiative created goodwill and bought time for the industrial countries to reappraise their strategy and tactics. But most importantly it bought the time needed to let the process of *embourgeoisement* run its full course. 'Embourgeoisement', a term adapted to the international context by Roger Hansen, an official of the National Security Council, is the process whereby OPEC and other rapidly growing developing countries — in accumulating a larger share of the world's wealth — will (so the advanced countries hope) become less interested in a new international order and more interested in preserving their stake in the old order.[48] To encourage this process of embourgeoisement, the Trilateral Commission has made the specific proposal that 'such major new powers as Iran [the report came out *before* the Revolution], Brazil and Mexico be invited to join the OECD, and that Saudi Arabia, which now has the largest monetary reserves in the world, might be invited to meetings of the Group of Ten [the steering group of the IMF)'.[49] On this subject the report notes with satisfaction that the membership of the CIEC has already provided 'key developing countries with a role in the international decision making process which corresponds to their sharply increased importance to the system'.[50] And sure enough the developing countries delegated by the Third World to the preparatory conferences of the CIEC in Paris were Algeria, Brazil, Iran, Saudi Arabia, Venezuela, Zaïre and India. The wider delegation (nineteen countries) to the CIEC ministerial conference itself included, again, the successful mineral exporters and some newly industrialising countries. Meagher, whose detailed study of the NIEO documents have been a valuable guide to the present chapter, says:

> It is interesting to note that, although all of the developing countries which attended can be classified as less developed countries, the list contained none of the 25 countries designated as least developed of the less developed countries — but it does include four of the 41 countries classified as most seriously affected [MSA countries].[51]

At this point one may well wonder where the Soviet Union and other Eastern European countries figure in the North–South dialogue. The very formulation 'North–South' had been chosen specifically to invite the socialist bloc to participate in the New International Economic Order discussions,

and every main document of the growing NIEO literature
ritually enjoins the socialist countries to increase their trade
with the South, too. However, other than voting in favour of
the *Charter*, the socialist bloc has played a minor role in the
debates concerning the NIEO. The reasons for this low pro-
file were aptly stated by the Chairman of the Soviet delegation
at the Seventh Special Session:

> It is not the Soviet Union who for ages used to plunder the
> national wealth of former colonial possessions which
> nowadays have come to be sovereign states. It is not the
> Soviet Union who used to exploit their population for
> centuries. Therefore, the Soviet Union does not bear — I
> specifically underline it — does not bear any responsibility
> whatsoever for the economic backwardness of the develop-
> ing countries, their present hard situation, particularly
> under the conditions of the aggravation of the economic
> crisis of the world capitalist economy.[52]

So what has emerged from the NIEO discussions? I do not
wish to harass the reader any further with the tedious details
of the fruitless North—South dialogue that has followed the
Seventh Special Session. It suffices to quote at length a summary on the 'progress towards NIEO', published by *Development Forum*, a semi-official UN publication, on the eve of
the Eleventh Special Session of the UN General Assembly.
This session (the third on the topic of the NIEO) was held in
August 1980 'in order to assess the progress made in various
forums of the UN system in the establishment of the New
International Economic Order, and on the basis of that assessment, to take appropriate action':

> In some areas there has been progress, but in most others
> achievements have been disappointing. There has been
> *agreement in principle* on a programme to regulate trade
> in commodities. An agreement has also been reached on
> how to deal with some of the 'restrictive business practices'
> injurious to economic development, and once this is en-
> dorsed by the General Assembly the stage will be set for
> implementation by governments. In shipping a Code of

Conduct on Liner Conferences is expected to come into force as soon as a number of countries in Europe fulfill the requirements to become 'contracting parties'. Several developed countries have written off the official debts of a number of developing countries. Other than this there is little that can be called progress towards the New International Economic Order. In monetary and financial areas talks have continued and minor adjustments made within the International Monetary Fund (IMF). There has been little change in the rules and structures governing industry, transfer of technology, transport or communications.[53]

To break the deadlock in the negotiations towards the NIEO, proposals were made for an intensive 'global round' of negotiations in 1981. At the time of this book going to press, a very reluctant and hostile US government was finally persuaded to attend a mini-summit of twenty-two representatives from rich and poor countries, in Mexico in October 1981.

Equity in the South: from Global Keynesianism to Global Social Democracy — the Basic Needs Strategy

As the NIEO debate got into full swing and the North re-examined its strategy and its options for a globally managed 'interdependent' world, a third key element was injected into the northern strategy and rapidly gained importance: internal reform and redistribution in the South. This was seen to take two forms: redistribution of resources between the countries of the South, more particularly a transfer of wealth from the oil-exporting to the oil-importing developing countries;[54] and internal domestic redistribution within developing countries. Increasingly developed countries began to take the view that the *Charter* had rather one-sidedly emphasised the obligations and duties of the rich countries, and that the poor countries themselves had responsibilities too. There was a link, it was argued, between international redistribution and internal reform.[55] Indeed, without internal reform international redistribution could neither eradicate world poverty nor promote the further economic development of the developing countries. The ultimate logic of this argument was to propose that concessions of international redistribution should be made conditional upon internationally recognised measures of internal reform adopted by the developing countries. This argument, for example, was put forward in the Brandt Report.[56]

What we are witnessing here is a very interesting evolution in the northern strategy from global efficiency and global Keynesianism to what one might term 'global social democracy'. It is interesting to note that the main ideological impetus for this evolution derives from an alliance between progressive elements within the Third World countries and certain enlightened, 'internationalist', political opinion-makers in the advanced countries. Neither of these groups as a rule wields direct political power inside its own national community. Rather, they converge in the secretariats, commissions, and *ad hoc* groups of experts and 'eminent persons' of the international organisations. In these organisations they themselves do not even have voting power. Yet they establish the parameters of the discourse, because it is they who prepare the documents and the background papers that ultimately inform the various 'resolutions'.[57]

Radical Third World writers, many themselves staff members of various international organisations,[58] have long since combined a radical analysis of the world economic structure with a critical analysis of the domestic socio-economic structures of Third World countries. As we shall see in Chapter 6, they have made it a central point that the unequal pattern of income distribution inside Third World countries is generated by its manner of insertion into the total world economy, and that this in turn presents bottlenecks for further economic growth of Third World countries.

In the late 1960s and early 1970s this radical Third World perspective fused with the global management and redistribution perspective (global Keynesianism) which was already gaining ground amongst the progressive thinkers of the North, including the highest echelons of the World Bank and, a little later, the Trilateral Commission. It had already been clearly understood in these progressive 'internationalist' circles that liberal aid and trade measures on behalf of the developing countries were not only necessary for moral, humanitarian reasons, but also because the developed world increasingly needed the developing countries as sources of raw materials and as export markets.[59] This is the essence of global Keynesianism. Now it also became recognised that the present rapid pace of industrialisation in some Third World countries, coupled with the highly unequal domestic structures inside these countries, would render international redistribution measures ineffective. The lack of domestic markets inside the rapidly growing Third World countries would either hinder further industrialisation (and hence restrict their function as markets for Western technology and consumer goods) or increasingly deflect this industrialisation into export-led growth.[60] The latter indeed was already happening and had in turn sparked off a growing protectionism, both formal and (more usually) informal, against manufacturing imports from the developing countries.[61]

In my view it is these concerns that have led to, for example, the World Bank's shift in orientation from 'bottom line' to 'bottom billion',[62] from 'growth' to 'redistribution'. In hot pursuit of the theme that there is no necessary link between inequality and growth (as had been previously argued by mainstream development economists) it now became official World Bank gospel to preach the opposite, namely that in the contemporary developing world objectives of growth can and must be pursued by strategies of redistribution, by 'poverty-focussed' strategies.[63]

Meanwhile, the ILO had initiated an important programme of studies on one key element of these strategies: employment. Employment was seen to link redistribution with growth. Precisely because the industrialisation experience of most rapidly growing countries had involved capital-intensive foreign imported plant and machinery, the labour-absorption rate of their manufacturing sectors had lagged far behind the growth rates of these sectors, leaving large masses of the population unemployed. It was advocated that a pattern of 'self-reliant' industrialisation and small-scale agriculture involving greater utilisation of local materials, local markets and local skills would create greater employment opportunities. These would in the long run also benefit the growth of the economy through 'trickle-up' effects of greater productivity and purchasing power of the poor.[64]

From a concern with relative poverty, international development assistance has shifted its attention to the eradication of absolute poverty. The reasons why this is so are not really clear, unless one adopts a critical Marxist stance, as we shall do at the end of this chapter. World Bank officials writing about this very important shift suggest somewhat lamely that the relative distribution policies just described seemed not to have the 'required effect'. But, surely, hardly any time had been allowed for such policies to have an effect!

> It was soon seen that, on the one hand, unemployment, in the sense that the term is used in the developed countries, was not the problem in the developing countries, and that, on the other hand, redistribution from growth only yielded very meagre results. Furthermore, it is clear that mass poverty can exist with a high degree of equality and reductions in absolute poverty are consistent with increases in inequality. The concern has shifted to the eradication of absolute poverty, particularly by concentrating on basic human needs.[65]

The *basic needs strategy* was a logical outgrowth and an extension of the new development strategy which had already replaced the emphasis on economic growth with an emphasis on redistribution and employment. However, it went beyond the new development strategy in that it no longer justified the distribution of income and the minimisation of *relative* poverty as a means to an end (namely, national economic growth) but instead aimed at the eradication of *absolute* poverty as an end in itself. Instead of the national economy 'it places man and his needs at the centre of development', according to World Bank officials.[66]

The basic needs approach is neither a coherent theory nor a methodologically clearly worked out development programme. Yet there is a loosely knit set of ideas, of common themes, that have surfaced time and again during the last decade in various international documents under the nomenclature 'basic needs approach'.[67] These common themes are:

(1)　A central emphasis on meeting the basic needs of the poorer masses within the shortest possible period.

(2)　A definition of basic human needs as consisting of:
    (a) minimum physical survival needs, i.e. food, shelter, clothing, access to water, hygiene, health; and
    (b) so-called 'non-material' needs, such as the need for education, for fundamental human rights, for participation — by which is meant both participation in economic development through employment and participation in political decision-making.

(3)　Attempts to operationalise basic needs in an effort
    (a) to define country-specific targets; and
    (b) to develop a measurement of comparative development performance.

(4)　The recognition that basic needs are not static but evolve over time in line with the growth of the economy and the aspirations of the people.

(5)　Although there are different views as to the methods appropriate to the basic needs approach, there is a common emphasis on the need for 'structural' transformation. The latter is seen to involve redistribution of assets and incomes not only through public policy measures but also through changing the patterns of demand, of consumption and production, e.g. through the utilisation of local resources, labour-intensive technologies, small-scale production, etc.

(6)　An acknowledgement that such structural transformation means taking actions that challenge existing class and power structures.

(7)　A realisation that the logic of a basic needs approach points towards policies of self-reliance, involving selected delinking from international production and marketing arrangements rather than the increased and improved forms of participation in the world economy implied by the NIEO demands.

It would be factually incorrect to suggest that the basic needs approach was invented by the World Bank. Indeed, part of its initial appeal to Third World participants in international negotiating fora was that it had originated as an authentically Third World perspective. The concept 'basic needs' was first coined by a group of radical Latin American scholars,[68] and the approach was officially launched at the ILO World Employment Conference in 1976, where it was endorsed by the Group of 77 as an alternative development strategy.

However, the basic needs approach was quickly 'appropriated' by the World Bank and, a bit more cautiously, by the DAC member countries (the donor countries of the OECD) as a focus for their respective aid policies.[69] It became the prevailing consensus (if not yet the actual practice) that concessionary resource transfers should be targeted on the least developed countries, while other forms of assistance should focus on the poorest segments of the 'middle-income' countries, and that donor countries should use their aid flows as a lever to encourage the adoption of 'basic needs'-type development strategies. Even the Trilateral Commission jumped on this social democratic bandwagon:

> much more must be done to assure that development efforts help the bottom 40 per cent of the population in the developing countries. Donor and recipient countries, working together in their mutual interest, should promote development programmes that stress not only increases in GNP but also the 'qualitative' aspects of development — the eradication of extreme poverty, a better distribution of income and wealth, the improvement of rural welfare, the reduction of unemployment, and broad access to education, health and social services.[70]

This misuse of the basic needs approach for interventionist purposes caused the Group of 77 scarcely a year later to attack the approach root and branch — as diversionary and unacceptably intrusive — in most international fora.[71] And although more recently still the Group of 77 have once more seemed receptive to 'basic need'-type aid (while still rejecting the terminology), their fundamental ambivalence towards the new strategy remains.

And this, indeed, is the paradox, or double-twist, in the development dialogue of the 1970s, namely that it took three decades of political independence of the colonial countries for the international community officially to recognise, and 'outlaw', the continuing economic colonialism of these

countries, only for this to be followed immedia[t]
denial of the relevance of the sovereignty of states i[n]
temporary world economic order generally. While re~~cog~~.... ~
the Third World countries' right to own and control their
natural resources and to determine their own economic affairs,
the basic needs approach yet queries the position of their
states as ultimate arbiters of human affairs. Rather, the
sovereignty of the individuals seems to precede that of the
state, and the individual's inalienable right to physical survival
and a life of dignity and well-being is thought to be better
protected by the international community.

And why should the international community all of a sudden be made 'responsible' for the poor of the world? Why,
indeed, should the World Bank, that standard-bearer of capitalist ideology, so dramatically redirect its aid policies that it
has even been accused of advocating 'socialism'.[72] Has the
World Bank at long last acquired a heart? Or has it perhaps
acquired a new insight into the present level of development
— and its contradictions — of the world capitalist system?
The latter interpretation we are more likely to find in Marxist
analyses of recent World Bank policies. Bennholdt-Thomsen,
for example, argues that the process of marginalisation
presently accelerating inside the Third World is not just a
consequence of capitalist penetration there, but also *functional*
to capitalist production.[73] To the extent that imperialist-
induced Third World capitalism typically can only engage a
relatively small sector of the active population and thus leaves
the rest of the population 'marginalised', the reproduction of
that marginalised population *outside* the capitalist sector
ensures — for the capitalist sector — an industrial reserve
army. The existence of such an industrial reserve army permits
both the suppression of wages within the capitalist sector,
as well as the reproduction of future generations to be 'fed
into' this sector. This Marxist interpretation of the phenomenon of marginalisation and poverty inside the Third World
sheds a critical light upon the World Bank's recent 'investment' in the world's poor, as the title of Bennholdt-Thomsen's
thesis suggests. Perhaps it is a testimony of the extent to
which capitalism has become truly international that the
nearest thing to a governing body of international capitalism
should now adopt a kind of international social policy designed

to assist the world-wide preservation of industrial reserve armies in countries where corrupt and repressive regimes are too short-sighted to carry out this task themselves.

The corollary of this thesis is that those bodies representing international capital's interests should now tend to direct their active (as opposed to rhetorical) concern for the world's poor only to those poor who live in the fast-growing Third World countries. There are indeed some empirical grounds for this suspicion. For example, in 1979 — ten years after McNamara's conversion — over half of all World Bank aid went to ten countries, only two of which are classified by the World Bank as belonging in the low-income group, namely India and Indonesia. These two were the top World Bank aid recipients in 1979, but the close runners-up after these two were Brazil, Mexico, South Korea and the Philippines.[74] Seventeen of the twenty-five least developed countries (by UN standards) received no World Bank aid at all in the past decade, and the least developed group as a whole received slightly less World Bank allocations in the period 1975—8 than in the period 1969—74 (1.4 per cent as compared with 2.8 per cent).[75] When it comes to *bilateral* aid from the OECD donor countries (the members of the OECD's Development Assistance Committee, DAC) this Fourth World (the least developed group) has fared somewhat better, receiving about one-sixth of all ODA allocations in 1979. Together with the rest of the poor world (DAC has a classification of *four* groups of developing countries, with the 'poorest' world comprising the bottom two) it received about half of all allocations. Even so, the writers of the DAC report of 1979 come to the conclusion that 'it is time for aid donors to stop rehearsing the reasons why provision of substantially more assistance to the [larger] set of the poorest countries is unfeasible, and to start figuring out . . . how to do it'. The writers of the report take some pains to dispel notions, current amongst donor countries, that the prospects of the poorest countries are 'hopeless' and that their capacity to absorb aid is 'limited'.[76]

Clearly, then, there *is* some tendency on the part of aid donors, in bilateral and more especially multilateral aid, to concentrate their aid efforts on the fastest-growing Third World countries and to neglect the rest of the Third World.

PART TWO
THEORIES

3

Social Evolution and Development: The Bourgeois Liberal Tradition

Scientific theories of development may be broadly classed into two groups: liberal and Marxist. Both are inheritors of a long-standing Western intellectual concern with progress. That concern, we all know, came fully into its own with the growth of science and technology, and the spread of industrialisation in Western Europe from the eighteenth century onwards. The irresistible conquest of man over nature, the resultant improvement in material conditions of life, and (above all) the economic and political power it permitted the European civilisations to wield over all other civilisations in the world, could not but have fed notions of progress and historical superiority into the philosophical reflections of the time.

. Yet the seeds of the passion for progress were planted much before that by the unique configuration of the Western European belief-system which combined a Judaic Voluntarist conception of man, a Christian eschatological view of history and an Aristotelian notion of imminent change. The conjoining of these three disparate cultural legacies fruited into a view of 'inevitable yet man-made betterment through the ages' and sponsored an enduring sense of historical destiny and human purpose that became one of the more stable elements of the European cultural tradition.[1]

The advent of the Age of Enlightenment merely turned the idea of 'inevitable yet man-made betterment' into a subject of systematic scientific enquiry. And, excepting certain isolated instances such as Malthus's population predictions, it overwhelmingly endorsed the idea of progress by replacing its metaphysical underpinnings with truly scientific ones. Eschatological beliefs and progress were thus transformed into theories of evolution.

Nineteenth-century Evolutionary Theories

Nineteenth-century evolutionary models grew directly out of attempts to obtain scientific understanding of social life generally. Envious of the successes of the natural sciences, students of human affairs sought to apply the scientific method to the study of society. Their somewhat uncritical adoption of the scientific method, which seeks to establish *general* laws of cause and effect governing the relationships between phenomena, and *general* laws of motion governing the change in phenomena, led — when applied to human societies — by implication to an imputation of continuity, of interconnectedness, in the historical process. After all, the very desire to generalise patterns of social change is intolerant of notions of chance, interruptedness, unrelatedness. A history that does not repeat itself is of no interest to the scientist. It denies prediction, that eagerly sought-after reward for scientific endeavour. Therefore, to understand today, with the scientific method, one is inescapably directed to the past, for causes must precede their effects in time. Human societies today are thus caused by, grow out of, those of yesterday. Moreover, in order to *generalise* the effect of today with the cause of yesterday one must go even further back in time and demonstrate similar cause-and-effect relationships occurring in chain-like fashion throughout history down to the beginning of time. It is not surprising that in order to identify this similarity of social changes in myriad historical events, nineteenth-century social scientists were driven to adopt very abstract categories indeed. In fact, they came up with only four: simple, complex, growth and specialisation. The development of human social life was presented as a progression from simple to complex forms by means of continuous processes of growth and specialisation. For example, Spencer's theory of evolution hinged on the following two propositions:

(1) That both in the development of organic life as well as in the development of human social life, there has been a process of diversification, whereby many forms of social life have developed out of a much smaller number of original forms.

(2) That there has been a general trend of development by which more complex forms of structure and organisation have arisen from simpler forms.

Having proposed the processes of growth and specialisation (more concretely, the division of labour) as the general laws of motion of social life, the early evolutionists devoted much of their intellectual energies to the classification of societies at the beginning and at the end of the evolutionary voyage. Simple societies, they said, differed from complex societies by the nature of the social bonds that held men together. In the former these bonds reflected the similarity of men's interests and experiences, in the latter — as a result of specialisation — these bonds were based on the differences between, and hence the complementarity of, men's interests and experiences. By logical corollary the evolution of human social life was marked by a process of increasing *individualisation*. In nearly all early evolutionist publications we come across the same twofold classification: Spencer speaks of *homogeneous* versus *heterogeneous* societies; Durkheim refers to *mechanical solidarity* versus *organic solidarity*; Henri Maine contrasts *status* with *contract*, and Tönnies *Gemeinschaft* with *Gesellschaft* ('association' versus 'organisation'). There is little doubt that the early classical thinkers evaluated the progression of general social life from simple to complex as a process of advancement, even though many of them, to be sure, were worried about the social problems and dislocations which this process had brought in its wake. Yet, as I have suggested before, neither the notion of continuity nor the idea of advancement was particularly new to the European cultural tradition. Indeed, nineteenth-century theories of evolution fitted the prevailing cultural ethos perfectly. What was novel was the attempt to award both notions scientific status. But this demanded more than the mere formulation of logically connected general propositions. It demanded also the testing of these logical propositions against empirical evidence. And here the whole exercise would have become unstuck — for where does one get empirical evidence from a distant and unrecorded past? — had it not been for the unique opportunities presented by the consolidation of European expansion over the entire globe which brought not only merchant travellers but also colonial administrators and men of learning into contact with overseas peoples, including remote and hitherto unknown isolated primitive communities. The often meticulous recordings of these peoples' customs and social institutions provided the documentary evidence which the scientific evolutionists needed to prove their general theories. For it was an ever-recurrent observation in these descriptive materials that primitive societies were indeed small in size, simple in organisation and exhibiting an all-pervasive and intense moral consensus.

For the evolutionists, who aspired to scientific status for their theories, this 'comparative method' was tantamount to an 'indirect experiment' which performed the same function as laboratory experimentation in the natural sciences.[2] It is a moot point of course whether the empirical descriptions of the first ethnographers were themselves not influenced by the evolutionary beliefs of the time: that is, whether they selectively recorded and interpreted those social features which confirmed the evolutionary scheme.

More questionable still was their assumption of unidirectionality and continuity of the evolutionary voyage. All human societies were assumed to follow a singular particular course between the two ideal polar types: from a simple 'primitive' to a complex 'modern' society. Perhaps the most explicit expression of this assumption was given by the anthropologist Morgan:

> Since mankind were one in origin, their career has been
> essentially one, running in different but uniform channels
> upon all continents, and very similarly in all tribes and
> nations of mankind down to the same status of advance-
> ment. It follows that the history and the experience of
> the American Indian tribes represent more or less nearly

the history and experience of our own remote ancestors when in corresponding conditions.[3]

For all its methodological weaknesses and theoretical inadequacies, notably the failure to describe the structures of 'in-between' societies on the evolutionary path, or indeed perhaps precisely because of this failure, the simplistic dichotomy 'primitive' versus 'modern' became a powerful paradigm nursing a strong Western social science tradition which for a long time exerted great influence on development policies.[4]

Twentieth-century Neo-evolutionary Theories

From Weber to Parsons, from Morgan to White, neo-evolutionary theory set out to elaborate the details of primitive (sometimes more benevolently referred to as 'traditional') and modern societies and even sketch the profiles of intermediate societies. The methodological preoccupation was materialistic, systemic and ahistorical. The centrepiece of social evolution was seen to be material, e.g. technological adaptability: man's mastery over the environment, which had enabled those societies that had won it to raise the material standards of living of the masses of their populations. The sociological problematic was therefore to examine which structural and cultural properties were responsible for this amazing feat. Paradoxically, although the listing of these properties entailed a recapitulation of the historical development of the West, the sociological theory of development that emerged from it yet became eminently ahistorical. Somewhere along the line of argument history became logic!

Neo-evolutionary theory took its cues from earlier evolutionary models — that social evolution was indeed a process of increasing complexity of human social life, a process now labelled 'social differentiation'. However, it improved on earlier models by suggesting that this process occurs in *stages*, each stage of differentiation earmarked by novel patterns of integration. What is this mysterious process of social differentiation? It is the process by which the

main social functions, e.g. economic, juridical, political,

cultural/religious, become disassociated from one another, attached to specialized collectivities and roles, and organized in relatively specific and autonomous symbolic and organizational frameworks within the confines of the same institutional system.[5]

It is the process of the division of labour in society writ large and in sociological jargon. Society is supposed to have four major functional or institutional spheres: polity, culture (religion), judiciary (integration) and economy, of which technology is a sub-sphere. In the over-all 'abstracted' history of human social evolution each institutional sphere differentiates, that is, it becomes autonomous, in turn, thereby each time progressively enhancing the over-all adaptive capacity of society, *provided* time and again new ways and means are found to integrate and co-ordinate the differentiated elements with each other and with the society as a whole. Thus each phase of social differentiation requires a new solidarity and integrity of the society as a whole, with both new common loyalties and new values and norms. The definition of such new common loyalties and the invention of new institutional means to co-ordinate the differentiated spheres of society, if successful, can graduate to become *evolutionary universals*. According to Parsons, the inventor of this concept, an evolutionary universal is 'an organizational development sufficiently important to further evolution, that rather than emerging only once, it is likely to be "hit upon" by various systems operating under different conditions'.[6] Indeed, once incorporated, evolutionary universals tend to become essential parts of later societies, and this also explains how they have come to appear on the check-list of 'structural and cultural properties' of modern societies, and why they have been presented as 'necessary requisites of development', by those development sociologists who stand in this tradition.

Which, then, are these stages of societal evolution? Talcott Parsons, undisputedly the most authoritative neo-evolutionary theorist today, and one moreover who presents a concise synthesis of the long tradition of Western evolutionary thought, distinguishes four stages beyond the primitive and *un*differentiated stage of kinship organisation, making a total

of five. Since I have given a detailed account of his theory in
The Sociology of Developing Societies it will be sufficient
here to present his paradigm in schematic form, listing the
stages of social differentiation, the attendant integrative
solutions (the evolutionary universals) and, by way of example,
the concrete historical societies representative of each stage
(see Figure 3.1 overleaf).

Note that integrative solutions actually consist of three
kinds:

(1)   There are co-ordinative devices. These are new norma-
      tive complexes designed to regulate and 'order' the
      relationships amongst the newly differentiated units,
      e.g. money, markets, property, contract, written language.
(2)   There are integrative devices proper. These are the
      definitions of the relevant societal community at each
      stage which legitimise the social order: 'kinship',
      'authority', 'citizenship'.
(3)   There are cultural symbolic representations, involving
      an appropriate rewrite, or reorientation, of world-views
      or religions.

There are three themes of particular note in this bourgeois
theory of evolution. The first is the conception that the
evolutionary process is one of increasing autonomy, of
independence and of freedom and individualisation on the
one hand, and — as a consequence — one of increasing
creativity, efficiency and generalised societal adaptability on
the other. All that the bourgeois theory effectively says is
that individuals perform societal functions (more especially
the economic and technological functions) more efficiently
to the extent that — in the course of the historical process —
these functions have become 'freed' from ascriptive bonds,
from political patronage, and from religious diktats.

A second important theme in bourgeois thinking is the
belief that the modern stage, which started in the sixteenth
century in Western Europe, earmarks the end of the human
evolutionary process. There is simply nothing after this.
There is no conception, or the possibility of a conception, of
a stage after the present one. Small wonder that writers

Stage of social differentiation

Integrative solutions or evolutionary universals

Evolutionary stages	Functional differentiation	Structural differentiation	Co-ordinative devices	Definition of relevant societal community	Constitutive symbolism
Primitive societies (Australian Aborigines)	None	Sex, age, descent	Religious ritual	Single affinal collectivity (kinship)	Conception of paradigmatic world 'myths'
Advanced primitive societies; archaic societies (Mesopotamian Empire, Ancient Egypt, Inca Empire)	Of the polity	King and court + religico/political elite; Ordinary men	Divination/revelation; written language (texts, scriptures)	Divine kingship + royal lineage; consanguinity with the gods	Cosmological world-view; polytheism
Historic societies (Islam, Buddhism, Confucian China, Roman Empire)	Of culture	1. Politico/military elite 2. Cultural/religious elite 3. Urban lower class 4. Peasant lower class	Administrative bureaucracy; Money and markets	Specialised cultural legitimation: the scholar official or 'priesthood'	Transcendence of supernatural from natural world; rational world-view
'Seedbed' societies (Greece, Israel)	Of integrative sphere, i.e. judiciary	Relatively egalitarian corporate community consisting of religious elites, political elites and functional/occupational groupings	Formal legal system	Corporate citizenbody with equality of franchise and basic rights before the law; 'citizenship' (in Israel) based on *voluntary* association	Transcendental; rational world-view
Modern societies (USA, USSR, Europe, Japan)	Of economy and technology	Pluralist egalitarian order based on functional/occupational differentiation	Formal legal system	'Citizenship'; democratic association with elective leadership and fully enfranchised membership	Rational, abstract, universalist value system

Loosely based upon Talcott Parsons's *Societies* and *The System of Modern Societies*.

FIGURE 3.1   *The stages of social evolution*

standing in this tradition often incline towards a doomsday position (cf. pp. 130ff).

The modern system of society is thought to have accommodated within itself all the relevant evolutionary adaptations of all previous civilisations. Each of the functional spheres of society, including the last one, namely the economy, are now autonomous, which is what makes them so efficient, and yet they are co-ordinated with each other and stably integrated into the society as a whole.

A third characteristic theme of the bourgeois theory of evolution is the notion of *structural compatibility*. In the course of the evolutionary process human societies are thought to have developed structural and cultural properties which are 'compatible'.[7] Like the pieces in a jigsaw puzzle, they fit each other perfectly.

The Modern Stage of Social Evolution

Consider the schematic presentation of the structural and cultural properties of modern societies, as presented in Figure 3.2. Above the double line are the primary qualities, below are the secondary consequences of the interaction of primary qualities. The arrows criss-crossing the diagram indicate the structural compatibilities of various properties with each other. Thus the differentiation of the economy with its resulting industrialisation and consequent improvement in living standards is made possible by the institutionalisation of money and markets as generalised media of exchange. These institutional complexes now permit the economy to operate on an autonomous principle: resources (both human and physical) from now on are 'freed' from ascriptive ties or political bondage, and can be allocated to wherever they can be best made use of, their sole criterion for allocation being the market price. The market price, however, cannot operate without a correlate market principle, namely profit maximisation as the dominant motive of all economic agents.

This principle of profit maximisation, or economic rationality, again, could never have become the dominant motive in the determination of human behaviour had it not been

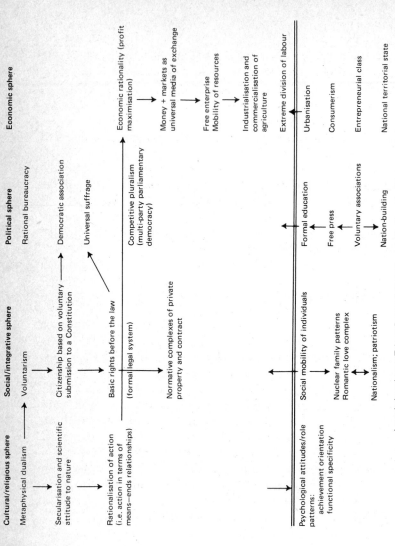

Loosely based upon Talcott Parsons's *Societies* and *The System of Modern Societies*.

FIGURE 3.2   *The structure of modern societies*

preceded by correlate changes in the cultural sphere. With Christianity, and especially with the Protestant Reformation, the wider cultural value system in Europe had become geared to *rational action* in the world, 'involving the explicit definition of goals and the increasingly precise calculation of the most effective means to achieve them, in contrast to action arising from habit or from traditionalism as principle'.[8] This value system, in turn, had blossomed as a result of preceding cultural/religious developments, notably the adoption of metaphysical dualism (with its notion of a transcendent God) which had encouraged the secularisation of both science and society.

The notion of a transcendent God, moreover, paves the way for *universalistic* application of values and norms, ultimately leading to social equality. For, in the eyes of a transcendent God everybody is equal, and every individual is in principle capable of salvation provided he subjects himself *voluntarily* to God's command. Thus metaphysical dualism and voluntarism make a handsome couple generating the principle of citizenship as the legitimising principle for the social order, e.g. for the inclusion of membership in the societal community. Equality in the eyes of God furthermore translates into equal rights before the law, which is a necessary juridical complex permitting the effective operation of the principles of private property and contract, which in their turn had been necessitated by the 'freeing' of the economy from ascriptive and political ties.

Political developments, notably bureaucratic administration (already developed to a pitch in previous civilisations) and democratic association complement developments in the cultural, economic and social spheres. The rational bureaucracy, with its separation of personal authority from authority in office, becomes a *neutral* medium of mobilisation and acquisition of resources in the interest of the collectivity, and as such provides a perfect organisational instrument for modern economic activities. Finally, in modern societies, argues Parsons, the completed differentiation of all functional spheres, including the economic-occupational sphere, has created such a multi-stratified, plural system of society that effective exercise of political responsibilities can no longer be accomplished without the mediation of consensus, both in policy formulation and in the exercise of power, on the part of all the differentiated sub-units of society. Democratic association, with its features of fully enfranchised membership and elected leadership, is therefore a final evolutionary universal and belongs to the modern stage. It differentiates within the body politic power from leadership, giving the power to those who are led.

Modernisation Theories

From neo-evolutionary to modernisation theory is but a small step. At the end of the Second World War the economic development of underdeveloped areas came to be regarded in some liberal-progressive circles as a necessary complement to the economic reconstruction of the war-ravaged industrial countries, and of a prosperous world capitalist economy based on free trade. In order to participate in world economic relations, either as efficient producers and exporters of crops and materials, or as consumers of Western industrial products and technology, or both, the underdeveloped countries now needed to travel speedily from the Stone Age to the twentieth century; they needed to 'modernise'. Economic development theorists were the first to put the finger on the intricate interaction between economic and socio-cultural factors in economic development, and soon sociologists jumped on this profitable intellectual bandwagon, ready with prescriptions to fill in the 'missing links' of development.[9]

As an explanatory theory of historical social change and development, neo-evolutionary theory had left much to be desired, but as a programme for modernisation it was eminently suited. For, as mentioned before, it had turned the abstracted, generalised history of European development into *logic.* By demonstrating the structural compatibility or 'correspondence' between certain advanced economic institutions (money, markets, occupational specialisation, profit maximisation) and certain Western, 'modern', political, social and cultural institutions, it turned the latter into necessary prerequisites or 'logical requirements' for economic development. And since there existed a fortunate collusion of interests between Western international capitalism and the ruling elites of the now ex-colonial territories — about which more in the next chapter — that dictated the goal of development to be economic, the wholesale adoption of the Western social, cultural and political structure became agreed official policy in most underdeveloped countries. Indeed, the *primary* properties of this structure were never even in dispute; they were the never-to-be-questioned legacies of colonial legislations. Rather, the energies of modernisation theorists and activists, international and national development planners, were concentrated mostly on the *second-order* consequences (see Figure 3.2, below the double line). These secondary qualities were seen to have been, in the now advanced modern societies, inevitable consequences of the emergence of the primary properties, and by the same logic of 'structural compatibility' were argued to be usable as facilitators of the successful introduction of the main modernisation programme.

Within the second-order consequences we can again distinguish between cultural and structural properties. The cultural properties usually refer to psychological aptitudes that individual members of modern societies are likely to have. Parsons had already argued that the modern economic/ technological complex, with its high degree of occupational specialisation and the principle of economic rationality, favours roles and attitudes that are functionally *specific achievement-orientated, universalistic* and *affectively neutral.*[10] These second-order consequences for individual values and attitudes have led some modernisation theorists to argue that successful modernisation is not a function of structural changes in society but rather of 'making men modern'.[11] Education, contact with mass media, and improved communication and transport, will all contribute to the instilling of such modern values and beliefs. Some authors even went as far as suggesting special training programmes for entrepreneurial elites in developing countries to imbue them with the appropriate 'need for achievement', a psychological motivational complex associated with the value of economic rationality and profit maximisation.[12]

Other second-order consequences, such as urbanisation,

social mobility, the emergence of voluntary/occupational associations and the nuclear-family pattern, are more directly structural. Modernisation theorists writing about these structural properties have been less concerned with implanting them (indeed, a rather improbable task) as with condemning the traditional opposites of these required modern forms (kinship/extended-family systems, rigid stratification structures, etc.) as obstacles to development, and with analysing as 'social problems' the structural discontinuities arising from a half-baked societal structure that combines modern with traditional elements.[13]

The logical connections between the primary and second-order characteristics have been thoroughly gone into elsewhere[14] and need not detain us here. The point that I wish to make here is that until the turn of the Second UN Development Decade one could trace a direct line of descent from classical evolutionary thought via neo-evolutionary and modernisation theories to internationally accepted lists of 'development indicators' and internationally sponsored development programmes.[15] Developing countries were compared in terms of their relative standing on any one of a number of social/economic/political indicators such as degree of urbanisation, industrialisation, political democracy, secularisation, social mobility, occupational differentiation, proliferation of voluntary associations, free enterprise, nuclear-family patterns and independent judiciaries.[16] The World Bank and other international organisations would outline to Third World governments the appropriate socio-economic programmes to be adopted if they wished to qualify for aid flows. Western technology, Western methods of production and Western economic enterprises were welcomed as important development agents. And so throughout the 1950s and well into the 1960s we encounter the modernisation theory and its underlying evolutionary paradigm as the dominant ideology legitimating the wholesale adoption by developing countries of what one critic has called 'Western patent solutions to basic human needs'.[17] In this way the theory has served well the implied commercial and economic interests of the advanced Western countries.

The success of this ideology in promoting national economic development has been claimed by many scholars standing in this tradition. The contributions in its main journal, *Economic Development and Cultural Change*, of late have shown a preoccupation with descriptive case studies of 'success stories', along with a marked decline of theoretical contributions. The guru of the neo-evolutionary perspective, Parsons himself, in a publication as recent as 1977 observed with satisfaction that it is 'only a slight exaggeration to say that all contemporary societies are more or less modern'.[18] Therefore, he concludes the world is now one system of modern societies. The future that lies ahead involves merely a completion of this system of one-worldness. There are more such optimists. Herman Kahn is another example. His latest book, *World Economic Development, 1979 and Beyond*,[19] describes the case histories of the success stories of national economic development (Japan, South Korea, Taiwan) and foresees a bright future for most, if not all, developing countries.

However, the very success of modernisation has *also* contributed to *reorientations* in bourgeois development thinking. First, anxieties about physical limits to world growth, and next about the economic limits of extreme inequality, drove progressive bourgeois thinkers into new directions, often radically different from the traditional modernisation theorists. I shall explore these new directions in the next chapter.

4

From Modernisation to Global Growth: New Directions in the Bourgeois Liberal Tradition

Early interest in the development of the underdeveloped areas had been a mixture of humanitarianism, ethnocentrism and economic expansionism. Economic development of the Third World was seen as both beneficial to the Third World and good for capitalist business. Modernisation theories merely provided the appropriate theoretical underpinning for comprehensive social and economic planning.

In the last decade, however, modernisation theories have become increasingly unpopular.[1] Their present-day eclipse owes as much to successful attacks from outside as to radical reflections from inside the bourgeois-liberal tradition. The attack from the outside came from the Marxist-orientated *dependency* theory, which offered a radically different explanation of poverty and underdevelopment. Attributing the present plight of Third World countries to European overseas expansion, it argued that modernisation programmes deepen the already existing patterns of economic and technological domination and dependency, and in this way make Third World countries even more underdeveloped. Dependency theory, about which more in the next chapter, gained in popularity in the 1960s, capturing the imagination of both the elites of the Third World and the more 'progressive' elements of the First World. It came to dominate the discourse on development in international organisations where the statutory contingents of Third World staff kept the dependency perspective alive and kicking. Even so, the reasons for its immense popularity, especially in the industrialised West, had not so much to do with its own merits as an explanatory theory than with the circumstances that its emphasis on the inequitable economic arrangements between the capitalist centres and the underdeveloped periphery corresponded to calls for international economic reform advanced by progressive 'liberal' thinkers. Their concern was less with the past economic injustices inflicted upon the Third World countries than with securing the future growth and stability of the global capitalist world.

In its original formulations modernisation theories had always assumed that the potential for economic growth and hence for human development throughout the world was infinite and that it could be pursued with impunity. In the late 1960s and early 1970s, however, several factors combined to corrode that happy assumption. The turn of the decade saw an end to the long period of post-war economic boom. *Economic recession* began to hit the industrial countries, sending its reverberations throughout the developing world. The post-war economic boom which had trebled the world's industrial product had succeeded in doing so only *by rapacious use of the world's natural resources*, including oil. After all, their colonial past had bestowed upon many countries of the Western world access to cheap supplies of Third World minerals. The terms of trade with which these Third World countries traditionally exchange their precious resources for the West's industrial products were deteriorating and thus contributing to a *widening* rather than closing of *the gap* between the First and Third Worlds. OPEC's decision to quadruple the price of oil in 1973 was a first instance of concerted *political defiance* on the part of the Third World. It furthermore deepened the economic recession and made double-digit *inflation* a permanent feature of the world economy. The economic stagnation, moreover, coupled with adverse weather conditions which brought disastrous crop failures in several parts of the world, pushed a delicate but so far positive balance between the world's food supplies and the world's population close to a negative one, and whipped up new Malthusian fears of *overpopulation*. The leading sector of world industrial growth in the post-war boom had been the *armaments* sector, and various localised struggles (Vietnam and the Middle East) acted as reminders of the potential for total destruction of which the super-powers were now capable. And, finally, the combined effects of world industrialisation, urbanisation and technological revolutions in agriculture on the environment erupted in a series of well-publicised *ecological imbalances*.

The coalescence of all these factors which more or less simultaneously (in historical terms) clamoured for the world's attention pushed liberal theories of development and evolution into novel directions. These new directions are at once global and futuristic, and involve an explicit or implicit use of a systems-theoretic perspective. Thinking about the future is now done from a global point of view. Third World growth and development are no longer seen as analytically distinct from First or even Second World developments, but rather as integral parts of it. The 'development problematic' is redefined as one concerning the possibilities or limits of the growth of the 'world system', of 'spaceship earth', as the favourite metaphor has it, and with the relative chances and conditions for the growth of underdeveloped countries *within* it. Unlike modernisation theories that had wished to model the socio-economic structure of developing countries after the historic example of the West, the emphasis is no longer on repeating the example but on filling in the gaps: on the Third World's complementarity to the First World's activities. The concern is with what role developing countries should and can play in future global economic arrangements.

It is, indeed, very interesting to see how the sudden awareness of the *global* interaction of physical variables such as economic growth, population growth, pollution, resource depletion, industrialisation, etc., has forced the idea of *geographical* interdependence and the need for a global political community to tackle global problems. Liberal thinkers have suddenly become conscious of the fact that it is not just the Third World that is dependent on the First World but that the relationship works the other way as well, and that there is a real threat to the future survival of the world capitalist system if, for instance, lack of international redistribution of resources leads to political violence on the part of Third World countries, or if, indeed, quite the opposite will occur and successful industrialisation on the part of all Third World countries leads to complete resource depletion of materials used by the advanced world. As we shall see below, it has led many of them to emphasise the 'organic' growth of the world system (Mesarovic and Pestel) and the 'functional interdependence' of its regions (Tinbergen).

World Futures Theories: Methodology

Before examining the substantive themes of these 'world-futures' theorists, first a word about their methodology.[2] Briefly, the methodology of the new approach involves a generalisation, and a globalisation of, *systems analysis*. Neo-evolutionary theory, in particular the final presentation of it by Talcott Parsons, had already characteristically involved systems theory. The *International Encyclopedia of the Social Sciences* provides a (somewhat wordy) definition:

> System is a concept that refers both to a complex of interdependence between parts, components and processes that involve discernible regularities of relationship and to a similar type of interdependency between such a complex and its surrounding environment.[3]

In neo-evolutionary theory the system was coextensive with the nation-state, and its interacting components were the subject-matter of the social sciences only: social, cultural, economic and political. But in world futures theories the 'system' is no longer coextensive with the nation-state but with, instead, the entire world, and the analysis of the system is now expanded to embrace the complex interaction of *all* known variables affecting this system: geological, physical, demographic and ecological, as well as social, economic, political and cultural. A prime characteristic of systems analysis as a methodology is the fusion of mathematical approaches with organismic approaches.[4] Systems analysis tries to *quantify* the interplay between a complex of interacting variables and its surrounding environment over time.

The actual method of the world futurists involves a sequence of intellectual steps:[5]

(1) A *model* has to be constructed. A model constitutes the definition of interrelationships amongst the components of the system as these are known at the present time. To take examples: economic growth will lead to population growth in the initial stages of a community's development until a certain average level of income is reached, after which population growth will decline; or the energy/GNP ratio tends to improve in the initial stages of economic development and then stabilise; or, more simply, industrialisation is associated with urbanisation; and so on and so forth.

(2) *Extrapolation* is the next step, and involves a process whereby the known behaviour of variables in the system under analysis is traced through time to a point in the future. To take examples: extrapolating current world population growth rates of 2.1 per cent will lead us to expect a doubling of the world population by the year 2010; or extrapolating the current increase of carbon dioxide in the atmosphere of 0.2 per cent p.a. will yield an increase of 50 per cent in atmospheric carbon dioxide by the year 2000.

(3) *Simulation*, next, is a computer method for analysing the behaviour of a system by computing its time path for given initial conditions and given initial values for the relationships between its components (e.g. existing ratios). In other words, in the simulation exercise are connected up all the 'extrapolated' curves in a manner prescribed by the initial definition of their interrelationships. This computation is then said to 'simulate' the system because it moves forward in time, step by step, with the movement of the system it describes.

(4) In a *scenario*, finally, certain basic assumptions of the original model are varied before the extrapolation and simulation exercises are carried out. To take examples: one might imagine that population growth rates will suddenly and dramatically decline as a result of, say, a major war or famine; or that the ratio between energy consumption and industrial

output will suddenly improve greatly because of a wonderful technological breakthrough that will make nuclear energy cheap, sound and safe; or that the economic growth rates of the poor countries will miraculously improve as a result of generous financial transfers from the rich countries; and so on and so forth.

Systems analysis has become a favourite method of social science research since the advent of the computer age, for the computer permits the processing of massive amounts of data series relating to a great number of variables, provided of course that these variables can be quantified. And it is not surprising that systems analysis, with its easy convertibility into computer language, has become even more keenly adopted in futures research, which precisely needs to analyse the interaction of a multitude of variables over a very long time period. It is a moot point, of course, whether futures research adopted systems analysis or whether systems analysis, with its associated computer mania, stimulated world futures research. There is at any rate a close 'technical' fit between the two.

With the application of systems analysis to world futures research a crucial methodological weakness presents itself. This is the problematic that systems analysis can only ever be used as a tool for decision-makers who are not themselves 'organic' variables of the 'organism', i.e. of the system one is analysing. Let me try and explain this in some detail, as it should lead us logically and unstoppably to the very heart of the subject-matter of this book, namely the fundamental difference between bourgeois and Marxist development theories.

The function of systems analysis is both normative and predictive: its ideal is for one to be able to make enlightened choices about the preferred future of the system. Applying systems analysis in an industrial enterprise one can calculate the effects of, say, the introduction of a new machine on (i) output and productivity, labour costs, raw-material costs, on shop-floor industrial relations; and (ii) on the negative (hindering) and positive (reinforcing) feedback effects of each of these on each other. Next, one can calculate the effects of increased output on sales, distribution and mar-

keting, and on the backward and forward linkages in the surrounding economic community, and next on the effects of
these in their turn on the level of income in the community
and the demand for the product; and so on and so forth. The
idea is that by studying 'if—then' sequences in a scientifically
valid manner, the decision-maker (in this case, management)
can make enlightened choices about the best options for the
system, in this case the enterprise. Best options are those
which ensure the long-term viability, or profitability, of the
enterprise. But this exercise makes sense only in so far as
management (the decision-maker) can be considered as 'tran-
scending' the system. Its own variability is neutral, held constant. Management is 'value-free', a mere technician. It has no
private interests or wants and needs at odds with those of the
system's ultimate goal. It is no accident that systems analysis
became a favourite tool of management science only when
two prior conditions had been fulfilled: first, when enterprises
had reached a size and level of technological development
where the future viability and growth of the firm had ousted
the search for immediate, short-term profits as the acknow-
ledged goal of the firm; and second, when the separation
between ownership and control of the enterprise had become
sufficiently complete for management (and theories of
management) to assume that corporate and private managerial
interests no longer conflicted. It was only when these two
conditions – in their conjunction – had been met that
managers could assume a role of decision-maker from a van-
tage-point outside the system they were to direct. It was only
then that the fiction of an abstract, neutral and dispassionate
decision-maker could be maintained.

Systems analysis, when applied to world futures research,
ostensibly serves the same purpose of enabling 'enlightened'
choices to be made. One may calculate, for instance, the
effects of various rates of economic growth on population
size, on industrialisation, on urbanisation, on pollution, on
resource depletion, on technological innovation, and so on.
One can then calculate the negative and positive feedback
loops within the system and assess the ultimate consequences
for the survival of the world system and for various sectors
and geographical entities (Third World) within it. The varia-

tions in the scenarios for the future are as many as there are
known variables and as there are different estimations of the
'known' interactions multiplied by the number of creative
suggestions for modifying the assumptions about these variables and their interactions. The professed aim of the world
futures theorists is again both predictive and normative. After
scientific exploration of the 'if—then' sequences one can
make intelligent choices for modifying the behaviour of
variables (e.g. reduce population growth, transfer resources
from the rich to the poor world, recycle petro-dollars or
mineral waste, etc.) so that one can arrive at the preferred
world of the future. But instead of arriving at the preferred
world of the future, we now arrive at the Achilles heel of
the world futures debate. For who is the 'one' who can make
the decisions? Who is the agent of social change? Which category of bureaucrat/technician is outside the world system?
God? Unable to cope with this dilemma, yet unwilling to face
it head on, bourgeois theorists appeal to either an abstract
entity such as 'mankind' or they underline the need for a
world community and a world government, or they naively
appeal to 'the leaders of the world'. Sometimes they simply
direct their pleas to the bourgeois intellectual elites of the
world.

Thus the weakness and at the same time the distinguishing
characteristic of all bourgeois world systems theories is the
completely ahistorical character of their analyses and their
scenarios. Ignoring the existence of historically determined
social relations, of conflicting interests and competing political entities, they seem to see the world as peopled by some
sort of clone, bereft of any real historical concrete interest,
yet endowed with common sense and a heart in the right
place. The task of the bourgeois theorists is to enlighten these
hearts and minds. Some writers do not even bother to appeal
to these good hearts and minds; they assume, in their scenarios,
and quite openly too, that the latter are already in control
of the world and are pursuing the same benevolent policies
everywhere.[6]

The problem with the bourgeois liberal tradition is that it
has always lacked a proper theory of social change (for a discussion, see pp. 146, 156). The tradition never went beyond a

formulation of the structural characteristics of different types of social organisation at different levels or plateaux of evolution. And it is for that reason that Parsons prefers to speak of an evolutionary *paradigm* rather than an evolutionary *theory*.[7] The legacy of this theoretical vacuum becomes painfully obvious in all liberal world models. There is no understanding of the forces of change, no conception of processes of change. Instead there is a somewhat feeble appeal to 'mankind', to men of goodwill, to act in concert for a change. Against this Christmas carol voluntarism, Marxists do have a theory of social change on offer, i.e. *historical materialism*. It is this historical materialism that makes their world systems theories the more credible — as we shall argue in the next chapter.

World Futures Theories: Themes and Issues

Turning now to a brief description of the substantive theories of contemporary bourgeois futurists, their methodological unity is forgotten, while, instead, I concentrate upon their kaleidoscopic diversity. Yes, surprisingly, there is found a remarkable range of both forecasts and scenarios spanning from Kahn's 'business-as-usual, more-of-the-same-worlds' to Herrera's radically 'new society'. While some see successful economic development of the Third World to be contingent upon the continued growth and greed of the advanced capitalist world, others see favourable prospects of poor countries precisely in zero growth of, and a generous redistribution of existing wealth by, the rich countries. The substantive differences in the world models do not just pertain to different conceptions *vis-à-vis* the role of inequality in world economic development — they also frequently gel with contrasting beliefs concerning the over-all capacity of the world economy for continued growth and the presence of global physical limits. That is to say, those authors who are concerned to point out the physical limits to global growth are also likely to favour solutions involving a radical rearrangement of global economic activities which will benefit poor countries. Over time, in the whole decade of the world futures debates, one notices a shift away from the question of global limits to the question of redistribution and re-structuring of international economic arrangements. As this is the case, an easy order of presentation of the various global growth models presents itself, namely one which is both chronologically correct and theoretically adequate.

The Global Growth Debate[8]

Up to the end of the 1960s long-term global forecasts were few and far between. They tended to express both a desire for continued economic growth and to attest to an un-shakeable belief in man's technological capabilities. A primer in futurology and a clear example of this technological optimism is Kahn and Wiener's *The Year 2000*. We are, so they argued, entering *la belle époche*, when man's capacities and commitment to economic development and control over his external and internal environment are increasingly seeming without foreseeable limit.[9] Continued economic growth will not only bring more wealth for all, it will also create the possibilities for new major technological innovations to bene-fit all humankind. The year 2000 will see the majority of people in the rich world enjoying a life of leisure, permitting themselves pleasant and increasingly unharmful indulgencies. They will be developing skills of interpersonal interaction and emphasising 'self-development' rather than having to toil for material reproduction. Thus, not only are Kahn and Wiener optimistic about man's technological abilities, they also wholeheartedly approve of the prospect of an even more materially affluent society than that which we in the rich countries already have. In this, their first major futurist work, Kahn and his co-workers are unconcerned with the Third World countries, complacently assuming that continued world economic growth will proceed along lines of increasing disparity of incomes between the affluent nations and the poor nations without this, however, becoming a problem for the rich ones, neither economically nor politically. First World countries do not need the Third World for their own economic development, and while the threat of nuclear war, they feel, has had a stabilising effect on the major powers, the poor countries do not possess the military resources to challenge successfully the existing world economic order. In response to their domestic insecurities poor countries are more likely to engage in an irrational attack upon one another.

Since the publication in 1972 of the first Club of Rome report on 'The Predicament of Mankind', called *The Limits to Growth*,[10] the tide, at least for a short while, turned in favour of the pessimists. Although widely criticised for the assumptions of their model and for their questionable use of statistics,[11] the authors of the report achieved what they had set out to do, namely to make wide sections of the literate public in the advanced countries concerned for the future of the world. Global modelling had come to stay. The predicament of mankind, according to the authors, is that at the present time and precisely as a result of mankind's great technological achievements and successful economic methods of production, we are coming up against a number of critical limits. These limits are physical, demographic, social, economic and psychological. But the crucial point is that these 'limits' or 'variables' interact and so reinforce each other, thus precipitating the arrival of doomsday. What are these critical limits?[12]

First there is the problem that world industrialisation and economic growth have led to an uncontrolled growth in world population, now expected to reach 7 billion in the year 2000. The more numerous the population throughout the world, the greater the industrial effort needed to satisfy the material needs of that population. For, at current rates of world and regional economic growth, we can expect the chances of satisfying *per capita* human needs to deteriorate. If we extrapolate the present relative growth rates of population and economic production in rich and poor countries, we discover that the gap between rich and poor countries will widen in absolute (not just in relative) terms. What can we do about it? Increase the *rate* of industrialisation?

Here the second problem arises. The industrial process has up till now been fed from sources of energy which are not in the main self-renewing. In a determinable space of time these supplies will be exhausted, and although their replacement through new sources of energy (e.g. nuclear power) is theoretically conceivable, this is not yet practically realisable. A similar problem arises with respect to the use of mineral raw materials, above all metals, which also are not self-renewing; their exploitation is advancing so rapidly that the exhaustion of deposits can be foreseen.

More critical still is the fact that the world's water levels are dropping. The water requirements of the industrial process have reached a point where they can no longer be satisfied by the natural circulation of water. As a result, the *Limits to Growth* report forecasts disturbances in the cycle of evaporation and precipitation which will lead to changes in climate. Desalination of sea-water would be a possible solution, but that solution would in its turn come up against the already critical limit of energy.

A further limiting factor is the production of foodstuffs. Here the report is particularly pessimistic, arguing (against the dominant beliefs of the time) that neither the area of land suitable for cultivation nor the yield per acre can for much longer be arbitrarily increased. For to do so would lead to new ecological imbalances, e.g. erosion, pollution through poisonous substances, reduction in genetic variability, etc.

'Pollution' of the earth itself, mainly as a result of industrial expansion, is another critical variable. There are two sub-problems here, one is that of irreversible waste, and the other is that of various forms of poisoning caused by harmful substances: physiological damage from pesticides, radioactive isotopes, detergents, pharmaceutical preparations, etc. The authors reckon that a world population of 7 billion at a level of *per capita* income comparable with that employed by North Americans today will pollute the earth ten times more than at present. It is not known at what point the critical limit of ecological balancing (e.g. the self-regulating capacity of natural systems) will be crossed. But one thing is certain, and that is that one special critical limit in the pollution category cannot be crossed, namely that of thermal waste. Heat is emitted by all processes involving the conversion of energy, and the laws of thermodynamics show that, even in principle, this limit cannot be crossed.

A final critical limit is presented by what is called *psychic pollution*. Under this heading come increasing exposure to excessive noise and other irritants, the psychical effects of overpopulation and other stress factors.

In short, in 1972 the Club of Rome expressed a neo-Malthusian fear that current production and consumption patterns of the advanced world would run into severe critical limits of resource depletion, overpopulation, pollution, or a combination of all these. This message, in outline, had already been communicated by a member of their team, Jay Forrester (in *World Dynamics*),[13] who was the first to spell out dooms-day prediction with the aid of a computer. The *Limits to Growth* was simply a more elaborated and popularised version which was particularly effective in terms of propaganda, because of its dramatic presentation of 'exponential curves' and 'positive and negative feedback loops'. It is the characteristic of exponential growth that the time needed to double a factor is progressively reduced. For example, imagine a pond in which there grows a water lily. The lily doubles its size every day. The lily will fill the pond in thirty days, suffocating all other forms of life in the pond. Now the dramatic issue is that for a while the lily will be quite unnoticed and small, and then, suddenly, when the lily has but filled half the pond, there is only one more day to go before the whole pond is doomed. Adding to this grim picture, *The Limits to Growth* drew attention to a point not made so clearly before, i.e. that of the mutually reinforcing nature of events because of the positive and negative feedback loops that connect up all the elements/variables in the world system.[14] This put the authors of the report clearly ahead in the 'doomsday league'. They showed very dramatically that attempts to improve or solve one problem would in fact only exacerbate another. For instance, it is well known that rapid industrialisation in underdeveloped countries is the only effective solution to population growth. Birth rates do come down and finally stabilise at a low level only when people have started to participate in the industrial/urban complex and have adopted nuclear-family patterns and materialistic life-styles which are predicated on the perception of children as costs rather than assets. However, increased industrialisation, on a world-wide basis, precipitates the depletion of resources, increases pollution, and aggravates the social disorientation and alienation associated with rapid urbanisation. Similarly, attempts to increase agricultural output, which itself is now quite feasible because of the 'Green Revolution', will aggravate problems of soil erosion, water pollution, etc. Again, tackling pollution requires a phenomenal increase in scientific research and technological innovation, which in turn depends on massive industrial and capital expansion; and so on and so forth.

This, to be sure, is the value of the method of computer-assisted systems analysis, namely that one can calculate the effect of one exponentially growing variable upon another. But the analysis has other, *theoretical*, consequences as well. For, seeing the entire world as a system of interacting variables, induces one to speak of 'equilibrium', of the 'danger of overshoot and collapse', and, next, of the 'responsibility' of the various components (e.g. geographical parts) towards the survival of the whole. Thus the Club of Rome argues that it may be unwise for the poor countries to attempt to industrialise because of the dangers of resource depletion and global pollution that this implies. They suggest that the rich—poor gap can only be diminished through redistribution and not through more growth. They advocate 'stabilisation' of the growth curves of 'spaceship earth' at current average levels rather than at growing levels of production and consumption. In a critical review of the ecology debate, Enzensberger has argued that this 'redistribution' talk is a mere sop, and reveals the ideological motives of the Club of Rome.[15] At what level is the world supposed to stabilise its production, when already the USA, with 6 per cent of the world population, rapaciously consumes 40 per cent of its energy and 35 per cent of its raw materials? Equalising the world's regions' use of resources at present average levels would entail such a *massive* amount of redistribution as to be politically quite out of the question. Therefore, the talk of redistribution which has today become so popular in circles of global capitalist institutions is mere rhetoric and designed to sugar the ideological pill of the 'spaceship earth' message, which is that 'The poor must not rock our lifeboat.'

Interestingly, Enzensberger's Marxist critique of the Club of Rome is echoed by that arch-conservative Kahn, who in a very recent work primarily addresses the anti-growth movement. He, too, is suspicious of the fact that the opposition to more world economic growth should come from people, classes and nations who are already rich.[16] And he not only dismisses the Club of Rome's finite-resources projections as being based on unsound assumptions and calculations, but he completely turns the argument around and upside down. The only foreseeable limit to *la belle époque* is not physical but social, namely the anti-growth movement itself. Neither resources nor pollution constitute crucial constraints for continued rapid economic growth, but rather slackening demand, changed values and changed attitudes — themselves a product of the anti-growth ideology. Our planet, he says, is like a muscle: the more you use it, the stronger it gets. There are no such things as finite resources because new sources and new kinds of resources arise from expanding use, not from standing still. The critical problems of our age (e.g. energy) can precisely only be overcome by *more* economic growth, by vast increases of capital expenditure and technological innovations.

The *Limits to Growth* predictions of doom and catastrophe which we are to expect soon after the globe has reached the year 2000 population of 7 billion have no place in Kahn's 'surprise-free' world of the year 2023, when he confidently anticipates a population of 10 billion and a gross world product of 20 trillion dollars. Widening gaps, too, hold no terror for Kahn. Not only are Kahn and his colleagues *in fact* more optimistic about the economic prospects of (most of the countries of) the Third World than either the dooms-day theorists now or they themselves previously were, but also *in theory* they embellish the conservative view that a *relative* widening gap is not only unproblematic for the advanced world but is also of positive advantage for the Third World. Rather than see the widening gap as an obstacle to economic development, they see it as a basic engine of growth in Third World countries. The widening gap is a force for transferring the benefits of economic development to the poor countries:

The great abundance of resources of the developed world — capital, management, technology and large markets in

which to sell — makes possible the incredibly rapid progress of most of the developing countries. Many of these
poorer countries are also developing relatively autonomous
capabilities at an increasing rate.[17]

Indeed, not only are they optimistic about the future, they
are also very satisfied with the progress of the Third World so
far. They point out that almost half of the world's population
now lives in countries that have progressed enormously in
acquiring wealth and have done so since the Second World
War.[18] The success of these capitalist middle-income countries,
and more especially of the newly industrialising countries
(Taiwan, South Korea) amongst them, owes much to their
untrammelled pursuit of an over-all economic growth strategy
in preference to a redistribution of income strategy. As is the
case between economies, inequality within the domestic
economy, too, serves as a powerful economic stimulant,
encouraging the talented, entrepreneurial elements to seize
economic opportunities and innovate, thereby increasing the
level of economic activity of the entire economy. It is true
that in contemporary developing countries the trickle-down
effect does not appear until very late in the development process, if at all, and that precisely because of this the middle-
group countries number as many poor as do the poor countries.
But this should not blind us to the 'genuine successes' that
these middle-income countries are enjoying. It would be
immoral to jeopardise the early prospects of a talented and
lucky minority — and the eventual prospects of the great
majority — in order either to preserve a relatively egalitarian
income distribution or to prevent the existing income distribution from being further distorted, as the basic needs
strategists advocate. Of course, the worst problems of the
'really' and 'remaining' poor should be alleviated, but in what
way Kahn does not tell us. This, however, is a moral objective,
not an economic or political necessity, for there is no evidence
that the poor people in developing countries hate or envy
their local rich. Inegalitarianism as a political issue is, again, a
Western prerogative.

Kahn's theories are interesting for their relief function:

they make the arguments of the more progressive liberals stand out more clearly. There are others within the bourgeois tradition who cling to the same perspective. Rostow's recent work also makes the point that the rich countries can help the poor countries only by growing still faster themselves.[19] His opinion of the *long-term* prospects of the world economy generally, and that of the Third World within it, is as optimistic as Kahn's. He is, however, more anxious about the immediate future. He views the last quarter of this century as a critical test, a crucial period on 'getting from here to there'.[20] Right now, he argues, the world economy is in the early phase of a fifth Kondratieff upswing, when — as in comparable phases of earlier long-term cycles — new sources of food and raw materials urgently need to be found. Such critical periods have always required an extra thrust of new inventions, innovations and enlarged investments, but the present period demands these innovative efforts for a longer list of basic commodities than ever before, that is, not just for food and raw materials but also for energy and energy conservation, pollution control, water supply, and so on. Neo-Keynesian economics is bankrupt: to restore the balance of economy in the USA and in the world as a whole, it will no longer suffice to 'focus obsessively on the indiscriminate expansion of effective demand'.[21] Instead we need enlarged investments in the top-priority areas of technology. But enlarged investment in these new frontiers of technology can only be successful if equal attention is paid to its foundation, namely the growth of the body of science generally. Most ominous of all contemporary gloomy world data for Rostow are not those on population, finite resources or pollution, but rather those that bear witness to the absolute and relative decline in R & D expenditure in the USA since the late 1960s.

If the salvation of the world economy lies in the expansion of R & D budgets (private, but especially public), by the same reasoning it lies in the acceleration of the growth rates of the already rich countries, namely the OECD nations. This will also help the Third World:

The maintenance of a high OECD growth rate is a more powerful instrument for sustaining progress in the developing world than either a 25% cut in the OPEC oil price or a radical liberalization of trade permitting an accelerated flow of manufactured exports from developing nations.

Thus argues Rostow and he conjures up some dubiously referenced World Bank data to back up this claim.[22] NIEO-type proposals for trade liberalisation and increased aid are fine but only if in return 'the South commits itself to maintain a regular flow of supplies, uninterrupted by political or quasi OPEC considerations'.[23] Rostow is all for a stable and effective partnership between the North and the South and for a 'common agenda' for the 'world community' provided this partnership and this community is organised and directed under the global leadership of the USA. In fact, Rostow quite openly pleads for a return to the USA's world hegemonic role – which he observes has declined in the 1950s and 1960s – because the USA happens to be the largest economy in a world of increasing international interdependence and at a time of structural change when the inputs to sustain industrial civilisation must be expanded.[24] This latter view contrasts sharply with that of the international Keynesians, who much prefer the 'world community' to be led by international political organisations and institutions, i.e. by a kind of 'supra-national state'.

International Keynesianism

The Club of Rome message has been repeated in various forms by other current writers: Schumacher,[25] Tinbergen,[26] Heil-broner,[27] The Ecologist team,[28] Barbara Ward.[29] The prescriptions only vary in the effect that they expect the world's 'limits' to have on the poor countries, in whether they anticipate 'nuclear blackmail' and 'wars of redistribution',[30] or whether they believe that some sort of redistribution deal can be worked out with at least part of the developing world. The latter solution has become the key concern of what may be termed the second-generation models, published since about the middle of the 1970s.

The second-generation models approach the issue of living

within our limits more constructively and less pessimistically. Both the problems of pollution and of resource depletion are now seen as being already technologically manageable, and in some of the most recent works even population is no longer reported as an urgent 'constraint', especially since the world population growth curve has started to level off.[31] The emphasis is no longer on zero growth but on redistribution, on international economic reform. The anti-growth movement has been replaced by international Keynesianism. The reasons for this reorientation are not hard to find. The first-generation models had come at the tail-end of a long world economic boom, the second-generation models are written during a deep world-wide recession. In a time of zero or even negative economic growth, when there is massive unemployment and widespread bankruptcies, anti-growth theories are not popular. Furthermore, the world economic recession has also brought the awesome additional insight that the advanced world may never recover unless at least part of the under-developed world can be brought up to a standard of life where people and nations can play a decent role as economic consumers. The need is therefore clearly not one of no growth, but one of new economic growth points, of a new international division of labour, a new international economic deal. At the political level the United Nations' adoption of the New International Economic Order action programme in 1974 — all too often mistaken for an exclusive product of Third World demands — provided the negotiation platform for working out this new economic deal. The second-generation models can be considered as the theoretical back-up service for this platform, designed to provide a rationale and a justification of the programme for public consumption in the advanced countries. To this end they have needed to pursue the logic of systems theory even further, and to postulate a world model where the regions as well as the 'limiting' variables are integrated.

The second Club of Rome report, this time written by Mesarovic and Pestel,[32] is a good example. Their major theme is the interconnectedness of world events, both physical and geographic, and therefore the need for global solutions. Coming hard on the heels of OPEC's successful price hike in 1974, their 'global' pleas acquire a special urgency and a new meaning. It permits them to point to 'the worldwide dependence on "common" [sic!] stocks of raw materials; the worldwide problems in providing energy and food supply; the sharing of common physical environment of land, sea and air'.[33] This global dependence and these global problems obviously require global solutions. In perfect accord with the nature of systems theory, they now openly plead for 'organic growth' rather than undifferentiated growth of the world; the latter would precisely lead to the kinds of exponential-curve disasters predicted in the first Club of Rome report. An organic-growth scenario for the world entails that 'all actions on major issues anywhere in the world . . . need . . . be taken in a global context and with full consideration of multi-disciplinary aspects'.[34] It also requires the balanced economic development of all regions. This in turn hinges upon worldwide industrial diversification, carefully planned with special regard for regional specificity. This calls for investment aid rather than commodity aid, except for food. But how do we get from here to organic growth? For that we need a viable world system, a 'one-world concept and a world community'. Therefore, Mesarovic and Pestel urge the shedding of narrow nationalism. They argue that a world system in which nations are increasingly interdependent is already emerging anyway. And they hope that the global world problems currently plaguing us will actually contribute to this one-worldness feeling. Actually, this particular report offers a rather unsubtle bargain-scenario. The advanced world's dependence on oil and other raw materials is traded for the Third World's food scarcity. Both problems are unceremoniously, and with no regard for their historical origins, uplifted to a 'common global level'. The idea is that the industrial countries will somehow solve the Third World's food problem, in return for which OPEC will continue to supply oil.

Professor Jan Tinbergen, one-time Nobel Prize-winning adviser to the United Nations and leading author of the third Club of Rome report, goes further still in the transition from global limits to international redistribution.[35] Although he admits that the planetary resource constraints are less severe than the previous Club of Rome reports had suggested, he yet begs us to abandon the mad pursuit of economic growth and material richness. Third World countries must give up the idea of 'catching up', while the advanced countries too should move from an over-all growth to an over-all welfare concept. For, in the current world economic order, maldistribution, both inside and between nations, is the more important aspect of the environmental crisis. Recognising that the institutional distortions of the free-world market system have been created by and work in favour of the advanced industrialised countries (costing the poor world an estimated 50–100 billion dollars per year)[36] and that the rich countries with 30 per cent of the world's population consume 70 per cent of all its resources, Tinbergen is haunted by the spectre of wars of retribution. OPEC's act of 'political defiance' in 1973 is hailed as both an omen and a moment of great historical portent. Normally, historical change is evolutionary, but now the constellation of events is such that we may expect a revolutionary change – when rich and poor countries realise that they have unparalleled problems that cannot be solved independently.

The fundamental aim of Tinbergen's new international order is a world where every individual has an unalienable right to a life of well-being and dignity. The latter two concepts are operationalised in a set of concrete rights: the right to survive, the right to work, the right to education, the right to recreation, the right to socio-cultural activities. The fundamental strategy for achieving the fundamental aim is redistribution, both at the international and at the national level. At the international level it involves a redistribution of growth, of jobs, of income. Here the Tinbergen project team explicitly embraces the NIEO demands and spells out the international measures of reform and the institutional changes necessary to implement it. This in fact was the task that the project team had been commissioned to do. The key strategy here is a new international division of labour, with rich and poor countries obediently following the law of comparative advantage specialising in those industrial activities which they are good at (metal work, electronics and R & D-intensive activities for the advanced countries) and abandoning 'inefficient' ones. At the same time, and contradictorily, poor countries have *also* to follow policies of self-reliance (including collective self-reliance) so as to overcome the relationship of dependency in which they stand *vis-à-vis* the advanced countries, and in order to attack their own problems of poverty directly. For policies of self-reliance serve to meet the requirement of domestic redistribution, and the satisfaction of basic needs, as they typically involve greater self-sufficiency in agriculture and maximum use of local resources (both of people and of materials) in industry. Tinbergen and his group valiantly struggle to square the circle of a preferred world where there shall in fact be more international trade, more international investment, and a greater interpenetration of different economies under the technology-spreading tentacles of multinational firms, and where — at the same time — there will be more *independence* and self-reliance for the two-thirds of the world that is poor. The way to square this circle is through a change of heart. Multinationals should adopt a code of conduct which permits their profit motives to be harmonised with the self-reliant interests of Third World countries. Similarly, the world's sky-rocketing expenditure or armaments which employs — they say — almost half the world's scientific and technological manpower should be directed to peaceful ends by a shift from a war to a peace mentality.[37] How simple! Now why did we not think of this before?

At the domestic level, too, the Tinbergen team attempts to square circles. On the one hand, they welcome the *Charter of Economic Rights and Duties of States*, which underscores the sovereignty of the national state, by attempting to give it real economic muscle, and on the other hand they undermine this sovereignty by ostensibly making the individual and the world's population, but *not* the nation-state, the primary subject of development strategies. To square this particular circle they propose a functional concept of 'national sovereignty' to accompany the observed functional interdependence of the present world sytem. There are some types of decision (e.g. those with consequences for people in other nations) which must be taken by international fora, representing the world's population. This requires a functional as opposed to a territorial interpretation of national sovereignty. It also implies a strengthening of existing international organisations.[38]

Several other international teams of experts have praised the virtues of global redistribution along the lines suggested by the NIEO demands: higher and stabilised prices for commodities from Third World countries, world-wide relocation of industry and massive financial transfers from the rich to the poor countries (see, for example, Leontief, in a study commissioned by the United Nations;[39] a Japanese team – again sponsored by the Club of Rome and led by Yoicha Kaya;[40] The Brandt Commission;[41] and, most recently, an OECD team of experts).[42] In sharp contrast to Kahn's and Rostow's proposition that Third World countries will grow if the rich countries grow faster still, the new orthodoxy advocates higher growth rates for Third World countries, coupled with moderate to lower growth rates in the advanced countries.

As the decade wore on and the recession deepened, the arguments in favour of this international Keynesianism became more candid. The Brandt Report is a good example. It states bluntly that the North 'needs' the South

> just like employers at the turn of this century had to be made aware that higher wages for workers increased purchasing power sufficiently to move the economy as a whole . . . the industrialised countries now need to be interested in the expansion of markets in the developed world.[43]

And in a passage that may do credit to any updated version of Lenin's *Imperialism*, it quotes the 1978 European Community *Annual Report*, which recognises that 'the equilibrium of the world economy *depends* on a continuing flow of private lending to the *non-oil producing developing countries* on a scale unheard of before 1974' (emphasis added).[44]

In concert with the other progressive liberal views just reviewed, the Brandt Report, too, sees the globalisation of problems and challenges, both economic as well as environmental, as a historical opportunity for selling the world-community idea and the need for strengthening the role and function of international organisations. I must profess to an uncommon flash of sympathy with the Conservative British Government when it commented on the Brandt proposals as containing nothing new. Indeed this is true. Excepting the relatively minor proposal of a tax on arms trade (on page 123), there is not one single new idea or argument in the report. It takes its place in a long queue of world development reports that started with the Third Worldist-dominated and controversial UNCTAD reports in the 1960s and grew into an avalanche of UN documents, official policy statements and commissioned world 'models' by reputed experts in the 1970s. So why has the Brandt Report become such a popular statement on the world situation? The answer is that this is what it was meant to be. It was clearly written as a public-relations exercise, and its good-quality journalism and popular presentation of facts as well as the careful choice of its main authors (elderly statesmen) reflect such. It is addressed to governments and 'open-minded responsible women and men all over the world',[45] and it has two main messages. One is directed to the working people of the advanced countries who have to suffer the adjustment problems associated with the world-wide relocation of industry, and possibly also the financial risks of a projected 300 per cent increase in (mainly commercial) lending to the newly industrialising countries.[46] They are told not to succumb to protectionist arguments. The other message is directed to the governments of the Third World, who are told to take policies of domestic redistribution seriously. The report lists a number of 'good' domestic policies, such as expansion of social services to embrace the poor, agrarian reform, increased development expenditures in rural areas, stimulation of small-scale enterprises, and better tax administration. These policies 'if widely adopted would signal to the international community a genuine commitment by developing countries to a more equitable sharing of the benefits of development as well as a determined effort to mobilize human and material resources for it'.[47] At the same time, and squaring Tinbergen's circle again, Third World countries are lectured on the differences between 'self-reliance', which is good and permitted, and autarchy, which is not:

The South needs and wants to be more self-reliant, to complete the process of political independence with economic dependence. But that does not imply separation from the world economy. It means rather the ability to bargain on more equal terms with the richer countries, to obtain a fair return for what it produces, and to participate fairly in the control and running of international institutions.[48]

Autarchy, by contrast, is a distinguishing feature of the Bariloche model and it may therefore come as a surprise to find this model also listed here amongst those of the progressive liberals. The Bariloche group is a group of distinguished Latin American social scientists who published the futurist document *Catastrophe or New Society?*[49] The idea for the work itself was sponsored jointly by the Club of Rome and the University of Argentina, and its aim was to build a model of the world that would reflect, in the first instance, the needs and development requirements of the Third World. These 'Third Worldists' had been particularly alarmed by the first Club of Rome's zero-growth suggestion, since (to be sure) that suggestion does not do much for Third World aspirations. So, therefore, the Bariloche group set out to prove that under *radically altered conditions* of global and domestic social and economic organisation, every single human being, whether in the bush in Malawi or in Manhattan, New York, can have an acceptable standard of living without this ever involving a trespassing of the so-called 'critical' physical or environmental limits. Their model is not meant to be predictive. It consists of a conceptual model which is a proposal for a *utopian* world, and a mathematical model which is the instrument through which the *material viability* of this utopia is demonstrated. The study does not explore the mechanisms or the processes of change through which the real world may reach the proposed objectives. The new utopian society is premissed on the following moral criteria: egalitarianism, full participation, non-consumer values, basic need satisfaction, and the use of a production function with substitution between capital and labour. It is clearly not a capitalist society, for resources are not allocated on the basis of profit, or via free-market mechanisms, but on the basis of social need.

Although the authors are a bit vague and woolly about the type of political organisation pertinent to the new society ('mechanisms of collective action'; 'and land and means of production are neither privately owned nor owned by the state'),[50] they do recognise clearly that the satisfaction of basic needs is incompatible with untrammelled international trade and economic interpenetration. Therefore, they propose to cut the world up into four autarchic regions based on geographical proximity: (i) developed countries, including socialist and capitalist nations, for (as a footnote on p. 43 quite innocently explains) socialist and capitalist countries are not differentiated, as all countries were supposed to follow the same policies after 1980; (ii) Latin America; (iii) Africa; and (iv) Asia and Australia. There is total collaboration within regions and a stabilising (not growing) level of international trade between regions. The satisfaction of basic needs is achieved in all regions with the use of almost exclusively local economic resources. But since international solidarity is also assumed as a moral premise, the rich countries will drastically reduce their growth rates and their non-essential consumption and transfer their resources to the poor countries through NIEO-type measures.

The Bariloche group has become famous for its concept of 'basic needs', which are operationalised in physical terms, e.g. number of calorie intake *per capita*, number of dwellings *per capita*, number of years of life expectancy *per capita*, number of years of basic education *per capita*, etc. The main conclusion of the report is that under conditions of egalitarianism, both international and national, the levels of GNP (and hence the growth rates) required for meeting basic needs is between three and five times *lower* than that required if current inegalitarian international and national income structures are maintained. It is the expressedly utopian character of Herrera's model that persuades me to classify it as a progressive liberal instead of as a Marxist model despite its very radical substantive themes. For the difference between bourgeois and Marxist perspectives, in my opinion, rests ultimately on the absence or presence of the *historical method*. Whereas the bourgeois systems approach negates such a method, the Marxist view embraces it.

Marxist theory, as we shall see in the next chapter, is in the first place the theory of historical materialism. It studies the process of historical change and predicts its direction by analysing the *logic* of human systems of production in each concrete historical period. This logic itself — as we shall see — is the logic of the dialectic: it expresses and brings forth growing contradictions between material forces of production and social relations of production.

Equipped with the conceptual framework of the historical method, Marxist writers will typically try to trace the *likely* course of social change. This involves first pinpointing the relevant and significant material contradictions of the present system of production (capitalism) and the corresponding loci of class conflict, both local and throughout the world. Next they will examine the ability of the system and its ruling class to overcome temporarily these material contradictions and to contain the class conflict by means of adjustment policies, both in the productive and the distributive spheres. Such adjustment policies typically involve shifting class alliances, again national and international. And finally, Marxist writers will often speculate on the probabilities of the final collapse of the system and its revolutionary change to an altogether new system of production.

The bourgeois theorists, by contrast, have no historical method and therefore no theory of social change. One may well ask: what about their theory of evolution, which states that human social evolution is a process of increasing specialisation and complexity (or differentiation and integration)? After all, meagre and unsatisfactory though it may be, it does outline two general laws of motion of human social organisation. This is true, but this theory of evolution fails the requirements for a theory of social change on two counts: first, it does not identify or wish to identify either sources or mechanisms of social change; and second, it does not conceive of a significant progression beyond the present social order of our modern society. With the arrival of the modern society we have arrived at the final destiny of human social evolution, as (for instance) Parsons is keen to point out. From hence onwards no movement is possible except geographically: the incorporation of the entire globe into the one modern world system. This leaves present-day bourgeois writers in a double bind: they can neither trace the logic of history into the future, nor do they have the conceptual equipment to look objectively and scientifically for likely sources of change, for main springs of future worlds. In such an intellectual vacuum they have but two options, both normative and not scientific, objective or predictive. Mechanically feeding existing data series into the computer they can come up with a world future projection that they either 'like' or 'don't like', depending on their own normative evaluations, their temperament, and so on. If they like it, as Kahn does his 'more-of-the-same, business-as-usual-world', all is well, but if they do not, as is the case with the various doomsday scenarios, their only recourse is to plead for mercy. And so they plead for 'political will', for 'good common sense', for a 'change of heart' or for a 'change of values', as in Laszlo's *The Inner Limits of Mankind*,[51] yet another Club of Rome report which spells out the new values 'mankind' must adopt if it is to avert catastrophe. These values are values appropriate to our 'global' age and include selflessness, internationalism, anti-consumerism, care for nature, and so on.

The kindest critique one can level at the bourgeois world development writers here reviewed is that, deeply hidden, they *do* have some sort of theory of social change. For, implicitly, they seem to adopt a voluntarist theory of social change. A voluntarist theory of social change assumes that

(a) men can change their behaviour at will; and that
(b) if and when all men change their behaviour at will and in concert, the course of history will be changed.

Accepting their works as *bona fide* expressions of their own good hearts and intentions, and not as some ideological expression of the interests of an international bourgeois class, one may thus justify the sacrifice of many valuable trees on the altar of their publications.

There is one group of writers, which I have kept to the last in this series, who make this voluntarist theory of social change *explicit* and who deliberately turn it into a comprehensive progamme of public education and media activation.

I am referring to the work of the World Order Models Project (WOMP) team of the Institute for World Order based in New York, but with affiliated experts such as Johan Galtung, Richard Falk and Ali Mazrui in respected academic institutions elsewhere. They, too, write scenarios of the future under the series 'Preferred Worlds for the 1990s'.[52] The central values of their preferred world order are, again, peace, well-being, basic need satisfaction, social justice, ecological balance and more such pleasing ideals. The institutional framework also is one of global integration through a central world authority responsible for global planning and the organisation of basic need satisfaction, distribution of food, ecological balancing, etc., but counterbalanced by regional and national cultural diversity (on the good liberal grounds that we are all equal but different). Incidentally, within WOMP there is some dispute between the world governmentalist (Falk) and the 'regionalists' (Galtung, Mazrui), who stress self-reliance. What is interesting about the WOMP writers is they they do not just stop at writing scenarios for the future; they sell them. Comparing their public education function with that of the abolitionist movement of the eighteenth and nineteenth centuries they aggressively popularise their 'World Order Studies' programmes in schools, in colleges and on television.

If the preferred world order is a 'must' for global survival, getting there takes time: twenty-five years (from 1975) is a nice round time-table for Richard Falk and his team.[53] The first ten of these are reserved for consciousness-raising, mostly about global limits, and the 'Apollovision' coined to express the spaceship-earth idea. The second ten years are devoted to the mobilisation of the masses of the population, and the remaining five to institutional reforms.

5

Theories of Social Evolution and Development: The Marxist Tradition

It has long been a point of controversy amongst Marxists whether Marx formulated, or even meant to formulate, a stage-like theory of human social evolution, as was the fashion amongst the liberal thinkers, and as indeed it became official Soviet ideology from Stalin's time. According to this Soviet interpretation, Marx was supposed to have delineated five progressive stages of human socio-economic formations: the 'classless' primitive community, the slave-based society of classical times, the feudal society based on serfdom, the modern bourgeois society based on capitalism, and lastly the advanced 'classless' society of the future, i.e. communist society. This unilinear schema was thought to be not only a logical but also a chronological progression of human social life. When applied to the now underdeveloped world, it permitted the Soviets to adopt an 'interventionist' view of social change in these societies, uncannily similar to that of the bourgeois modernisation theorists. Both Soviet and bourgeois theorists believed that the laws and generalisations derived from the past experience of the nations now affluent could serve as a lesson for the present and the future of those who were still poor. Just as modernisation theorists had considered underdeveloped societies to be suspended in a pre-modern stage from which they could progress only with assistance from the advanced world, so too the Soviets believed the underdeveloped societies to be locked in a pre-modern stage of 'semi-feudalism and semi-capitalism', from where advance was only possible (given the obstructive intervention by imperialist nations) if a strong nationalist state, based on a historically correct class alliance of bourgeois and proletarian elements, and supported by the already advanced socialist community, assumed state control of a capitalist economy.[1] As Wallerstein points out:

> this version of Marxist thought, so prevalent between 1945 and 1965, is a sort of mechanical copying of liberal views. Basically, the analysis is the same except that the names of the stages are changed and the model country has shifted from Great Britain to the USSR.[2]

In the West, and even more so in the Third World, the Marxist tradition has, however, *also* engendered a *contrary* perspective. This perspective (usually referred to as neo-Marxist) does not see nation-states as societies that have separate, yet parallel histories, but as parts of a single developing capitalist world economy. Nevertheless, even for this non-Soviet interpretation of Marxist theory the question of 'historical stages' has remained pertinent. In fact, recent years have witnessed a revival of neo-Marxist concern with 'stages' of human evolution. The reasons for this revival are very complex. One set of reasons stems from certain intellectual problems that arose within the neo-Marxist school of 'dependency and underdevelopment'.[3] In criticising the modernisation school, this 'dependency' school argued that the underdevelopment of the Third World was not a pre-modern stage, but that it was precisely a consequence and a complement of the capitalist development of the First World. However, one problem that presented itself around the turn of the last decade was that of the diversity of the 'underdevelopment' experience. Some countries were quite clearly undergoing some sort of economic development while others were not. As a result the theory of 'dependency and underdevelopment' had to be refined to permit an explanation of these different experiences. A closer look at the differences in 'pre-capitalist formations' *prior* to the penetration of capitalism was a logical next step in this theory's development. A second in-

tellectual problem arose in relation to their crude conception
of underdevelopment as 'stagnation resulting from exploitation'. How long can stagnation continue? And who exactly
is doing the exploiting inside these Third World countries?
And what form does this exploitation take? Is it, as earlier
forms of the dependency theory had argued, the expropriation of a country's economic surplus, either through looting
or through the mechanism of the world market? If so, then
surely the point would be reached when the surplus had
disappeared, and with it the rapacious interest of the capitalist
penetrator. Or were the conditions for exploitation through
dependency being *reproduced* through time? This, as we shall
see in Chapter 6, is the revised conception of more recent
dependency theorists. It has led them away from a concern
with *unequal trade* to a concern *with production*, and through
it to the social relations of production that exist in the countries of the Third World. These social relations are both more
complex and more varied than the relations of production in
the advanced capitalist countries, where (after all) capitalism
has long since become the dominant and the exclusive mode
of production. In the countries of the Third World, by
contrast, capitalist relations of production, such as wage-
labour, interact or 'articulate' with pre-capitalist relations
such as feudal – and communal – property relations, in a
manner that invites at once a more profound analysis of the
phenomenon of exploitation and an explanation of the
continuity of exploitation through time. Thus a recent textbook on underdevelopment presents as its main thesis that
we cannot understand contemporary reality in underdeveloped
countries unless it is analysed from within historical materialism as a social formation which is dominated by an articulation of (at least) two modes of production, a capitalist and
a non-capitalist mode, in which the former is, or is becoming,
increasingly dominant over the other.[4]

This new departure within theories of 'dependency and
underdevelopment' which has led them to examine world-
wide exploitation from the point of view of the coexistence
of different modes of production, was in its turn encouraged
at the theoretical level by the *new orthodoxy* in Western
Marxism. This new orthodoxy was formulated in the mid-

1960s by Althusser and his co-author Balibar in *Reading 'Capital'*.[5] The new orthodoxy reconstituted the concept of *mode of production* as central to the Marxist theory of society and history. According to this interpretation, human history was indeed seen by Marx as a succession of stages. But this succession was not a chronological progression of specific societies, but – and this is very reminiscent of neo-evolutionary thought – rather a generalised and abstracted evolution of human social organisation. This generalised process of human evolution may at the broadest historical level be broken down into a number of stages, each stage being characterised by a particular mode of production: the primitive or communal mode, the ancient or slave mode, the feudal mode, the capitalist mode and a communist mode (yet to come).

A few years earlier, in the United Kingdom, Hobsbawm had edited a collection of Marx and Engels's writings on *Precapitalist Economic Formations* wherein he had established the same perspective:

> The general theory of Historical Materialism requires only that there should be a succession of Modes of Production, though not necessarily any particular modes, and perhaps not in any particular determined order.[6]

The Concept of Mode of Production and Historical Materialism[7]

What, then, precisely, does this mysterious concept of mode of production stand for? By way of shorthand one might say that a mode of production is both a method of performing labour and a method of extracting labour.

The starting-point for Marx's theory of social and economic evolution is 'men performing labour'. 'Men create and reproduce their existence in daily practice,' he says, 'in breathing, in seeking food and shelter, in making love, etc.' They do this by operating *in* nature, by taking *from* nature (and eventually consciously changing nature) for this purpose. This taking from nature is called 'appropriation'. Originally, in prehistoric times, this appropriation involved no more than the taking by man of the ready-made consumer objects from nature (e.g. fish and fruit) but since that pre-historic stage man's appropriation from nature has involved the process of labour in which a determinate raw material is transformed into a determinate product for consumption. In other words, in Marx's theory, history only begins when men *produce for their reproduction*. In this process of productive appropriation three elements (*forces of production*) are combined:

(1)   The personal activity of man himself (i.e. work/labour).
(2)   The object of work (i.e. land).
(3)   The instrument of work. This includes the means of production (chemical, mechanical and technical aids in production such as shovels and picks, fishing nets, spinning wheels, assembly lines and micro chips). It also includes science and technology generally and even the manner in which (1), (2) and (3) are combined technically in the production process.

These forces of production are really of the essence: they refer to the way in which man relates to his natural laboratory, the earth and nature, and to the way in which he takes from nature what he needs to reproduce himself and to reproduce the objective conditions of his existence (like keeping some seeds to plant the crops for the next harvest, or saving money to buy a new tool).

In the beginning, says Marx, there is a *natural unity* between these three forces of production; there is a 'natural unity of labour with its material prerequisites'. But, being a social animal, man develops both co-operation and a social division of labour. This is made possible by, and in turn makes more possible still, the production of a surplus over and above what is needed to maintain the individual and the community of which he is a part. In this process of social division of labour the *natural* unity between the three forces of production is progressively broken up; production becomes increasingly a process in which the three elements are *socially* (as opposed to naturally), and at the same time increasingly more antagonistically, combined. They become more and more 'negatively related' to one another.

Different historical stages of evolution are marked by different social combinations of the three elements into concrete forms of co-operation and co-ordination of labour, and into concrete forms of articulation of the means and the object of labour. While the concept of *forces of production* refers to the three elements, land, labour and the means of production, including the manner of their technical combination, the concept of *relations of production* refers to the social organisation of this combination. That is to say, the concept of relations of production defines both the specific mode of appropriation of surplus labour and the specific form of social distribution of the means of production corresponding to that mode of surplus appropriation. The concept of relations of production thus becomes tantamount to both the concept of property relations and the concept of class relations. Thus capitalist relations of production define a mode of appropriation of surplus labour which works by way of economic means, namely commodity exchange (see pp. 159–60), but in pre-capitalist modes of production appropriation of surplus labour occurs by means of political domination (as in both feudal and slave-based societies) or by means of ideological control (as in primitive or 'communal' societies). The corresponding class relations are: bourgeois and proletariat, landlord and serf, free citizen and slave, official and peasant.

Thus for Marx the distinctive structural characteristic of each historical epoch lies in the manner in which surplus labour is appropriated and distributed (i.e. through ideological, political or economic means); to this, in turn, corresponds the manner in which the forces of production are socially and technically combined. In this way it may be said that particular forces of production and particular relations of production together form a particular *mode of production*.

Marx and Engels describe four such historical modes of production up to the present: primitive or communal, ancient or slave, feudal, and capitalist. A fifth mode of production, the final outcome of human evolution, is yet to come. And what precisely is the purpose of man's evolutionary voyage through these stages? In close agreement with their bourgeois counterparts, Marx and Engels firmly believed this to be *progress.* More, they defined *the content of* progress in very similar terms, namely as the growing emancipation of man from nature, resulting in man's increasing control over nature. They, too, saw the development of economy and technology as the 'freedom-giving agency' in this process, and the individualisation of man as a logical corollary of it. As did Parsons later, they furthermore recognised that in the course of human social evolution each one of the structural levels of society (the ideological, the political and the economic) becomes dominant *in turn* (and in the same order), and that the most advanced stage to date is that in which the economic structure of society provides the organising principle for all human conduct and for the entire social fabric.

To the extent that there is indeed this similarity between the two traditions, criticisms as to their euro-centricity are fully justified.[8] Indeed, it is remarkable to observe how the respective development theories derived from these traditions simply cannot handle (nor indeed could predict) the success of, for example, the Islamic Revolution in Iran. For neither tradition has the conceptual tools to recognise a lasting reassertion of the religious or ideological level in developing countries. Economic development subjected to religious procedures and values is anathema to both traditions; and human development is simply not definable in terms other than principally economic ones. Therefore, both traditions are driven to dismiss the Islamic Revolution as an expression of anti-imperialist, nationalist sentiments only.

One is thus perfectly justified to conclude that both traditions have a materialist interpretation of human progress. But where the bourgeois theories simply do not go beyond this materialist preoccupation, the Marxist tradition has another ace up its sleeve. While for Parsons and the bourgeois tradition progress has been evenly accumulated by mankind throughout its history, we learn from Marx and Engels that the whole of history and each of the stages of human evolution up to and including the present one are but necessary, materially progressive, yet at the same time dehumanising, preludes to the final advanced epoch yet to come. This final advanced stage is that stage of evolution, the communist stage, when human freedom and dignity can finally catch up with all the material benefits acquired in previous periods of *un*freedom.

For, indeed, the modes of social organisation of human activity thus far — while absolutely necessary for the development of the forces of production — are a testimony to increasing exploitation and human misery. The very same 'evolutionary universals' which Parsons praises as appropriately 'integrative' devices corresponding to each phase of the social division of labour, Marx and Engels denounce as ever so many cultural, legal and religious disguises for increasingly 'negatively related' forces of production. Where for Parsons the societal community harmoniously widens to embrace, in progressive stages, kin, subject, 'gent' and finally 'citizen', for Marx and Engels it divides ever more viciously between exploiting and exploited groups, between oppressor and oppressed.

And so we reach the heart of the matter, which is the difference between the two traditions. Since for the bourgeois evolutionists human progress consists exclusively of material progress made possible by the successive invention of integrative cultural symbols and organisational devices, it is not really necessary for them to concern themselves with the causes of social change. They do not need a theory of social change. For, ultimately, human progress involves a cumulation of 'good' ideas, and there is no reason why these ideas cannot be passed on through the ages either by accident (as in the past) or by design (as today, in the 'modernisation' period). One does not really need to know *how* things came to pass; all one needs to know is which cultural and social ingredients are compatible with each other at any particular stage of social differentiation. Because social change is therefore in the last analysis conceived as a *logical* process, it can be presented as a product of an *intellectual insight.* Moreover, since there is never any question that those social and cultural forms that are appropriate in any one historical epoch are more appropriate to some classes or groups than others, and serving the needs of some better than others, but are instead thought to be universally valid for all, social change can be invoked by intellectual appeal. We have seen in Chapter 4 how this bourgeois, formal, epistemological conception continues to impede the writings of those who stand in this tradition, even when they are 'radical' by any other definition, and truly concerned with, for instance, the inequality between nations, the vested interests of the rich and the plight of the poor. They fail utterly to make the transition from a bourgeois to a Marxist analysis of human history. Although — as I have argued — Marx and Engels did outline a history of human progress in stages, it would be contrived and misleading to present these stages in the schematic form that we used to present Parsons's stages of evolution (see p. 12). For such schematic presentation cannot convey the more essential message of Marx and Engels's theory, which is that of the *dialectical* nature of historical change. In contrast to the bourgeois theories which do not formulate a theory of historical change but merely outline a taxonomy of human social organisation along some logically perceived stepladder of evolution, Marx and Engels are primarily concerned — not even with a description of stages — but with an analysis of the forces of transformation within each stage.

Their description of the structural characteristics of various historical stages (a description that is scant in the case of primitive and ancient modes, though very elaborate in the case of the feudal and capitalist modes) is *subordinated* to a dynamic analysis of the forces of change. In the most general terms these forces of historical change are reflected in the struggle between emerging and obsolete relations of production, consequent upon the quantitative growth and qualitative change of the forces of production. This is the kernel of Marx and Engels's historical materialism. At each historical stage, haves and have-nots, exploiting and exploited classes, are pitched against each other owing to the contradictions inherent in the manner in which production is organised. These contradictions become aggravated as a result of the development of the forces of production to a point where these can no longer be usefully contained within the existing relations of production. They then lead to class conflict, revolution and ultimately a historical transformation of the mode of production.

How soon and how successfully these contradictions lead to conflict and revolution depends very much on the degree of the consciousness of the oppressed class, and this in turn is a matter of political organisation, leadership and the mass circulation of a historically correct analysis: that is, an analysis of the method of appropriation of surplus labour, and of the growing contradictions of this mode of appropriation; an identification of the historically relevant classes and a formulation of the progressive development of the class struggle. Therefore, a truly Marxist analysis always requires a *revolutionary praxis*. It demands active participation on the side of the oppressed by those who make the correct historical analysis in the first place. A truly Marxist analysis means taking sides, and taking to the streets. It means combining one's intellectual activity with political grass-roots work.

Obviously, many 'Marxist' writers who analyse developing countries today do not adhere to this puritanical interpretation of the methodology of Marxist analysis — they still prefer to do their analytical work from behind their desks. And yet, as we shall see in the next chapter, one recent development within the Marxist tradition demonstrates, alongside a revived interest in the concept of mode of production, a renewed faith in the orthodox epistemology of the Marxist tradition, namely that a historical analysis is nothing if it is not about exploitation in production and about class conflict, and if it is not expressing a commitment to further the class struggle. And thus, in diametric contrast to the bourgeois tradition, which forever tries to formulate and assert intellectually 'logical fits' or 'structural compatibilities', the Marxist analysis does exactly the opposite: it seeks to trace the contradictions engendered by any mode of production, to clarify and deepen them.

The Capitalist Mode of Production

In line with the presentation of the bourgeois tradition, I shall here also merely give the briefest possible outline of the capitalist mode of production. For we are interested in the capitalist stage only in so far as the Marxist analysis thereof has fed into Marxist theories about the Third World, just as we were only interested in a brief description of Parson's 'modern stage' because it had inspired bourgeois theories about the Third World; i.e. modernisation theories.

The dissolution of the natural unity between the forces of production, says Marx, becomes complete with the arrival of the capitalist mode. Having already lost his control over land (the object of work) in previous historical epochs, man now loses control over the instrument of his labour (the means of production) and, with the establishment of machine-dominated production in mature capitalism, one might even say he loses control over his own labour. At this penultimate stage of evolution, beyond which the bourgeois theorist desires neither to think nor to speculate, we find man at his most exploited: stripped of his dignity and pride – a mere possessor of labour-power.

There is a continuing debate about what exactly are the essential characteristics of capitalism. Some consider the essential characteristic of capitalism to be 'generalised commodity exchange',[9] while others insist that its essential characteristic is the normal condition of free contractual labour.[10] Again others define capitalism in terms of private ownership of the means of production.[11] Which of these is central to the definition of capitalism is of course crucial in deciding whether or not capitalist development is or is not taking place in contemporary developing countries.

In keeping with the method of characterisation of modes of production generally I take the definitive characteristic of capitalism to be its method of surplus appropriation. This method of surplus appropriation is *economic*, operating as it does through the mechanism of commodity exchange and the organisation of forces and relations of production by means of that exchange. But this requires precisely the presence of *all* three characteristics in conjunction: namely, generalised production for the market, the presence of free contractual labour, and private ownership of the means of production, which entitles the capitalist to ownership of the final product.

In pre-capitalist societies things are produced, and indeed exchanged, but there is no commodity production or commodity exchange, because things are not produced primarily for exchange, nor are they produced as a result of the process of exchange. There is a market-place but not a market principle, one might say. Nor, again, are the relations between the people in the society, and between those who are co-operating in production, determined by the exchange. But under capitalism the forces of supply and demand in the market-place, by determining the price of the produced goods (market principle), in turn determine the relative value of the three factors of production and so turns them into commodities too.

As commodity owner, the worker is free to sell or not to sell his labour as he chooses, and he is subject only to the economic constraint imposed by the exchange of commodities. That means that 'only' the whip of hunger, as even Max Weber had to admit, will force him to offer his labour. But this, precisely, is in sharp contrast to other modes of production where the worker does not possess such freedom but rather is made to work by some extra-economic means. Now, this fact, coupled with the third characteristic, the capitalist's ownership of the final product, means that any surplus product (i.e. the exchange-value of the product minus the cost of the wage) can be appropriated by the capitalist on the basis of *apparent* freedom, according to the economic laws of commodity exchange. This, in fact, makes capitalism the more 'efficient' method of surplus appropriation. In the commodity form of labour on which capitalism is premissed is implicated a dissolution between labourer and labour-power: the capitalist hires the latter but not the former. Therefore, the reproduction of the *concrete* labourer, and the cost of it, is none of the individual capitalist's business or responsibility (unlike the case in the feudal or slave-based modes). All he is concerned with is the cost of labour-*power*. But this is both an abstraction and an average, namely the average cost of the labour-time 'socially necessary' to produce it. This, in turn, is reflected in the 'average' wage level. Marx agreed with Ricardo that under the pure free-market conditions of capitalism this average wage represents the minimum living costs of the labourers in any one concrete historical period. It changes, of course: upwards with advances in the productivity of labour, i.e. with general progress. Marx's labour theory of value is predicated on this distinction between labourer and labour-power on the one hand, and on the distinction between the use-value and the exchange-value of labour-power on the other. The theory states:

(1) Labour is the source of all value.
(2) All commodities, including labour-power, have an exchange-value which is the equivalent of the labour-time socially necessary to produce them.
(3) The use-value of labour-power is always greater than its exchange-value (i.e. the wage) or else there would be no point in capitalists hiring labour.
(4) The capitalist, having bought the labour-power of the worker for a certain period, is entitled to appropriate the entire production of the worker including the surplus-value (i.e. the difference between the value produced by the worker and his wage).

This labour theory of value has re-emerged recently as the *dominant* component of theories of contemporary imperialism (cf. p. 200). Instead of arguing — as classical theories of imperialism did, and which were correct at the time —that the imperialist expansion of capitalism was due to its internal contradictions (e.g. the falling rate of profit at home, see p. 164) some now argue that the differences in the 'average' wage levels pertaining in rich and poor countries cause capital to flow from one to the other.

Let us now turn to the *laws of motion* of capitalism. The capitalists extract surplus-value, not to enjoy luxury but to accumulate more the means of increasing employment so as to extract still more surplus. They are driven to do this because of the competitive nature of the free market which rewards enterprises that are technologically ahead and penalises those that are behind. Every capitalist enterprise is thus forced by competition to aim for greater profits, for this is the only way it can constantly improve its technology and its labour productivity. In this manner entrepreneurs are forced to invest their profits into forever newer investments, or into 'expanded reproduction' as Marx called it. And this, in turn, is the reason why capitalism more than any other mode of production develops the forces of production while at the same time more than ever antagonistically setting up the relations of production one against the other. For it is not only a *prerequisite* of capitalism that the society should be marked by severe social inequality, concentrating the means of production in the hands of a single social class, the bourgeoisie, while leaving the mass of the people with no possessions or means of subsistence other than the sale of labour-power, it is furthermore an *outcome* of the inner logic of this mode of production that the conflicts between these two classes should forever deepen. For one thing, the competitive struggle between the capitalists leads to concentration of capital into fewer and fewer hands, and the consequent proletarianisation of a part of the bourgeois class. For another, concentration of capital itself reflects an increasingly higher organic composition of capital (with machines replacing human hands) in economic activity accompanied by the progressive expulsion of more sections of the proletariat from that activity. This leads to periodic crises of 'overproduction' and testifies to *capitalism's inherent contradiction, which is the tendency of the rate of profit to fall.* In the course of its history capitalism has time and again overcome its own natural limits first by branching out into new areas of activity and creating new wants and needs, and second by extending geographically into new areas. The latter phenomenon is better known by the term *imperialism*, to which we shall turn next.

Theories of Imperialism, Dependency and Underdevelopment

Theories of imperialism

It is as well to make the point at the outset that theories of imperialism are not exclusively the product of the Marxist tradition. In the nineteenth century the concern with 'empire' and with 'making the empire bigger' had encouraged the formulation of apologetic bourgeois theories of imperialism as well as critical Marxist ones.[12] 'Imperialism' then was not the dirty word that it is now. In the minds of classical, liberal economists an aggressive colonial policy was a necessary complement to the creation of a perfect international division of labour in which each area of the globe, each region or country, would specialise in what it was good at and would thus cash in on Ricardo's theory of comparative advantage. The classical model saw colonisation as a means of imposing on underdeveloped countries a specialisation of production that would eventually benefit them. Since the classical economic theorists were at the same time staunch supporters of 'free trade', the *continuation* of colonial rule with all its petty restrictions and protectionist devices presented them with a real dilemma. As there was no way they could defend the phenomenon on theoretical economic grounds, they soon developed *political* and even *demographic* explanations, e.g. national rivalries between the European powers, excess population in Europe, etc.[13] Over time, when the direct political subjugation of overseas peoples ('colonialism') was no longer seen to serve any useful purpose in the continuation of existing world economic relations, liberal economic thinkers preferred to regard imperialism as a thing of the past, and they filed away the concept in historical archives.

Marxist writers on imperialism, on the other hand, have experienced no such intellectual difficulty, as to them the essence of imperialism had always been *economic* domination and subordination, while 'colonialism' was only regarded as a historically specific political complement of imperialism.

Marxist theories of imperialism, moreover, are theories of *capitalist* imperialism because essentially they regard imperialism as a necessary expansive phase of capitalism. Marxists, since Lenin, exclusively reserve the concept of imperialism to denote a necessary stage in the development of capitalism, and only of capitalism. However, it would not be correct to say that Marxists were the only writers to connect imperialism with the dynamic development of capitalism. Paradoxically, the foundation of the theory of capitalist imperialism is equally credited to two writers, V. I. Lenin and J. A. Hobson,[14] the latter of whom was not a Marxist but a liberal. The argument which both developed and which may be considered the centrepiece of the theory of capitalist imperialism is that the rate of profit in capitalist societies over a long period tends to decline because the very process of capitalist accumulation increases the amount of fixed capital per worker and increases productivity. The declining rate of profit leads to crises of overproduction and underconsumption. To counter the declining rate of profit at home entrepeneurs will export capital abroad, and colonial expansion, defined as direct political domination over areas where capital is invested, will follow. Thus the essence of imperialism is the export of capital rather than of commodities. Since the need to export capital, by the logic of capitalist development, occurs when a certain degree of capitalist accumulation and concentration has been achieved, imperialism as a necessary expansive stage of capitalism coincides with the monopoly stage of capitalism. Although both Hobson and Lenin attributed the exodus of capital to declining investment opportunities at home, Hobson's remedy was to improve living standards at home, especially of the rural population, who had lost out in the uneven distribution of the benefits of capitalist progress. This remained the favourite prescription of liberals and of various shades of West European social democrats for decades to come. By contrast, its impossibility under capitalism became one of the leading tenets of Marxism.

The very emphasis of classical theorists of imperialism such as Lenin, Hilferding and Bukharin on the dynamics of capitalist development in the advanced countries as the *source* of imperialism made them neglect the study of the *effects* of imperialism in the overseas territories to which capital was being exported. If they expressed any thoughts about the colonies at all, these displayed a naive conception of the uniformity of the overseas experiences and of the synonymity of capital with capitalism. It was taken for granted that the penetration of capital would inevitably work up the same social-structural forces and tensions as the emergence of capitalism had already done at home. It was assumed that under imperialism capitalism would spread across the globe, and that in so doing it would turn the whole world capitalistic, and hence ripe for world-wide socialist revolutions. The only notable exception was Rosa Luxemburg, who — much before her time — made the point that the capitalist mode of production depends precisely for the production of surplus-value on an exchange with non-capitalist modes of production.[15]

Theories of dependency and underdevelopment

If modernisation theories were the bourgeois theorists'
answer to the plight of the underdeveloped countries, dependency theory was the product of the application of Marxist
theories of imperialism. From about the late 1950s theories
of imperialism began to address popularly the *effects* of
imperialism on the overseas territories in an attempt to explain
the roots of backwardness. The dependency theory that
emerged from this exercise thus became a counterpart to
Marxist theories of imperialism. Imperialism is seen from the
standpoint of the subordinate nations.[16] It has been observed
by several commentators, critical and sympathetic, that
'theory' is probably not an apt description of the type of
work carried out under the name. What surfaced was more of
a 'perspective', a 'paradigm', or a 'school' of thinking which
brought a wide variety of Marxist and non-Marxist radicals
together under one banner.[17] The dependency perspective
which these thinkers, and development strategists — for many
were employed as policy-makers/advisers to international
organisations and governments — came to share was sufficiently potent to act as a classificatory principle, distinguishing
the dependency theorists from the bourgeois modernisation
theorists. Indeed, the genesis of dependency thinking and its
continuing qualifying essence was its criticism of bourgeois
modernisation theory.[18]

The original version of 'dependency and underdevelopment'
theory, as outlined by first Paul Baran,[19] and next more
popularly and grandly by André Gunder Frank,[20] concentrated on locating the cause of backwardness of Third World
countries, more especially of Latin America, within the dynamic growth of the world capitalist system. Underdevelopment — as distinct from *un*development — it was claimed, is
not due to some 'original state of affairs', as bourgeois theory
has it, but is the result of the same world historical process in
which the now developed capitalist countries became developed. Thus, from the very beginning, the dependency approach
has been a *world-system* approach, explicitly rejecting the
concept of the unified state as actor and the notion of the
global system as a collection of nation-states.[21]

Baran was the first to make the point that 'development and underdevelopment' is a two-way street: the advanced capitalist countries had become developed by expropriating economic surplus from those overseas countries with which they first traded and which they later colonised, while the overseas countries became underdeveloped by aiding the ascendancy of the West. For their intense economic interaction with the industrialising capitalist states left the overseas countries with a narrowly specialised, export-orientated primary production structure which found its handmaiden in a frozen internal class structure dominated by a small, landed and mercantile ('comprador') elite whose economic interests became increasingly intertwined with those of the advanced capitalist states, and whose cultural life-styles and tastes were a faithful imitation of the same. This is the essence of 'dependency'. The imposed specialisation of production and the continued coincidence of interests between the imperialist states and the ex-colonial elites even after *inde*pendence blocked any attempt at industrialisation and internal social transformation (e.g. a bourgeois revolution). Over-all economic stagnation and extreme pauperisation of the masses was the result. Thus, in contrast to Marx's own optimism regarding the historically progressive role of capitalism everywhere, Baran demonstrated the impotence of the imported variety.[22]

André Gunder Frank expanded and formalised this substantive theme into a theory of underdevelopment, postulating three 'laws' of motion of the process of development and underdevelopment and coining the twin concept 'metropolis—satellite' to characterise the nature of imperialist economic relations.[23] He went little beyond Baran's masterpiece when he traced the metropolis—satellite contradiction beyond the international into the national—local sphere. The ties of dominance and dependency, he said, run in chain-like fashion throughout the global capitalist system, with metropolitan states appropriating the surplus from the satellites, their towns removing the surplus from their hinterland, their landlords from the peasants, their merchants from shopkeepers, and finally, the shopkeepers from the customers. Frank's mixing of spatial with social metaphors gave his image of the chain of metropolis—satellite contradictions rather more ideological than scientific value. At any rate it was soon criticised for being un-Marxist because of its identification of the mechanism of economic surplus extraction with the capitalist market.[24] Thus it located 'exploitation' in the sphere of exchange rather than production. Nor was it made quite clear how exactly this exchange led to exploitation.[25]

Now, the structural link between the development and underdevelopment of different world regions had already been postulated before by others, more especially by the scholars from the Economic Commission for Latin America. The notion of dependent external-structural relationships particularly was associated with the name of Raoul Prebisch, one-time founder and president of UNCTAD, whose centre— periphery model antedated Frank's metropolis—satellite model of world capitalist relationships by over a decade.[26] Where Paul Baran and André Gunder Frank transcended the ECLA analysis was in defining this structural link in *politico*-economic terms, rather than in strictly economic terms. Prebisch and ECLA had put the underdevelopment of Latin America down to its unequal trade with the industrial world arising from two historical distortions of the world *market* system. The first was the international division of labour which had reduced colonial countries to being specialist producers and exporters of raw materials and foodstuffs, while encouraging the industrialised world to produce and sell manufactures. ECLA presented the by now well-worn technical economic arguments why such a pattern of international trade tends to favour the industrial over the primary producers in both the distribution of the benefits arising from such trade and in the general developmental impetus generated by it. The second historical distortion of the international market was that factor and commodity markets at the centre of the world capitalist system had become more monopolistic and oligopolistic than at the periphery. In the long run this affected the terms of trade for the periphery unfavourably.[27]

Thus the ECLA and Prebisch formulations had sought to establish the cause of underdevelopment in *external*, global, structures and dependent relationships, and their development strategies derived directly from this analysis. They prescribed a policy of inward-directed development for Latin America based on the twin principles of state-protected industrialisation and import substitution under the aegis of foreign investment. Such a policy, it was believed, would at one and the same time stimulate economic growth in Latin America and reduce Latin America's dependence on the advanced world.

At the time this analysis was thought to be extremely progressive, and it was even accused of being Marxist, no doubt because its emphasis on industrialisation indirectly threatened the traditional imperialist—feudal alliance. The irony was, however, that the imperialist—feudal alliance was never directly and openly attacked. Had that been the case, it would have alerted the ECLA intellectuals to the notion of class alliance itself and through it to the *dynamic* interaction between external and internal structural factors affecting Latin American development processes.

It is only when the ECLA policies failed in their objectives, that is, when the balance-of-payments problems were not eased but in fact worsened as a result of 'import substitution', — when real wages did not rise sufficiently quickly to stimulate domestic demand, when unemployment grew more acute and income distributions more unequal, and when, as a result, industrial production became increasingly concentrated in products typically consumed by the elites, it was only then that the intellectual climate finally ripened for class analysis.

Both Baran and Frank helped this process by emphasising the complicity of local elites in the transfer of economic surplus from subordinate to imperialist countries. Frank, moreover, in a later work, was now able to 'explain' the failure of ECLA's policies by pointing to the same external/internal dynamic link: industrialisation, which was to have been a panacea of all dependency ills, itself had become increasingly dependent on the capitalist metropoles for financing, marketing, for capital goods, technology design, patents, trademarks, licences, etc. The very process of industrialisation had led to a deepening of dependence and to further underdevelopment.[28] Why was this so? Frank's argument is that the previous, colonially imposed, class structure had rendered a

highly *unequal income distribution.* This unequal income
distribution severely limits the internal domestic market. And
this, in turn, has two corellate effects: on the one hand, it
ushers in the process of industrialisation by way of production of luxury/consumer durables, and such a pattern of
production, by its very own nature, involves a heavy reliance
on imported producer goods, spare parts, technology, etc. On
the other hand, the increasingly severe balance-of-payments
problems resulting from this pattern of industrialisation leads
to the pursuit of even greater dependency: foreign firms are
now invited to invest their producer-goods/technology locally.
Now, the combination of a limited domestic market and the
presence of foreign industrial subsidiaries encourages a
grotesquely inefficient system of production and a net out-
flow of resources: the Latin American subsidiaries have
become the dumping-ground for either obsolete foreign
equipment or foreign plants that have obsolescence deliberately built into them;[29] their capacity is grossly under-
utilised, and their labour absorption rate minimal. Over time
remitted returns on foreign investment have come to exceed
by several times the net inflow.[30]

By emphasising how external dependency interfaces with
the internal structure of extreme income inequality, which in
its turn distorts the industrialisation process, Frank has invited criticisms to the effect that his is a 'mechanical', economistic deterministic explanation of dependency and underdevelopment.[31] The national bourgeoisie is seen as a rather
passive instrument of foreign domination unable to dis-
entangle the national economic good from its own interests,
which are solidly locked in with foreign capital (e.g. as
partners/managers of foreign firms, as subcontractors and
distributors and as consumers of the luxuries). 'Dependence,'
Frank claims, 'is indivisible and makes the bourgeoisie itself
dependent.'[32] And this is why his solution to Latin America's
problems is a radical break with the world capitalist system.
Replying to his critics, Frank has also stressed the *active* role
of the national bourgeoisie in its articulation of government
policies that facilitate dependency and underdevelopment —
government policies such as the liberalisation of import con-
trols for capital and intermediate goods, repeated currency

devaluations, a halt to agrarian reforms, and fiscal policies. 'In this manner,' he says, ' "lumpendevelopment" is promoted by a "lumpenbourgeoisie".'[33]

It seems to me that Frank continues to miss the point made by his critics. The critical issue surely is *not* whether local elites consciously or unconsciously collaborate with foreign interests, but whether or not 'social classes are seen as completely derivative of economic forces, and whether these economic forces appear to be having a "necessary logic", thus denying the possibilities of struggles against imperialism'.[34] This is the critical point made by Colin Leys in a summary review of dependency theories generally. Remedies like a radical break deny such revolutionary potential, he continues, adding somewhat cynically that such denial is not just theoretical, it is also political, for both dependency theories and dependency theorists have been nicely 'co-opted' by the central institutions of global capitalism, notably the World Bank and the various UN organisations.[35] Having arisen as a criticism of bourgeois development theory, dependency theory has now itself become bourgeois: it is no longer radical because it fails to appeal to the masses of peasants and workers.

6

From Dependency to Global Political Economy: New Directions in the Marxist Tradition

The imperialism and underdevelopment thesis which we discussed in the previous chapter had run out of steam by the early 1970s. The changing capitalist world economy, with its increasing internationalisation of production, permitting the rapid economic development of some Third World countries within its widening industrial embrace, while at the same time excluding and marginalising others, the OPEC rebellion, the post-Vietnam dollar crisis and the apparent decline of US hegemony, these all posed fresh and *contentious* issues which the Marxist tradition had to resolve at the theoretical level. But in particular the nature of Third World economic development needed to be defined: was it capitalist development or was it not, and consequently did it or did it not open up the possibility for revolutionary social and political movements to develop *locally* without any prior 'radical break' with the world capitalist system, as Frank had advocated. In its original form the Frankian dependency paradigm had categorically denied the possibility of any capitalist development anywhere or at any time in the periphery of the world capitalist system. Such theoretical denial not only came up against empirical economic realities; it also rendered the analysis of dependency and underdevelopment static and ahistorical.[1] By locating the root of underdevelopment in the transfer of 'economic surplus' from the periphery to the centre capitalist countries, via the mechanism of the world market, the Frankian thesis could not satisfactorily explain why and how the conditions for further exploitation were renewed and reproduced through time under historically altered conditions. Once the economic surplus had been expropriated, what mechanisms and/or forces made for the reproduction of economic surplus to be expropriated in the next historical period?[2] And what about the problem of over-accumulation in the centres? What explained *their* needs to continue their rape of the Third World? Rather, such explanation, Frank's critics would claim, required an analysis of production (class) relations inside the Third World countries, and not merely an analysis of commodity (market) relations.

As we shall see in this chapter, much of the post-Frankian Marxist debate concerning Third World development and/or underdevelopment has got bogged down into precisely this controversy, that is, whether the genesis and the continuity of Third World exploitation is to be located in 'imperialist-dominated' production relations inside the Third World itself, or whether it is to be sought in world capitalist market arrangements. It is a controversy between 'productionist' and 'circulationist' conceptions of exploitation. And the logic of each position dictates its own political *praxis*: those writers who now focus on imperialist-induced internal class structures inside Third World countries perceive great scope for local class struggles, for articulating defensive class alliances which may redefine and 'improve' the links of dependency with the world capitalist system and which can 'construct paths to Socialism' (although, to be honest, no descriptions of such socialism within the world capitalist orbit are ever presented).[3] It is a line of argument often preferred by Third World, especially Latin American, writers themselves. It is an argument that has a voluntarist emphasis, an almost Gramscian inspiration. It neither blindly follows the laws of motion of the world capitalist system — the centres of which are, after all, out of reach of the Third World — nor does it advocate a radical break from it, which is in any event unrealistic in the case of most Third World countries. It believes in fighting for national social progress within the constraints, and even taking advantage of, the penetration of world capitalism. And thus it ultimately asserts the belief in the *national development* of Third World countries.

By contrast, the logic of the circulationist position leads to a world system perspective whose prime unit of analysis remains the world capitalist system, its historic-logical progression and its inner contradictions. This view, inevitably, sees whatever happens in the Third World countries – be it industrial development in some, or further stagnation and decline in others – as derivative of the logic of capitalist accumulation in the capitalist centre countries. In the extreme form this perspective denies the people in individual Third World countries the theoretical possibility for national-socialist struggles now. For these writers, the socialist transition remains something that can only be attained at a world level, namely when the world capitalist system has run out of tricks to overcome the inner contradictions of its over-accumulation and underconsumption. When driven to declare a position in respect of *political* struggles, these writers will call upon not national but *world* class struggles, and they will advocate the solidarity of the international proletariat.

Of course, this is an extreme simplification, a caricature, of the post-Frankian debate. There are a host of brooks flowing into and out of each mainstream, and writers differ to the extent that they either acknowledge or ignore the insights of their opponents. But a simplification of positions is in my view justified on didactic grounds. It is a *device* to pull out the main themes, organise and systematise them. For within each main angle of vision answers are developed not only about the nature of capitalist development in the Third World, and its prospects for national-socialist transformation, but also, contingent upon these views, there are answers to related questions concerning the relative position and the role of rapidly developing Third World countries within the world economic hierarchy, the need for and prospects of Third World solidarity, the value and meaning of the NIEO and the directive tendencies of imperialism.

It may well surprise the reader to find that in the following survey of the post-Frankian literature I have none the less organised the text around *three themes* rather than around the above two schools of thought. This is a complication forced by the actual chronological history of ideas. For the post-Frankian debate originated with one particular Marxist critique of Frank's concept of capitalism, and this critique was wrapped up in the Althusserian concept of mode of production. Subsequently, since it was such a useful tool, it was seized upon by both schools, though for different purposes. In each case the meaning of the concept was reduced to fit the prevailing theoretical orientation. The concept suffered a double reductionism at the hands of 'circulationists' and 'productionists', an economic reductionism in the case of the former and a class reductionism in the case of the latter.[4]

Re-examining the Concept of 'Exploitation': the Articulation of Modes of Production

In a by now classic article which appeared in 1971 Ernesto Laclau criticised Frank for equating capitalism with commodity exchange, and thus — by logical corollary — locating the cause of satellite exploitation in the sphere of *exchange* rather than in the sphere of *production*.[5] Laclau's refreshing article has had implications that go far beyond those of a criticism of a trend-setting scholar. His criticisms coalesced with an otherwise quite unrelated tradition, that of the radical French anthropologists[6] and Althusserianism, and the two helped inspire a new direction in Third World studies, one which tries to understand poverty and exploitation in underdeveloped countries as a result of the articulation of capitalist modes of production with pre-capitalist production. As we shall see below, this theoretical notion has the additional advantage of facilitating a diachronic theory of imperialism.

Frank had argued emphatically that Latin America had been made 'capitalist' right from the early settler days in the sixteenth century, and although he never gave a precise definition of 'capitalism' it was clear from several paragraphs in his *Capitalism and Underdevelopment in Latin America* that he equated it fully with 'production for profit which is oriented to the [world] market'.[7] Since in Latin America this profit was first in the hands of settler landlords and foreign companies, and next of a Westernised elite, and since moreover the trade imposed on Latin America was a mono-polistic form of trade controlled by metropolitan capital, Latin America's insertion into the world market acted as a drain on its 'economic surplus'. Thus in Frank's and the earlier dependency paradigm 'exploitation' came to take on the meaning of a unilateral transfer of economic, i.e. investable, surplus by means of an unfair world market system. Viewed from this point of view, Frank's position does not seem to go much beyond that of the ECLA analysis and neoclassical theories of international trade generally (see p. 167), a point made by several of his critics.[8]

Laclau accused Frank of an 'unmarxist' conception of capitalism. Capitalism, according to Marx (as we have seen), is a *mode of production* rather than a mode of exchange. The peculiarity of the capitalist mode of production is that under it the forces of production are combined and organised by means of commodity exchange. That is to say, under the capitalist mode of production labour and land as well as capital become commodities freely exchanged in the market, where their relative value (the price) is determined by forces of supply and demand (see pp. 159–60). In other words, free wage labour and freely transferable property rights are essen-tial conditions of capitalism as a mode of production. Now, as Laclau points out, the whole point about imperialist 'ex-ploitation' is precisely that metropolitan capitalism did not establish capitalist relations of production when it brought the world market to the satellite countries. Rather, it brought about an alliance between capitalist relations of production and existing pre-capitalist relations of production; it articu-lated capitalist modes of surplus appropriation (e.g. com-modity exchange) with pre-capitalist modes of surplus appropriation (tribute collection, servile exactions, use of slave labour). In this way capitalism overseas came to have the best of both worlds: it introduced commodity exchange all over the globe arranging for an international division of labour most suited for its own needs, and at the same time it could get the overseas products at prices which were obtained through extra-economic means. It is this exploitation through extra-economic means that explains the low wage costs and the low ground rents which obtained in the underdeveloped lands and which, when encapsulated in final commodities for international exchange, explains the low price level of these commodities in relation to those from the advanced countries for which they were traded. Examples of such articulation of capitalist with pre-capitalist modes with reference to Latin America are somewhat briefly given by Laclau: feudal relations were intensified with production for the world market. The feudal regime of the 'haciendas' tended to increase its servile exactions on the peasantry as the growing demands of the world market stimulated maximisation of their surplus:

> the labour exacted was often equivalent to that of a permanent worker while the traditional rights of the peasant were simultaneously reduced, especially his right to *talaje* or pasturage. The money wage he now obtained was lower than that of a day labourer or a journeyman. It would be a mistake to see in this process the emergence of a rural proletariat. If this had been the case, the wage should have become the major part of the *inquilinos'* means of subsistence. But all the signs show that, on the contrary, the wage was merely one subordinate element in a subsistence economy based on the land tenancy. That is to say, we are faced with a peasant subjected to servile obligations, and not with an agricultural wage earner, who completes his income with customary privileges and a piece of land.[9]

It would be a mistake to believe, as some do, that the presence of feudal relations of production with their depressing effects on wages in an otherwise 'modern' capitalistic sector is a thing of the past. Ernest Feder's book *The Rape of the Peasantry* testifies to the persistence of feudal relations in Latin America in an age of legal freedoms and democratic rights:

> Nothing characterizes the autocratic nature of a *latifundio* agriculture better than the fact that on many large estates and plantations the authority of the landlords and the ad-

ministrators is reinforced by strong-arm men — a private police force. They make the workers 'toe the line' through intimidation, terrorization and corporal punishment. At times they kill.[10]

The terms and conditions of work of the *campesinos* do not approach anything like a legal agreement between freely contracting parties: oral agreements rather than written ones prevail, and where there are written ones there is only one copy (for the employer). Furthermore, the contract is open-ended to allow subsequent imposition of terms more unfavourable for the worker than anticipated. One may retort that similarly unfavourable conditions of work and of legal abuses by employers existed in Europe in the nineteenth century, yet no one would deny the existence of the capitalist mode as a dominant and exclusive mode in that period. This raises two important theoretical issues:

(1) The Althusserian Marxist analysis places the watershed between historical modes of production in terms of the type of surplus extraction — ideological, political or economic. Social formations, to an extent, are always mixtures of several modes. But what classifies a period is the mode which has become dominant and exclusive. In Europe in the nineteenth century there were still feudal vestiges, even in the patron's own work-place. These elements of 'extra-economic' coercion kept wages low. It was only when the working class had socially organised itself sufficiently that it could avail itself of its existing legal rights and thus ensure the proper workings of the capitalist mode in respect of the commodity 'labour', that is, an establishment of the wage rate by purely economic means (i.e. the market). And, as both Ricardo and Marx argued, it is only when the wage is the *only* income responsible for the worker's (and his family's) reproduction that it will stabilise at the socially necessary labour-time (i.e. a wage at subsistence level). Further developments of labour emancipation and trade-union organisation have progressively redefined and improved the 'socially' necessary labour-time to one which now, in the advanced countries, includes about 40 per cent worth of social provisions (health, unemployment benefits, etc.). By contrast Third World countries — even the most

advanced amongst them — *characteristically combine elements of extra-economic with economic surplus extraction*. And this is precisely what depresses wage levels in even their most 'modern' capitalist sectors. This has nothing to do with their (supposed) transition from traditional to modern societies, or from one mode of production to the next. Rather, it has to do with the class alliance between their traditional feudal overlords, or their contemporary bureaucratic military overlords on the one hand, and imperial capital on the other. Today, authoritarian and repressive regimes in many successfully industrialising Third World countries perform a function in relation to the world capitalist centres comparable with that of the feudal overlords and slave owners of a century ago: they *make available* to the overseas investor both a docile, stable and unorganised work-force, and the monopolistic rights to the use of land and natural resources; it is their *political* presence and their *political* domination which permit the capitalist production of commodities in the overseas countries, and also guarantee that the conditions for reproduction of land and labour remain 'pre-capitalist'. In this way they permit the super-exploitation of human and physical resources in the Third World.

It is not difficult to see that the injection of the concept of 'mode of production' in the post-Frankian development literature greatly encouraged those who wished to take a more voluntarist, a more local, class-struggle-orientated stance. For, indeed at one level, but only at this one level, the concept calls attention to production relations, and hence to class structures. But the concept also, and equally, calls attention to the articulation of economic systems: to forces of production.

(2) And this is the *second* important difference between Europe in the nineteenth century and Latin America (and all the Third World) in the twentieth, namely that in the latter we find besides an articulation of 'relations of production' also an articulation of entire modes, or — as Laclau prefers to call it in a recent postscript to a reprint of his 1971 article — *economic systems*.[11] Up to this day, in the Third World, the pre-capitalist subsistence sectors are used to subsidise the reproduction of labour in the capitalist sector. On the planta-

tions in Latin America, for example, the landlord uses 'access to land', i.e. a tiny plot upon which the *campesino* is allowed to grow his own food, to manipulate terms of employment to his own advantage, including the level of the wage which the *campesino* receives for working the landlord's hacienda.[12] To the extent that this 'access to land' (a feudal notion of 'tenure') continues to be a significant part of the *campesino*'s reproduction, we can speak of a situation where a pre-capitalist subsistence economy subsidises the low wage level, and thus the price of the export commodity, in the capitalist sector.

The subsidising role of pre-capitalist subsistence economies is dealt with more elaborately by Claude Meillassoux, one of the French radical anthropologists close to the Althusserian radicals. Basing his conclusions on African studies, he claims that there is always a *process of transfer of labour-value to the capitalist sector through the maintenance of self-sustaining domestic agriculture.*[13] In fact, he argues that under colonialism the Europeans themselves were very keen to preserve native authority, native kinship and tribal life. They were eager to preserve the organisation of domestic subsistence production because that meant that commodity production (on their plantations and in the mines) would not have to lead to full proletarianisation (as it does when capitalism becomes the exclusive and not just a dominant mode of production). For full proletarianisation means that wages need to be sufficient to reproduce labour and the family (wife and children), i.e. the future generations of labour. It was therefore quite convenient for the Europeans to make cash wages only a sort of target wage for the worker: a target for three things, to pay the colonial taxes, to have a little extra to buy European commodities, and to pay the bride price. Since the elders in the community controlled the bride prices and the brides, this was in their interest as well: monetisation of the bride price meant that they could buy fancy European commodities, and become richer all the time. (This, in *strictu sensu*, is an instance of articulation of pre-capitalist with capitalist *relations of production*.) In this manner, the cash wage became a mere supplement to and an entitlement to family income in the villages; the cash wage was not meant to be sufficient to reproduce wage labour itself. The empirical indicators of this articulation between capitalist and pre-capitalist economic systems were seasonal withdrawals and high rates of turnover of labour, as well as frequent migrations between rural villages and the capitalist sector. As Meillassoux says:

> It was also the policy of the Europeans whenever practicable to leave the care of the destitutes and the disabled in the hands of the tribal clan and the family organisation which had traditionally accepted this responsibility . . . preservation of the relations with the village and the familial community was an absolute requirement for the wage earners and so was the maintenance of the traditional mode of production.[14]

This system of articulation of modes of production has been perfected in the South African *apartheid* regime. It is what *apartheid* is all about.

Back to theory. In so far as the here described transfer of labour-value from the subsistence to the capitalist sector is 'embodied' in the commodities which the latter sector exports to the advanced capitalist countries in exchange for commodities from the advanced countries which do not embody such 'hidden transfers', one can therefore with justification also speak of *exploitation through unequal exchange*. In the bold terms of Phillippe Rey, 'behind every exploited worker in the Third World stand 10 exploited peasants'.[15] Now this, precisely, is the point made by the world system theorists (see below). World system theorists speak of 'accumulation on a world scale' through the domination and the superimposition world wide of the capitalist mode of production upon pre-capitalist modes through the economic mechanism of capitalist commodity exchange. We can thus see that the mode of production (MOP) approach was also fed into the circulationist argument. These twin errors of reductionism (class reductionism and economic reductionism) to which the MOP approach has been subjected in the respective post-Frankian camps has occasioned Laclau, in his postscript in 1979, to denounce the concept MOP (which he himself introduced in the debate in the first place) as 'inadequate'.

Somewhat condescendingly he observes 'that Marxist thought in Latin America has found considerable difficulty in moving *simultaneously* at the level of *modes of production* and that of *economic systems*, and that its most frequent mistakes derive from a unilateral use of one or other of the two levels' (emphasis in original).[16]

One may consider this lengthy treatment of the MOP theme disproportionate in the context of a general introductory text. My reasons for giving it so much space is not only because it happened to be the first most influential post-Frankian concept, and one which helps us to tease out some differences between competing theories, but also because the concept of MOP can advance the development of a *diachronic* theory of imperialism. I have said before that the Frankian thesis could not satisfactorily explain why and how the conditions for further exploitation were renewed and reproduced through time and under historically altered conditions. The MOP approach, by contrast, facilitates such understanding: it pinpoints the logical necessity for capitalist imperialism through time. The problem with the reformist/liberal bourgeois analyses of international exchange, and even of Frank's analyses, is that even when they are able to tell us how the exchange between rich and poor countries 'happens' to be an unequal one, their location of the source of this inequality in the sphere of circulation prevents an understanding of the rich countries' *need* for such inequality. The rich countries are seen as lucky beneficiaries, the poor countries as unlucky victims, of a natural accident. They cannot see the exploitation of overseas countries as systematic, i.e. as a requirement for the continued expansion and reproduction of centre capitalism.

Classical writers on imperialism, as we have seen before, had of course argued the need of mature capitalism to export capital on grounds of a declining rate of profit (Lenin), or on grounds of the need for higher rates of return (Bukharin) which could be obtained in places where the organic composition of capital was lower (than in the centre countries). Those, to be sure, were adequate explanations for the export of capital (i.e. for imperialism) in the colonial period. But what about the modern world, when — and this is agreed by all writers, both bourgeois and Marxist — there is no difference in the organic composition of capital between the advanced capitalist sectors of the Third World countries and the organic composition of capital in the metropolitan countries, when, in other words, productivities tend to equalise between the countries of the centre and those of the periphery, and when, therefore, one would expect the profit rate to equalise between centre and periphery? This is where the MOP approach comes into its own: it explains the need for centre capitalism, at all stages of its development, to exchange with pre-capitalist modes of production overseas.

Rosa Luxemburg was the first to make this point, namely that exchange with pre-capitalist modes was necessary at all stages of capitalist development both for reasons of accumulation (investment) and for reasons of realisation of surplus-value (seeking market outlets). She thought, however, not in terms of a *preservation* of pre-capitalist modes but of a conquering and a destruction of pre-capitalist modes. The recent MOP writers make the same point, and go one step further: the expansion of industrial capitalism in the metropolitan countries necessarily depends on the *maintenance* of pre-capitalist modes of production in the peripheral areas. The theoretical argument is best put by Laclau. The process of capital accumulation depends on the rate of profit. The rate of profit in turn is determined by the rate of surplus-value and the organic composition of capital. As the latter rises, as it is bound to in capitalist development, so it increasingly needs the rate of surplus-value to rise too, in order to offset the decline in the rate of profit. An expansion into peripheral areas where an alliance with pre-capitalist modes permits super-exploitation of land and labour allows absolute surplus-value to increase. Laclau continues:

> In this way the world economic system is capitalist to the extent that the law of motion of the capitalist mode of production — that is to say, the fluctuations in the rate of profit (which is a strictly capitalist category, $s/(c + v)$, since it presupposes the existence of free labour) — has come to be the law of motion which articulates the system as a whole. It is this that permits the coexistence of various

non-capitalist modes to be articulated within the world capitalist system . . . the structural changes which the capitalist mode of production has experienced in the metropolitan countries can in many cases contribute to a strengthening of extra-economic exploitation of labour in the peripheral areas.[17]

Finally, the concept of mode of production in theories of imperialism can also be helpful in analysing the differential development experiences of different peripheral regions and areas, as well as the differential development experience in different historical periods. Under colonialism, capitalism would sometimes destroy indigenous societies (settler colonies); in other cases, when focusing on labour expropriation, it would do its best to preserve native authority, institutions and social organisation; again, in others, when it was interested in a particular region for reasons of raw-material extraction or large-scale commodity production, it would cement, fossilise and at times even introduce feudal forms.

The differential interest of centre capitalism in various overseas regions during the colonial period may continue to affect the type of relationship that these countries have with foreign capital today. In a very perceptive article Massiah maps out the manner in which different profit strategies of different transnational corporations press for different class alliances in the Third World.[18] Noting the over-all process of the development of centre capitalism, he points to the over-all tendency of overseas investments away from raw-material extraction and towards manufacturing industries or branch plant activities. Multinationals differ in profit strategies and in their preferred class alliances according to their different dominant activity. MNCs that engage in raw-material extraction are interested in access to land and physical resources. They are not necessarily interested in cheap labour or markets. These MNCs will therefore prefer to ally themselves with feudal types of social structures, and encourage the preservation of the power of landlords, the dispossession of the peasantry and extremely unequal distributions of income. The level of development of centre capitalism during the colonial period made this kind of profit strategy the prevalent one. MNCs which are interested in manufacturing industry, on the other hand, tend to have different profit strategies, and consequently seek different class alliances. They may seek to exploit cheap labour for a specially labour-intensive part of the production process and/or they may be interested in creating a fast-growing market. In the case of the former strategy an alliance with a military/bureaucratic regime capable of fierce industrial repression is in order; in the case of the latter an alliance with the local bourgeoisie and more democratic forms of proletarianisation which involve improving standards of living and creating effective demand is called for.

Thus different MNC activities and different MNC profit strategies, coupled with different types of Third World class alliances, accompany different manners of insertion of Third World countries into the world capitalist economy. The problem of development and the class struggles hence appear as qualitatively different in resource-based Third World economies such as Indonesia, Bolivia and Southern Africa, from labour-intensive industrialising countries such as South Korea, Singapore and Taiwan, and again are different from domestic-market-orientated industrialising economies such as Mexico, Argentina and Brazil.

In this way — and we now come full circle to the 'productionists' again — the MOP approach offers an opportunity to raise practical revolutionary questions and devise historically concrete revolutionary strategies. Instead of having a blanket response of 'anti-imperialism and anti-capitalism' the approach invites one to examine the locally relevant patterns of exploitation and of existing class relations consequent upon the locally and historically specific form of imperialist penetration. This is the theme taken up, as a primary concern, by the post-Frankian *dependista* writers.

The 'Productionist' Argument: Dependency-associated Development, Historical Specificity and Class Reductionism

By the early 1970s, and in contrast to the dependency and underdevelopment theories of the Baran–Frank variety, some

Latin American scholars — notably Cardoso and Faletto[19] — started to take a more optimistic view of the penetration of industrial-financial capital in Latin America. This optimism, coupled with a class-reductionist interpretation of the MOP approach, has led them to emphasise the *political* character of the process of economic transformation.

They believe there is no denying it: capitalist industrialisation is not only taking place in Latin America but it does create new productive forces (however high the rate of obsolescence); it does accumulate capital locally, and it does employ wage labour, thus generating — and this is the crucial point — new social interest groups, new rising expectations, new contradictions, new class struggles. The internal structure is not as lifeless and stagnant as Frank would have us believe. It is moving all the time in dynamic response to new external impulses:

> The system of external domination reappears as an internal phenomenon through the social practices of local groups and classes, who share its interests and values. Other internal groups and forces oppose this domination and in the concrete development of these contradictions the specific dynamic of the society is generated.[20]

They argue that just because the social costs of dependent capitalist development, in the form of highly unequal income distributions, authoritarian-repressive regimes, marginalisation of the masses, etc., are very high, that is no reason to complain that capitalist development is not taking place. It is precisely because it is taking place that these social costs are being incurred. In any case

> it is not realistic to imagine that capitalist development will solve basic problems for the majority of the population. In the end, what has to be discussed as an alternative is not the consolidation of the State and the fulfillment of 'autonomous' capitalism, but how to supersede them. The important question is how to construct paths to socialism.[21]

The contribution that the *dependistas* can make in respect of this question is to identify the structural possibilities for change and point out alternatives to dependency at any one historical moment. The skill here lies in the application of a dialectical methodology which brings together both external and internal factors.

What is argued is that each expansive phase of capitalism created new forms of economic dependency, new ways in which the Latin American economies were inserted into the world capitalist economy; but in each phase this new insertion brought forth new class contradictions, required new class alliances and ended in new forms of state organisation. Thus Latin America's insertion as producer of export crops demanded the hegemony of the landed oligarchy over the enclave economy; next, the new dependent role of Latin American economies as import-substitute markets for manufactures was consolidated in the national/populist alliance of practically all sectors against the feudal/imperial alliance. What is specific *today* to Latin American economies is the *new* dependency created by foreign penetration and control over the *industrial producer-goods* sector, which increasingly has to rely on an alliance with the *state* as direct agent of production in the public sector. In countries like Brazil, Chile, Colombia, Peru, Mexico and Venezuela, the public sector now contributes more than 50 per cent to the annual formation of capital, with the remainder contributed by private national and foreign enterprises.[22] The counterpart of this process is the expulsion of increasing sectors of the national bourgeoisie as well as of the working class (marginalisation). In this way the state apparatus is forever becoming more divorced from the nation, from civil society. And yet the very expansion of industrial dependent capitalism (to which the state/imperial alliance is committed in the present stage) needs the members of the civil society as both producers and consumers. At the present historical juncture, therefore, it is claimed, there is greater scope than ever before (say, during the export-enclave economy period) for various social and political movements to develop and to influence both the concrete conditions of the dependency links and the nature of the regime types. An empirical, concrete, analysis of the specific situations of dependency and class and state in Latin

America reveals a wide range of historical options that apparently suit the imperial/state alliance equally well. There are, for example, the torturing autocratic regimes of Brazil and Chile, but *also* the 'restricted democracy' regimes of Venezuela and Colombia, and — better still — there is the benevolent bureaucratic/authoritarian regime of Peru which 'whilst not revolutionary, is not income concentrating . . . and whose policies are oriented toward the incorporation of the masses, or at least toward the partial consideration of peasant and popular interests'.[23] In other words, there is plenty of choice and scope for political action. The task of the *dependista* writers is to identify the structural limits posed, on the one hand, by the new forms of dependence, and on the other by the new appropriate class alliances (appropriate in the sense of being able to reproduce the dependence) *while these are still being formed.* In this way *dependista* writers can help to strengthen 'defensive' alliances and pose political alternatives at the precise historical juncture. This requires a passion for the 'possible' rather than a 'catastrophic version of history' (a jibe at the deterministic world system theorists) or a 'permanent indefinition'.[24]

This sounds fine, but let us not get carried away by this passion for the possible. In the long run the *dependistas*, naturally, wish to construct paths to socialism, but at the present historical juncture their aspirations are limited to a 'substantive democratisation'[25] and an increase in the material benefits of Latin America's rapid economic development for the mass of the people. To this purpose better deals with the transnationals which would eliminate or decrease dependency are in order — especially as an option for collective action (by the Andean Pact countries, for example). As it happens, at the present geopolitical juncture there is real scope for such negotiation of better dependency terms. For, so they argue, the 1970s have witnessed a decline of US hegemony and an increase in inter-imperialist rivalry. This, by corollary, has improved the capacity for action of various Latin American states, both in their relation to the transnational corporations, and in relation to foreign policy. In this, therefore, they are also less dependent than they were before.[26]

With this positive appraisal of dependency-associated

development we are moving back to a more orthodox Marxist position, of which Bill Warren has been an early protagonist amongst Western writers.[27] Warren was the first to expose the notion of 'dependency and underdevelopment' as a 'Third World nationalist-populist myth'.[28] As early as 1974 he had claimed that imperialism was precisely doing what Marx had predicted it would, that is, both develop the forces of production and spread capitalist relations of production inside the (ex-)colonial countries. Recently he has exposed the 'illusion of underdevelopment' still further, pointing to the

> titanic strides forward in the establishment, consolidation and growth of capitalism in the Third World, with corresponding advances in material welfare and the expansion of the productive forces.[29]

He admits that this capitalist development has been uneven as between countries and also that its material benefits have been unevenly distributed inside these countries. But he, too, claims that this is only to be expected of capitalism, and that moreover there is no evidence to support the thesis (still held by all *dependistas*) that Third World capitalist development is associated with *ever-growing* inequalities and marginalisation. Such inequalities as there are are as much causes as consequences of rapid economic growth (a view ardently shared by bourgeois writers of the Rostow and Kahn variety). Ignoring the growth of international monopolies, he even dismisses the notion of the detrimental effects of technological dependency. The increasingly competitive conditions of a world where distribution of economic power is becoming less concentrated (in Warren's eyes) make such technological dependency actually a requisite for greater independence. The recent wave of nationalisations of foreign direct investment testifies — in Warren's view — to ever greater autonomy and control by Third World countries over their own destinies.[30]

Neither Warren's empirical analysis nor his conclusions differ in any way that I can see from the conservative bourgeois position as held, for example, by Kahn. Where he goes

beyond the bourgeois writers, and once more steps into his
Marxist shoes, is in the assertion (and the desire) that the
success of capitalism inside the Third World will facilitate, in
fact is a necessary condition for, its transition to socialism,
for with the spread of capitalist production relations enters
the Marxist dialectic of the class struggle that will usher in
the socialist future. In this way imperialism, by helping to
establish capitalism overseas, is yet fulfilling its historic
mission. The failure on the part of the earlier dependency
theories to recognise the progressive nature of imperialism
has helped to disarm the working class of much of Asia,
Africa and Latin America in its struggle for political and cultural independence from the bourgeoisie. Thus dependency
theory can be blamed for subordinating the working class and
the socialist movement inside the Third World to 'ideologies
of nationalist, anti-imperialist unity' and to 'induce them to
bow to undemocratic regimes'.[31]

The 'Circulationist' Argument: Deepening of the World System Perspective and Economic Reductionism

While it was always characteristic of the dependency school
to view 'development and underdevelopment' as two sides of
one global-historical process, one line of argument now takes
us further still by analysing successive patterns of dependency
as following and in turn affecting successive transformations
within world capitalism. Mindful of the recent facts of the
internationalisation of production and of the growing importance of multinational corporations, the world system is seen
as more closely integrated than ever before, now including in its
nucleus certain capital-accumulating centres in the periphery.

Sunkel, for example, argues that with the emergence of the
transnational corporation as the dominant organisational
form of capitalism, the structure of world capitalism has
changed world wide. Transnational integration has increased
at the expense of national disintegration.[32] While an international nucleus of 'modern' activities, regions and social
groups of varying degrees of importance in each country are

becoming more and more integrated, other 'backward' activities, regions and social groups both within the developed and the underdeveloped countries become more and more marginalised. The difference between developed and underdeveloped countries exists merely in the extent to which modern activities, regions and social groups prevail in the former, while backward activities, regions and groups prevail in the latter. At the same time international polarisation between countries still continues because the transnational corporate strategy centralises the more rewarding activities of research and entrepreneurial decision-making in the centre countries, while it farms out subsidiary activities of production and distribution to the 'peripheral' countries. But also, at the same time, the integrating forces of the MNCs effect a levelling of income between the centre states' recipient social groups and the social groups and regions linked closely to high-productivity activities in the underdeveloped countries. Thus, within the transnational corporate strategy, the interests of Third World bourgeoisies are harmonised with those of the middle classes in the advanced world. And whereas there is increasing transnational linkage of activities and social groups which are advanced, there is no such transnational linkage of the marginalised groups. Disarticulation or disintegration of the periphery (and, although to a lesser extent, the centre) goes hand in hand with marginalisation of the masses. Rather contradicting his own belief in the twin logic of transnational integration and national disintegration, but probably influenced by his Latin American *dependista* colleagues' 'passion for the possible', Sunkel's policy options are that rather than resist the present developments (i.e. no radical break), it is in the national(?) interest of Latin American countries to pursue a policy of hard bargaining with transnational corporations. As is the case with the *dependistas*, and Bill Warren's views, the potential for such hard bargaining lies in the inter-imperialist rivalries between transnational corporations from different centre countries.

Probably the fullest, and ideologically most consistent, exposition of the present world-system perspective comes from Immanuel Wallerstein. Reaffirming Frank's original thesis, Wallerstein boldly states that the capitalist economy was a world capitalist economy from the very beginning – namely, from the sixteenth century. Instead of talking about national capitalisms and about national capitalist development, he says, we should examine the laws of motion and the historical development of the world capitalist system. 'Neither the "development" nor the underdevelopment of any specific territorial unit can be analyzed or interpreted without fitting it into the cyclical rhythms and secular trends of the world economy as a whole.'[33]

A world system, according to Wallerstein, 'is a single division of labour comprising multiple cultural systems, multiple political entities and even different modes of surplus appropriation' (i.e. feudal, slave mode, wage labour).[34] Like Frank, Wallerstein is able to redefine the boundaries of the capitalist system and postulate them to have been world-wide from the beginning because of his own – some would say unmarxist – definition of capitalism. Instead of taking 'free labour' or 'capitalist relations of production' to be the determining features of capitalism, he defines it simply as 'production for sale in a market with the object to realize maximum profits'.[35] Appropriation of this profit is either on the basis of individual or of collective ownership. This definition casts a net so wide that even the USSR and all other so-called 'socialist' countries in the world can be seen to belong to the world capitalist economy, something Wallerstein is eager to assert.

In respect of the problem of development and underdevelopment, and of imperialism and dependency, Wallerstein develops an argument that can be thought of as intermediate between circulationist and productionist conceptions. For, as Brenner notes, he explains the putative transfer of surplus from periphery to core areas in two different ways: one economic and one political.[36] On the one hand he argues that the division of labour in the world economy 'naturally' develops a hierarchy of occupational tasks in which tasks that require higher levels of skills and greater capitalisation are reserved for higher-ranking areas. Since a capitalist world economy essentially rewards accumulated capital, including human capital, at a higher rate than 'raw' labour-power, the geographical maldistribution of these occupational skills involves a strong trend towards self-maintenance. Therefore, over time exchange becomes unequal and remains unequal as a result of different wage levels operating in different regions and nations. This is indeed the new orthodoxy since Emmanuel first belaboured it in his *Unequal Exchange* in 1974.[37] In other words, the global distribution of wealth and poverty is seen here as a result of market forces reinforcing an accident of history which gave a headstart to the European nations. But there is also political interference in the market. While the single world market rewards some activities and penalises others, the actors can and do interfere with the operation of the world market by appealing to their nation-states to interfere on their behalf. And once we get a difference in strength of the state machineries, we get the operation of unequal exchange imposed by strong states on weak ones, and — by logical corollary, since strong states tend to develop in core areas and weak ones in peripheral areas — by core areas on peripheral areas. In this way capitalism involves not only appropriation of the surplus-value by an owner from a labourer but an appropriation of the whole world economy by core areas.[38]

So far it would seem that the dice is doubly and permanently loaded in favour of the core areas and against the periphery. Is there then no movement possible, does the world system not change? If that were the case, the system would soon have run into insurmountable contradictions created by its own unequal exchange. But it is precisely the strength and the vitality of the capitalist world system that it has a *dynamic* structure with differently placed groups and nations jostling for different positions all the time. First of all, from the beginning the world economy has been stratified into three, not two layers: core, periphery, and, in the middle, semi-periphery. The reasons for the emergence of the semi-peripheral areas, which Wallerstein dates no later than 1640, are firstly and primarily *political*. In Galtung's terms semi-peripheral nations are go-between nations.[39] A system based on unequal rewards must constantly worry about rebellion. To avert this 'middle sectors' are created which tend to think of themselves primarily as better off than the lower sector rather than worse off than the upper sector. They thus perform a similar function as do the middle classes within national stratification systems. This proposition about the political mediating role of the middle-income countries is not as entirely speculative as Wallerstein himself presents it. There is an interesting study by Selcher, for example, on Brazil's multilateral relations between the First and Third Worlds that offers plenty of documentary evidence that Brazil's official foreign policy is predicated on the self-perception of that nation as both an economically intermediate and a politically mediating nation.[40]

Within the world system the go-between nations also assume an economic role: standing between exploiters and exploited, they themselves are exploiting and exploited. The semi-peripheral nations seek trade with both core and periphery, exchanging different kinds of products with each and achieving intermediate wage levels and profit margins. For example, the middle-income countries import advanced technology from the core countries, and export semi-processed products to them, while obtaining raw materials from periphery and exporting finished manufactures to the periphery.

The dynamic quality of the world system which allows for the upward and downward mobility of nations is a function of the cyclical nature of the capitalist mode of production but is made possible by precisely the very fact of unequal wage levels (and hence unequal exchange) coupled with relative rigidities in national wage levels. The latter argument, which is central to the whole thesis, Wallerstein too adopts from Emmanuel: in the core countries high wage levels, once achieved, are not easily relinquished even in a recession. And so during world economic recessions most of the relative shifting of positions occurs. The chain of events is as follows. As a result of development in the core countries, the rising wages of the workers, combined with the increasing economic disadvantage of the leading economic producers (for instance, steel and automobiles), leads to an inevitable decline in the comparative costs of production:

> For individual capitalists, the ability to shift capital from a declining leading sector to a rising sector is the only way to survive the effects of cyclical shifts in the loci of the leading

sectors. For this there must be areas able to profit from the wage-productivity squeeze of the leading sector.[41]

Those areas are the semi-peripheral countries. It is in this light, for example, that we must understand the recent sale of the German Volkswagen plant (trade-mark, technology, plant and machinery) to Brazil or the transfer of the Vespa rights to India. Whereas steel and automobiles are the declining leading sectors in the core countries, they are the rising leading sectors of the semi-peripheral countries – a point, of course, which has not escaped the attention of the multinational corporations, whose special talent it is to manipulate the locations in which they realise their world-wide profits. Today the multinationals can more effectively and efficiently than ever affect the world-wide redistribution of surplus-value, expand the world market and open up the 'charmed circle' of world centres of capital accumulation.

While it is possible for semi-peripheral countries to improve their standing, especially during periods of recession, and for peripheral countries to graduate to become semi-peripheral, it is theoretically not possible for all states to develop simultaneously. It is in the nature of the capitalist system that there is only limited room at the middle of the hierarchy and even less at the top. Therefore, the rise of some countries occurs at the expense of others.

So what is it that determines the successes of some and the failures of others? This question is especially interesting in view of the recent emphases on class struggle and on a more voluntarist, less fatalistic, conception of development. It is therefore particularly disappointing that Wallerstein does not answer this question at all satisfactorily, mainly because he poses it loosely and without the necessary theoretical rigour. For example, he fails to ask: Are the determinants of success 'external' or are they 'internal'? To what extent does success itself present problems or prospects for the later transition to socialism? Even so we can try to cull his answers from a free interpretation of his disorganised text. The determinants are partly external and partly internal, and sometimes they are more external, at other times they are more internal. This gives rise to different success strategies. There is 'promotion by invitation' when a country becomes the preferred location for a multinational's subsidiary activities, either because of its natural endowments or because of its local political factor endowments (the latter is partly, of course, also an instance of internal factors, i.e. of MNC-preferred class alliances). Then there is a 'self-reliant' strategy, of which Wallerstein seems to think Tanzania is a prime example (which it surely is not, nor indeed is it a success story). The determinant for this strategy, oddly and paradoxically, is also external. Tanzania has been permitted to be self-reliant by the grace and whim of the core countries: 'both Tanzania's poverty and her rarity amongst Africa's regimes stand her in good stead of thus far minimizing pressure brought to bear against her economic policies'.[42]

Finally, there is the 'seizing the chance' strategy, to which Wallerstein devotes most attention. It has the ringing sound of an internally propelled development strategy:

> By seizing the chance, we mean simply the fact that at moments of world-market contraction, where typically the price level of primary exports from peripheral countries goes down more rapidly than the price level of techno-logically advanced industrial exports from core countries, the governments of peripheral states are faced with balance-of-payments problems, a rise in unemployment and a reduction of state income. One solution is 'import substi-tution' which tends to palliate these difficulties. It is a matter of 'seizing the chance' because it involves aggressive state action that takes advantage of the weakened political position of core countries and the weakened economic position of domestic opponents of such policies.[43]

The disadvantage of this 'successful' strategy is that it is *unsuccessful* from the point of view either of achieving national economic independence, or nationally integrated economic development, for reasons spelt out by the Latin American *dependistas* and Gunder Frank, and from the point of view of (let us say) the participation of the masses in the nation's success. To the contrary, it leads to marginalisation of the masses as a necessary condition for a country's upward mobility. *At the national peripheral level the problem is re-latively insoluble*, says Wallerstein, and can at best be mini-mised:

> But it also points to one of the long-run contradictions of the system as it presently exists: for one day, the 'demand' of these marginalized workers will in fact be needed to maintain the profit rates. And when that comes, we will be faced, *in a way that we are not now*, with the question of the transition to socialism (emphasis added).[44]

In short, the problems of the transition to socialism are – in Wallerstein's view – neither the concern of the national liberation movements, nor indeed of the here and now. There is still a lot of life in the world capitalist system, and it may last well into the next century before it collapses under the weight of its own inner contradictions. This is not to say that Wallerstein has no time at all for liberation movements, for forces of change. With typical deterministic emphasis, he declares that 'they come in precisely as not totally coherent pressures of groups which *arise out of* the structural contra-dictions of the world capitalist economy' (emphasis added).[45] These struggles take place all over the world, in the core areas, the semi-peripheral and in the peripheral areas, and they sap the dominant forces of capitalism. Even Third World national liberation movements contribute to this process. But at the same time they come up against the adjusting forces of order of the world capitalist economy. Their regimes become co-opted, and 'one can ask if the net result has not been in part further to integrate these countries – into the world capitalist economy'.[46]

If Wallerstein, in concord with the *dependistas* and Warren, does credit the semi-peripheral countries of the Third World with a real economic advance in position within the world capitalist system, Ernest Mandel, another world-system writer, does not. This just goes to show how totally fragmented the Marxist analysis of contemporary Third World development/ underdevelopment is. Mandel is a world-system writer in that he, too, believes that the world capitalist economy is the prime unit of analysis: 'A capitalist world economy is an articulated system of capitalist, semi-capitalist and pre-capitalist relations of production, linked to each other by capitalist relations of exchange and dominated by the capitalist world market.'[47] Because he locates the dynamic of the system only in the economic laws of the capitalist mode of production, he therefore sees developments in the Third World as secondary, subordinated to and derivative of the laws of motion of capitalism in the *centre* countries. For these reasons he cannot credit the industrialisation of some Third World countries as anything other than a temporary and relative improvement in national income.[48] It is an industrialisation dependent upon and subjected to the world-wide profit strategies of the metropolitan multinational firms (the dominant organisational form of the capitalist MOP in late capitalism)[49] and these strategies change with the further 'organic' development of capitalism. This is more especially the case in those economies of South-East Asia whose industrial growth is export-led, labour-intensive, and under partial or complete control of metropolitan monopoly capital. Curiously, the very same inter-imperialist rivalries which have incited the *dependistas* and Warren to optimism arouse Mandel's profound cynicism, for the sharper these rivalries over labour-intensive production facilities in these countries become, the likelier the outcome of increasing rationalisation and automation, thus wiping out the temporary advantage in production costs resulting from the difference in wage levels that these countries now enjoy.[50] This explanation, of course, does not hold water in the case of Latin American domestic-market-orientated processes of industrialisation. But these, too, Mandel dismisses as 'relative' progress only: 'The decisive fact continues to be the impossibility of any thorough industrialization of the underdeveloped countries within the framework of the world market, in the age of late capitalism and neocolonialism, just as much as in the age of "classical" imperialism.'[51] What is the answer then? A radical break!

liberation from the capitalist world market by socialization of the major means of production and the social surplus product makes it possible to solve the agrarian problem and to launch full-scale industrialization. *The building of a socialist economy can, itself, of course, only be completed on a world scale* (emphasis added).[52]

The Global Political Economy of Samir Amin

The last of the world-system theorists which I shall discuss here is Samir Amin. In some ways it may not seem fair to put Amin in the same camp as Wallerstein and Mandel, since in recent years his works have strained to straddle both a determinist and a voluntarist perspective: a world system and a national liberation approach. Unlike Wallerstein and Mandel, Samir Amin believes not just in the possibility but in the necessity of the socialist break of the peripheral countries *now*.[53] Moreover, he puts forward a highly complex and anti-eurocentric theory of imperialism which argues that the movements for *national* liberation in the periphery were and are ever so many moments in the socialist transformation of the whole world. His is a world-system perspective in that it acknowledges the world capitalist system as the prime *unit* of analysis. But the prime-*mover* of this world capitalist system is no longer its laws of motion as these arise out of the contradictions of the centre countries (falling rates of profit, over-accumulation, etc., as Mandel believes, for example) but rather the contradiction which world capitalism has created in the periphery ever since imperialism began. Imperialism constituted a qualitative break in the history of world capitalism.[54] And since that time all the initiatives for the further development of world capitalism have sprung from rebellions in the periphery. Each time these rebellions have forced world capitalism to reorganise and readjust itself, and in so doing it has (thus far) reached ever higher stages of advance and accumulation. So far it has been a process of *reculer pour mieux sauter*: first the national liberation movements which ended colonialism; next the various revolutionary struggles in South-East Asia, Cuba, etc.; and today the OPEC revolt of the oil bourgeoisies and the demands for NIEO. Now, of course, these varying degrees of resistance to world capitalism did not and do not constitute 'socialism' or even a 'transition to socialism', only a 'break towards

socialism'.[55] But 'to the extent that the periphery offers
different degrees of resistance, then imperialist capital is
forced to transfer the contradictions to the metropoles, thus
reducing the objective basis for social democracy and strengthening the tendencies toward renewed revolution'.[56] This is
how the world-wide socialist revolution has already begun.

So here we have a genuine Third Worldist world-system
perspective. Samir Amin, in my opinion, is an insightful –
at times brilliant – writer whose hurried prose and whose
very prolificacy nevertheless give one the impression that his
pen moves faster than his thoughts. This is a pity, because
there is much he has to tell us, though not quite as much as
his publications record might lead us to think and purchase.
On the other hand, this makes the task of a summariser like
myself a rewarding one. If in the next pages I yet present
his theory in greater detail than I seem to have done in the
case of any other writer, it is because I do believe that Amin's
work offers a genuine attempt to synthesise all that was good
and lasting in the dependency and underdevelopment literature
from Baran onwards. He strains to reconcile circulationist
with productionist conceptions of exploitation, just as he
strives to transcend both a one-sided determinism and a one-
sided voluntarism in Marxism. For these efforts he rewards
us with a theory of historical materialism that truly does go
beyond Marx's and Lenin's time and leads us to where we are
right now.

Like other theorists of imperialism, Samir Amin, too, starts
his analysis of imperialism and underdevelopment with an
examination of the laws of motion of capitalism. But unlike
Lenin, and more recently Laclau, he does not see the cause
of imperialism in the tendency of the rate of profit to fall.
To be sure, there is a process of centralisation and of concentration of capital, and a consequent rise in organic composition of capital, but the 'pure' capitalist mode of production
as it originally developed in the centre countries could and
should have been perfectly able to overcome this tendency
internally. For, and this is a crucial step in Amin's argument,
what characterises the process of capital accumulation in
these centre countries is precisely that it is an autocentric
process: their economies are integrated economies.[57] This is

manifested in the simultaneous development of departments
II and I, i.e. of consumer-goods production and of capital-
goods production, and in the simultaneous development of
agriculture and industry. Social division of labour as well as
productivities, profitabilities and wage rates tend to equalise
between these two departments and between these two sectors of the domestic economy in the centre countries. As a
logical corollary there is a necessary, objective relation between the rate of surplus-value (and its obverse, the wage
rate) and the level of development of the productive forces.
This necessary objective relationship, which was theorised by
Karl Marx, has time and again been empirically realised
through conjunctural fluctuations.[58] In short, according to
Samir Amin, who here follows Emmanuel, in the centre
autocentric capitalist countries, wage levels have kept pace
with the development of the economy.

Now, the reason for the expansion of capitalism overseas
in both colonial and post-colonial periods is not because of
any declining rate of profit at home but because, when a certain level of development of productive forces and, indeed, of
wages, had been reached, it became obvious to the competing
national capitalists in the centre countries that more profits
could be made overseas. How? By creating an export sector
over there, and thus obtaining from the overseas countries
products which are the basic elements of constant capital
(raw materials) and of variable capital (food products) at
production costs lower than those obtained at the centre for
similar products or their substitutes. Why will these costs be
lower? At this crucial point in the analysis, Amin combines
and transcends the lines of argument developed by Emmanuel
on the one hand and by Meillassoux and Laclau on the other.
With Emmanuel he agrees that one reason for the differential
rewards for labour between rich and poor countries is the
rising wage levels in the centre countries, where (as we have
seen) wages keep their pace with productivity. The other
reason is the one advanced by the 'articulation of modes of
production' theorists: in overseas countries the price of labour
is continually kept low because domination by centre capital
ensures that the entire social formation (including the pre-
capitalist modes, which are kept backward for the reason)

will by every means, both economic and non-economic, be made subject to the periphery's function of providing cheap labour for the export sector.[59]

As a result of this 'super-exploitation' the commodities which the Third World countries exchange with the advanced countries embody within their physical form hidden 'transfers of value' from the periphery to the centre which Amin estimates to amount to 22 billion dollars annually, twice the amount of aid and 'private' capital that the periphery receives. While this amount is negligible from the point of view of the centre countries (a mere 2 or 3 per cent of their gross internal product), it *is* significant from the point of view of the peripheral countries (constituting 20 per cent of total GNP) and from the point of view of the centre countries' giant firms who are the main beneficiaries.[60]

In this way, Amin argues, *unequal exploitation leads to unequal exchange* ('unequal' as between centre and periphery conditions of exploitation). It is because of this unequal exploitation that Third World countries have typically found their 'terms of trade' deteriorate. But the story does not end here. *Unequal exchange in its turn leads to unequal development*, for it shapes a structure of economy and society in the overseas countries which continually *reproduces* the conditions for renewed unequal exchange in new historical periods and circumstances. The world-wide unequal exploitation at the level of production in being transformed into exploitation at the level of exchange also has consequences for the structure and further historical development of the world capitalist system itself. I now look at the flow of this argument.

Having been subjected to a specific form of international specialisation under colonialism and to a specific function (provider of cheap labour for the export sector) for central capital, the overseas territories develop (in this colonial period, 1890–1950) a specific structure of economy and society which Amin calls 'peripheral capitalist', the laws of motion which are distinctly different from those pertaining to centre capitalism.[61] The structure of the economy is characterised by a distortion towards exports (extraversion), a bias towards tertiary (unproductive) activities and a distortion towards light branches of industry. In contrast to the autocentric capitalist countries, productivities between sectors of the peripheral economy are extremely uneven (the pre-capitalist sector being deliberately kept backward), as are incomes and profitabilities. Furthermore, the integration of the peripheral economy with the centre economies (extraversion) occurs at the cost of *dis*articulation of the various sectors within the peripheral economy itself. At the social-structural level this integration/disarticulation contradiction is mediated by a class alliance of land-owning/commercial elites with foreign capital on the one hand, and the marginalisation of the masses on the other: 'The marginalisation of the masses is the very condition underlying the integration of the minority within the world system, the guarantee of increasing income for this minority which ensures the adoption, by this minority, of European patterns of consumption.'[62]

From here Amin's analysis of the laws of motion of peripheral capitalism begins to resemble Frank's analysis of dependency (see p. 169): the extremely uneven income distribution inhibits the development of an effective domestic market and dictates import-substitute industrialisation of elitist consumer goods which deepen technological dependency on foreign capital goods, and so on and so forth. This law of motion of peripheral capitalism effectively reproduces the conditions of unequal exchange necessary for the (re-)integration of peripheral countries in the *next*, the neo-colonial, period (1950–67).[63] In this period their new function is mainly that of importers of industrial equipment. Class alliance shifts from landowners to national bourgeoisies *as a result of national liberation struggles*, but the disarticulation of the economy and the marginalisation of the masses continue unheeded. At this stage of diversification and reinforcement of underdevelopment there are appearing, he says, new mechanisms of domination/dependency, cultural and political mechanisms, but also economic ones: technological dependence and domination by the transnational companies. The latter increasingly take advantage of the widening gap between centre and periphery by installing manufacturing industries for re-exportation to developed countries and even a capital-goods sector in countries with a potentially large enough market (e.g. Brazil, Mexico). This is the second historical stage within the neo-colonial period: differentiation within the Third World and the rise of 'sub-imperialist states', 'staging posts' or 'relay stations'.[64] It heralds a new international division of labour which, however, remains unequal, in the sense that the periphery inherits industries that have a limited scope for expansion (hardware), while the centre keeps back for itself those with the highest potential for progress (software). But the countries in the periphery are highly unequal candidates for this new division of labour. Some which are best placed as regards their economic potential (i.e. abundant natural resources, more advanced proletarianisation) and a certain extent of 'political solidity' could advance faster on the path of new dependence if they also had markets in the less developed countries and if they could have direct and cheap access to their supplies of raw materials and food. This is the scenario for the rise of 'sub-imperialisms' within the present world capitalist system.[65] *Like Wallerstein, Amin believes that these sub-imperialist states could provide an economic and political balance for the world capitalist system.* From the point of view of the world revolutionary struggle waged by the worker and peasant alliance *such a scenario is much to be preferred* over its alternative in which all international division of labour is excluded and in which both the new-technology industries as well as the 'standard' industries would all be concentrated in the centre, while the whole of the periphery would be really marginalised. This prospect, says Amin, would necessarily involve the genocide of the peoples of the present Third World who would become completely useless and even dangerous for the reproduction of the capitalist system.[66]

It is in the context of this dialectic development of the world political economy that we should place both the Third World bourgeoisie's demand for a New International Economic Order, the energy and raw materials 'crisis', and the ideological efforts of the more far-sighted bourgeoisies of the developed world (Brandt, Tinbergen, etc.).[67]

What are the features of the present crisis of world capitalism? The laws of motion of the capitalist mode of production, we have seen, are increasing concentration and centralisation of capital, coupled with increasing rising organic composition of capital. What this means is that we are forever witnessing a development of the productive forces (capital accumulation), but at the same time these productive forces become more social in character, while the production relations (the class relations) become forever narrower. Time and again in the history of capitalist development the development of the productive forces (the process of capital accumulation) comes up against the structural limitations of the narrowing production relations, as these were organised during, and suitable for, the previous period of capital accumulation.

It has become fashionable for current Marxist writers (and Amin is no exception)[68] to delineate long phases of capital accumulations alternated by periods of structural crises during which adequate responses to the limitations of existing production relations are found. In opposition to a vulgar Marxist, economistic interpretation, Amin sees these periods of structural crises as periods of intensified class struggle in which the initiative for the rearrrangement of the production relations can come from either the capitalists (as, for instance, imperialist expansion overseas) or from the exploited classes (exemplified in national liberation struggles). Since the advent of imperialism all struggles have originated in the periphery.[69] Each structural resolve permits a period of renewed expansion, but the ultimate crisis can thereby only be postponed, for the underlying trend towards the ever-growing social nature of the productive forces and the ever narrowing production relations continues. According to Amin's calculations, about 90 per cent of the entire world population is now exploited, while only 10 per cent constitutes the parasitical world bourgeoisie.[70]

Imperialism, both in the colonial period which started in 1890 and in the neo-colonial period which ended in 1967, was characterised by a geographical expansion of the capitalist mode on a world scale. Geographical expansion permitted capitalism time and again to overcome its problems of narrowing production relations by encroaching and dominating fresh pre-capitalist areas which, in Rosa Luxemburg's terms, could be used for purposes of primitive accumulation. What characterises the present crisis is that there are simply no more 'fresh' pre-capitalist areas available for further geographical expansion. So capitalism this time has to overcome its present crisis without resort to imperialism. Now this is perfectly possible, for, in Amin's theory, imperialism was neither a necessary nor an only solution anyway. It was just one amongst several, of which the permanent arms race, for instance, is another.

In the history of capitalism thus far each phase of expansion (of capital accumulation) has had its own propelling industries, its own particular organisation of international specialisation, its own pattern of distribution of the social product, its own form of unequal exchange and its own international class alliances.

The present structural crisis is characterised by the following traits:

(1) The fact that the propelling industries of the previous phase of expansion, i.e. car and steel industries, and industrial-goods industries generally, have run out of steam. They now suffer from declining profitabilities in the centre, where up till now their principal markets were located. So they have to find new markets in the periphery, but there is a second bottleneck here.

(2) The fact that the international division of labour of the previous era, with its attendant class alliances and pattern of unequal exchange (the Third World countries still principally exporting 'undervalued' primary goods with which their bourgeoisies now have to import industrial equipment to propel their import-substitute industrialisation) blocks this. Therefore, one of the ways of overcoming this crisis is to *'reshuffle the cards and revise North–South relations'* (my emphasis).[71] The way to do this is to include mining rents in the prices of the products exported by the countries of the Third World. This will improve the financing capacity of their bourgeoisies and enable them to enter a new stage of industrialisation based upon the exportation of industrial products to the centre. This strategy will suit the alliance of sub-imperialist bourgeoisies and monopoly capital, but will be directed against the workers and peasants of the entire

world, including the working classes of the centre who will have to bear the brunt of industrial relocation and rising raw-material prices (industrial relocation will increase the reserve industrial army, thereby once more raising the rate of surplus-value at the centre itself). It is at this very point that Amin's attempt to reconcile world system and national liberation perspectives becomes tortuous and uncertain. It is true that the present crisis of contemporary capitalism originates in the periphery, and the revolts of the periphery (OPEC and the NIEO demands) are genuine political struggles. But it is *also* the case that these very demands by the Third World bourgeoisies offer the world capitalist system precisely the structural means to overcome the crisis, and it is also true that the far-sighted bourgeoisies in the centre will (and do) attempt to seize these means and in the process successfully co-opt the Third World bourgeoisies once more (as they did before, after the anti-colonial liberation struggles) and re-integrate them once more into the system:

> there is no doubt in theory that this rebellion can be coopted. But in theory only; for what counts in history are the accidents along the way, and some serious ones can occur in the peripheries and the centers during the contra-diction-filled transition from the second to the third phase of imperialism.[72]

Right now we are at the crossroads, and we do not know for sure whether the system will succeed in co-opting this rebel-lion, or whether some serious accidents will happen. If the former scenario materialises, then there is no doubt that the NIEO will simply herald yet a new international division of labour, this time based on the export of cheap manufactures by the periphery. This would simply perpetuate and aggra-vate the system of unequal exchange. It would continue the path of 'extraverted' development in the periphery, for which the Third World peasants and workers pay the price, though increasingly so *also* will various disaffected groups within the centre countries. It would also, and inevitably, involve the breaking up of the Third World bloc as the contradictions between the sub-imperialist Third World and the marginalised Fourth World deepen.[73]

But the accident scenario, too, is also a real possibility at the present historical juncture. In fact, one might even argue, as Amin seems to be doing in his most recent work, that the world capitalist system is becoming *more* accident-prone.[74] For the accumulated rebellions in the periphery (from anti-colonial struggles to OPEC and the NIEO) have made the centre countries more dependent than was ever the case before on an alliance with the bourgeois *states* in the Third World (think, for example, of the state as the legal owner of national-ised foreign companies and of its participation in the produc-tive sector of the economy). At the same time, the state bourgeoisies appear ever more visibly as oppressors, as strangers in their own country. In the widening gulf between state and nation (which, one will remember, the *dependista* writers too see as a fertile ground for political action) the revolutionary bloc 'can form more easily and in the framework of a general strategy of uninterrupted revolution by stages, create effec-tive tactical alliances likely to erode the hegemonic bloc'.[75]

Ultra-leftists in the West who resist the NIEO demands on grounds that these will benefit the Third World state bour-geoisies only precisely miss the point of the 'imperialist' break in the development of capitalism. That is, that the initiatives for the world socialist transformation *have* to come from the periphery. And that while it is true that each partial victory of national liberation creates the conditions for the deepening of capitalist development, it also, at the same time, aggravates the contradictions between the popular masses and imperialism:

> A gigantic struggle has begun, pitting the bourgeoisie against the proletariat of these nations, and the outcome will be decisive for socialism. As national liberation cannot be achieved under the leadership of the bourgeoisie, it must be carried out through the stages of development of the imperialist system, until the moment when the proletariat succeeds in taking over the leadership and when the achieve-ment of national liberation creates the new problems of the socialist transition. It is thus that socialism makes its way, a way which cannot be predicted in advance.[76]

Conclusions

I would have considered it perfectly proper to end a survey of theories on the uncertain note of the last quote of the final chapter. However, some people insist that books must have conclusions. Now, what if one does not have any? Does one make them up? Or does one select a point of view already current on grounds of its popularity, its logical consistency, its predictive value, its capacity to strike a chord in one's heart? And what if one changes one's views in the course of one's intellectual development? In a previous work I boldly came forward with some very interesting conclusions which I would now denounce as a naive exposition of a progressive liberal fantasy! Such experience is sobering and makes one cautious.

Even so, there may be some value in completing this book with a number of critical comments on the nature of the theoretical debate and on the relevance of this debate in relation to the facts presented in Part One of the book. In the course of this critical commentary my own transitory views may become transparent, and my reasons for ordering facts and theories in the manner that I have done clarified.

First, the theories. I have said in the introduction that today it is more common to find a threefold classification of development theories: conservative, reformist and radical. I have defended my own bipolar classificatory scheme (bourgeois versus Marxist) on methodological grounds. What is fundamental as a classificatory principle is not the substance of the utopian vision (everybody fed, clothed and happy) but the approach to historical change. And whereas Marxist writers will always ground their analyses in the *historical* development of forces and relations of *production*, bourgeois writers are concerned with neither history nor indeed with production. Unlike the Marxists, bourgeois writers do not study the world economy as one particular historical formation, with its own laws of motion, its inner contradictions, and its generation of wealth and poverty as *necessary* manifestations of its historical progression. Rather, the world economy (the word 'capitalism' is studiously avoided in all bourgeois literature) appears as a *natural*, timeless phenomenon: production for· profit instead of for human needs, and competition in the market, are the natural, unquestioned attributes of 'rational' modern man. The *progressive* bourgeois writers, it is true, worry a great deal about world poverty, and about the 'unfair' *distribution* of global resources. But this distribution is not seen as an *inevitable* outcome of the historical development of the capitalist system of production — rather, it is regarded as a natural, indeed even as a historical, *accident*, a malfunctioning of the system, a 'kind of madness' which a spirit of global political will and co-operation can set right.

The progressive liberal's concern for the poor, meanwhile, is genuine, whether this concern is prompted by fears of wars of retribution, or by humanitarianism, or by an enlightened Keynesian insight into global demand economics. It has helped propagate an ideology of humanity, of human rights, human dignity and global human equality (world citizenry) which is *ethically* incomparably superior to the ruthless conservatism of Kahn or the 'America rules okay' scenario of Rostow. It is, furthermore, a necessary voice of protest to the extremely reactionary ideologies of those who have now gained command over the *political* order in some Northern nations, and whose narrow perception of the national interest may stop not even short of nuclear war. However scathing I may have been about the progressive liberals' 'one-world' vision, their 'global government' fantasies, and in particular about Mesarovic and Pestel's 'oil for food' bargain-scenario, they have my full support when — as now — the alternative is the sending of rapid deployment forces to secure the North's access to 'vital' interests in the South. It is precisely in this restricted sense that I consider the Brandt Report as a 'programme of survival', for it is a programme that buys time.

At the same time, along with Marxist writers generally, I critically interpret the 'global redistribution' pleas of the progressive liberals as 'appropriate' responses of the centre capitalist countries at the present historical juncture. 'Appropriate', that is, in the sense of being able to overcome the present world economic crisis and to reproduce the conditions for the further survival of world capitalism, and hence for further exploitation, deepening global inequalities, and so on and so forth.

Since I am partial to a world-system perspective, and one moreover which quite blindly follows the laws of motion of capitalism, I am reasonably optimistic that the progressive liberal views will yet win the day. The observant reader may have noticed that in a previous paragraph I was careful to say that it was over the *political* domain that the reactionary forces in the Northern countries had gained command; the economic order both inside and outside these countries remains firmly in the hands of international capital, that is, the large multinational corporations and the international banks. These two forms of international capital are presently committed to a course of action which — in Amin's words — 'will reshuffle the cards and revise North—South relations', or at any rate relations with that part of the South which their profit strategies have selected as areas for investment and expansion.

In the 'facts' part of this book I have described the intricate connection between, on the one hand, the NIEO rebellion of the bourgeois Third World states (which include, *inter alia*, the right to nationalise foreign enterprises and easier access to international financial markets), and on the other the process of internationalisation of production coupled with the injection of international finance capital into this process of internationalisation of production. Thus we are dealing here with a *triple* alliance between international *finance* capital, international *productive* capital and the *states* of the fast-growing Third World countries. This triple alliance, I have argued, has been greatly strengthened by the recycling of petro-dollars through the international financial markets since the OPEC rebellion of 1973, which itself was a manifestation of national self-determination on the part of the

Third World. It does not require a theory of conspiracy to believe, as I do, that even if the initiative for the OPEC price increases came from the oil-producing peripheral countries (a point which in any case is debateable),[1] the fact that OPEC has been permitted to get away with it, is entirely due to the positive economic and financial consequences of the OPEC action for international capital. And just as it was, at that time (1976), the interest of international capital which influenced and moderated the North's reaction to both OPEC and the NIEO, it will now again be the interest of international capital that will bring recalcitrant Northern governments to toe the line of 'global redistribution'. For the present extent of the exposure of international finance capital inside selected Third World countries is — in the words of a *Financial Times* (30 March 1981) correspondent — 'one of the greatest single difficulties facing international banks today' (i.e. 1981). Therefore, First World governments — however reluctant — will be forced to support their bankers' overseas adventures with massive injections of aid and public lending to those areas where international capital is most at risk.

My survey of theories in the (neo-)Marxist tradition has brought to the attention of the reader both the very great diversity of positions within that tradition, and my own view that the deepest crack causing fragmentation within the Marxist camp remains the century-old controversy between 'freedom and necessity' within historical materialism. Economic determinism still rivals with voluntarism, i.e. the view that the irresistible flow of history yet permits political struggles and political choices at every historical juncture. When applied to the problem of Third World development, this century-old controversy synchronises with the 'world-system' versus 'national liberation and development' controversy. I have already professed to a personal preference for economic determinism and for the world-system perspective. I really do believe that our scope for influencing the course of history is extremely limited. Why, then, do I join practically every march that is going, park myself and my posters in front of foreign embassies, write letters to the press, my MP and even generals of military regimes in remote countries? The answer is simple, but does not really warrant any sophisticated construction of a new theory: I do it to save my soul. I believe that we must fight, not in order to win (I do not think we can) but in order to retain our human dignity.

And what do the theories have to say about the facts? Do the theories surveyed in Part Two address the facts in Part One at all competently and comprehensively? Here the answer is a disappointed 'Not really'. I have said before that economic facts always move faster than either political responses or theoretical explanations. I have attributed this in part to problems of communication, of information-processing and of the circulation of ideas. The resulting time lag, however, is an attenuating circumstance only. For theories have roots that stretch deep and far into past realities and the theoretical explanations of such past realities. These define, as it were, the parameters of the discourse, and these tend to direct attention selectively to what appears as 'salient' from within a dated perspective. For these very reasons I have found it necessary to preamble the contemporary theories in Chapters 4 and 6 with their historical forerunners in Chapters 3 and 5.

Let us examine this in more detail. The survey of economic facts in Part One uncovered the striking difference in national economic progress between those Third World countries which continue to have something to offer in the world economy, and those which have not. This fact, striking as it is, indeed penetrated all theories as the crucial 'problematic' of Third World development in the 1970s. Some theories have tried to explain, others have tried to explain away, this economic progress. They have asked: What is the nature of this progress? Is this genuine economic development, dependent capitalist development, sub-imperialist development, relative and temporary economic development? And so on and so forth. Yet I have also pointed out that the much improved economic performance of these countries was attributable to very *different* forms of continued participation in world economic arrangements. Some countries are resource-based economies whose critical or strategic mineral wealth attracts overseas *extractive* investments; others are labour-based economies whose favourable political climate

attracts *labour-intensive*, export-orientated industrial investment; and again others are relatively populous countries
which had already experienced a sustained period of import-
substitute industrialisation and which are now passing on to
a second stage of industrialisation, namely that of producing
capital goods to satisfy *domestic* markets. None of the
theories surveyed has addressed these differences at all
satisfactorily; most have tended to ignore them or relegate
them to subsidiary clauses. The reason, I think, is that bourgeois and Marxist writers have been constrained by the limits
posed by their past theoretical heritage, in particular the
generalised category of 'Third World'. And while for the
bourgeois writers 'economic development' simply covers
any increase in national income wherever it comes from, for
the Marxist writers 'dependency' and the 'imperial alliance'
remain the dominant defining categories. This lack of differentiation — at the theoretical level — of the various forms
of dependency makes it difficult to direct and organise locally
relevant political protests and class struggles, both in the
periphery and in the centre countries. For example, should
the people of Northern Nigeria, whose oil-fuelled pattern of
industrialisation involves no significant exploitation of labour,
demand to be treated like their South-East Asian colleagues?
And should we in the centre countries support the importa-
tion of textiles from South-East Asia because of (or in spite
of) the fact that they have been produced through 'super-
exploitation', but not the leatherware from Brazil on grounds
that there it should have been produced for the home market?
Clearly, none of the theories surveyed can give any answers
to such very practical questions. Such lack of differentiation
at the theoretical level is particularly disappointing in the
case of Samir Amin, whose writings, as the observant reader
may have noticed, have had a formative influence on the
present text. For Amin's insistence on the essential unity of
the 'peripheral' capitalist countries makes him, too, disguise
the real economic differences between various Third World
countries and hence ignore the political implications of these
differences.[2]

Next, there is the intimate connection between the present

internationalisation of production and the petro-dollar-financed 'debt explosion' of certain Third World countries. This, too, has yet to massage the brains of our theorists. The debt problem continues to be cast in terms of the need for 'aid' and 'transfer of resources'. However, the present nature of the debt problem puts an entirely novel complexion on the relationship between the taxpaying peoples of the advanced countries and the 'exploited' peoples of the Third World. What is the purpose of foreign aid when our public money is to be paid to Third World governments only to be used to service loans to our banks?

And finally, there is the Fourth World, the widening gap and that appalling figure of one billion poor people in the world. Having established the widening gulf between the Third World and the Fourth World, precious little attention is paid by *any* theorist to the Fourth World, where, as we have seen, nearly 80 per cent of the one billion people classified as 'below the poverty line' live (if that is the word). Progressive liberalism, to be sure, has done as much if not more than the Marxists to put the world's poor on the map. And yet their policy recommendations – I have argued – remain focused not on *all* the world's poor but only on those who live in the fast-growing Third World countries. This focus they share with their Marxist colleagues, whose concept of 'marginalisation' equally applies only to those people who live in 'dependency-associated', developing, or 'sub-imperialist' states. The Marxist preoccupation with 'dependency' and the 'imperial alliance' leaves no room for addressing the problems of those countries whose states are not invited to play any part in the imperialist alliance, because neither their people nor their natural resources are worthy of exploitation.

This, I think, is a sad reflection on the nature of theory. Unable to free ourselves from the chains of the capitalist world economy, we cannot or will not concern ourselves with the plight of those who are increasingly expelled from that same world economy. We may try to understand, and improve, the conditions of life of those who live *within* our world system, we cannot even think about those outside it.

Notes and References

Chapter 1

1. Part of the problem arises from the fact that official exchange rates (on which GNP and GDP calculations are based) do not measure relative *domestic* purchasing power because a large portion of marketed GNP does not enter into world trade. This problem was first discussed in a seminal paper in 1954 by M. Gilbert and I. Kravis in *An International Comparison of National Products and the Purchasing Power of Currencies* (Paris: OECD, 1954). Since then Kravis and his team, now working for the World Bank, have tried to improve the measure of international comparisons of GDP. Their calculations involve direct binary comparisons of physical quantities for sixteen selected countries ranging from the USA to India and Kenya and crude interpolations using these countries as a yardstick. See I. Kravis *et al.*, *A System of International Comparison of Real Product and Purchasing Power* (Washington: IBRD–UN, 1975); I. Kravis, A. W. Heston and R. Summers, 'Real GDP Per Capita for More than One Hundred Countries', *Economic Journal*, June 1978; and I. Kravis *et al.*, *International Comparisons of Real Product and Purchasing Power* (Baltimore: Johns Hopkins Press, 1978). More seriously, the GNP calculations of course do not measure income distribution. GNP *per capita* is a statistical average which in view of the enormously unequal income distributions especially characteristic of developing countries cannot strictly speaking be acceptable as a statistical measure of a central tendency. Efforts to complement GNP measures with indexes of 'levels of living' and of 'levels of welfare' which do include a distributional component have none the less come up with the surprising finding that there is after all a close correlation between such levels of living indexes and GNP *per capita*; cf. Jan Drenowski and Wolf Scott, *The Level of Living Index* (Geneva: UNRISD, 1966). See also the comment made by Bill Warren, *Imperialism, Pioneer of*

Capitalism (London: New Left Books, 1980) pp. 224ff. More recent data on basic needs performance, which may be argued to have (indirectly) a distributional component, also suggest a close correlation between the monetary GNP *per capita* and the substantive indicators of welfare and well-being. See Glen Sheenan and Mike Hopkins, *Basic Needs Performance: an Analysis of Some International Data* (Geneva: ILO, 1979).

2. *World Development Report 1980* (Washington: IBRD, 1980) p. 158.

3. R. McNamara, *Address to the Governors* (Washington: IBRD, 1980) p. 35.

4. Lester B. Pearson *et al.*, *Partners in Development: Report of the Commission on International Development* (London: Pall Mall Press, 1970) p. 29.

5. Ibid, p. 29.

6. UNCTAD *Document TD/B/288* (Geneva: UNCTAD, 1970). This was the report of the first group of experts convened by UNCTAD II in 1968. This report was the first to identify the 'least developed country' category.

7. Committee for Development Planning, Report on the Seventh Session 1971, *Document E/4990* (New York: United Nations, 1971). The Committee, acting upon the recommendations of the first group of experts (see note 6 above), laid down the criteria for identifying least developed countries. At first, the list of criteria contained some eight items. These were next simplified to three on the argument that 'arbitrary though it was, the distinction and its simplified method was necessary if a concrete expression was to be given to the political will to implement special measures in their favour'.

8. *Report of the Secretary-General* (Paris: OECD, 1979) p. 19.

9. Ibid.

10. *World Development Report 1979* (Washington: IBRD, 1979) p. 87.

11. Ibid, p. 5. The World Bank's projected estimate here is that by 1990 the developing countries will have captured 16 per cent of the world's trade in manufactures.

12. *World Development Report 1978* (Washington: IBRD, 1978) p. 10.

13. *International Trade 1977–8* (Geneva: GATT, 1978) p. 24.

14. *World Development Report 1979*. See especially the argument which is presented on pp. 100ff.

15. Cf. G. K. Helleiner, 'Structural Aspects of Third World Trade, Some Trends and Some Prospects', Paper submitted at the 25th Anniversary Conference 16–20 December 1977, The Hague, Institute of Social Studies, p. 2.

16. *International Trade 1978—9* (Geneva: GATT, 1979).

17. The notion that successful economic development in developing countries is closely associated with the degree of their integration into patterns of world trade and international capital movements (in short, the world economy) has long since been the conventional wisdom of the World Bank. The notion was empirically verified in a study by H. Chenery (Vice-president) and M. Syrguin, *Patterns of Development, 1950—1970* (Oxford University Press, 1975).

18. Cf. Warren, *Imperialism, Pioneer of Capitalism*, p. 198. See also Lars Anell and Birgitta Nygaren, *The Developing Countries and the World Economic Order* (London: Francis Pinter (Publisher) Ltd, 1980).

19. The 1967 figures are based on data presented in the *World Bank Atlas 1968*; the 1978 figures are based on data presented in the World Bank's *World Development Report 1980*.

20. There are really thirty-eight blocks here, but for reasons of comparison I have rounded them off to thirty-seven. This is permissible, I think, because the margin of error is negligible, as Kuwait's income is only just within the thirty-eighth interval anyway.

21. Anell and Nygaren, *The Developing Countries and the World Economic Order*, p. 69.

22. Keith Griffin and A. R. Khan, *Poverty and Landlessness in Rural Asia* (Geneva: ILO, 1977). This widely quoted ILO study showed that for a large number of developing countries recent growth has been accompanied by an increase in the absolute poverty of the bottom 20 to 40 per cent of the population.

23. Cf. Stephen Hellinger and Douglas A. Hellinger, *Unemployment and the Multinationals* (New York: Kennekat Press, 1976) esp. chs 1 and 2. The authors estimate that by 1967, in Latin America as a whole, industry was absorbing only 31 per cent of the total non-agricultural labour force as compared with 35 per cent in 1950.

24. This point was made by ex-president of the World Bank, Mr R. McNamara in his address to UNCTAD II, Santiago, Chile, on 14 April 1972. McNamara told delegates that after ten years of the Brazilian miracle the share of national income received by the bottom 40 per cent of the population had declined from 10 to 8 per cent while that of the top 5 per cent had risen from 29 to 38 per cent. Quoted in Orlando Letelier and Michael Moffit, *The International Economic Order, Part I* (Amsterdam: Transnational Institute, 1977) p. 52.

25. Fishlow estimates that 50 per cent of the Brazilian population lives below a poverty line of 75 dollars per annum. See A. Fishlow, 'Equity in North—South Relations', in A. Fishlow *et al., Rich and*

Poor Nations in the World Economy (New York: McGraw-Hill, 1978). For the 80 per cent estimate see Th. Dos Santos, 'The Crisis of the Brazilian Miracle', mimeograph (Toronto: Latin American Research Unit, 1977). Dos Santos here quotes the Brazilian demographic census as saying that 80 per cent of the population in Brazil barely achieves minimal survival levels, and furthermore that it has decreased its already low share of GNP from 45.5 per cent in 1960 to 36.8 per cent in 1970.

26. M. Ahluwalia, 'Income Inequality', in Hollis Chenery *et al.*, *Redistribution with Growth* (Oxford University Press, 1974) pp. 13ff.

27. S. Kuznets, 'Economic Growth and Income Inequality', *American Economic Review*, 45, no. 1, 1955, pp. 1–28. See also S. Kuznets, 'Quantitative aspects of Economic Growth of Nations III: Distribution of Income by Size', *Economic Development and Cultural Change*, 11, January 1963, pp. 1–80.

28. R. McNamara, *Address to the Massachusetts Institute of Technology* (Cambridge, Mass.: 28 April 1977) p. 35. The World Bank's shift from 'bottom line to bottom billion' thinking may be officially dated with the publication of the then president's book in which he outlines and advocates the new policy: R. McNamara, *One Hundred Countries, Two Billion People: the Dimensions of Development* (London: Pall Mall Press, 1973). For a thorough and critical review of the reorientation of the World Bank's ideology and its lending policies, see Aart v.d. Laar, 'The World Bank and the Poor', thesis, (Amsterdam: Vrije Universiteit, 1979).

29. The distinction between absolute and relative poverty became current within World Bank circles in the mid-1970s; cf. v. d. Laar, 'The World Bank and the Poor', p. 122.

30. R. R. Fagen, 'Equity in the South in the Context of North–South Relations', in Fishlow *et al.*, *Rich and Poor Nations in the World Economy*, p. 175. Another, equally vague definition of absolute poverty is also current in circles of international organisations, namely 'absolute poverty – as a condition of life so limited by malnutrition, illiteracy, disease, high infant mortality and low life expectancy as to be below any rational definition of human decency': R. McNamara, *Address to the Board of Governors* (Belgrade, Yugoslavia: 2 October 1979) p. 19. Exactly the same definition appears in J. Tinbergen *et al.*, *Reshaping the International Order*, Second Report to the Club of Rome (New York: Dutton, 1976) p. 66.

31. v.d. Laar, 'The World Bank and the Poor', p. 122.

32. Tinbergen *et al.*, *Reshaping the International Order*, p. 66.

33. Cf. McNamara, *Address to the Board of Governors*, p. 19; and R. McNamara, *Address to the University of Chicago*, 22 May 1979,

p. 4. The one billion figure for people living in absolute poverty is also used in the Brandt Report: *North—South: A Programme for Survival*, Report of the Independent Commission on International Development Issues under the Chairmanship of Willy Brandt (London: Pan Books, 1980).

34. *World Development Report 1980*, p. 35.
35. Cf. Kravis *et al.*, *International Comparisons of Real Product and Purchasing Power*.
36. That is to say, we take 80 per cent of the bottom group who receive 40 per cent of GNP of that bottom group + 40 per cent of the next group who are said by McNamara to receive typically 15 per cent of GNP, etc., until we have a total number of people equivalent to 40 per cent of the free world's population. This was not done for the top 20 per cent. Here one simply looks at the richest countries and counts their populations multiplied by GNP *per capita* until one reaches a number of people equivalent to 20 per cent of the free world's population. I have excluded China from this particular calculation since we are dealing here with a historical comparison, and 1967 dates China back to when it was truly outside the free world economy.
37. OECD, *Economic Outlook* (Paris: OECD, 1980) p. 121.
38. Bank for International Settlements, *50th Annual Report* (Basle: BIS, 1980) pp. 84—5.
39. OECD, *Economic Outlook*, p. 121.
40. Saudi Arabia, Libya, Kuwait, Iraq, Iran, United Arab Emirates, Qatar.
41. Initially, all payments for oil were in dollars and sterling, the world's convertible currencies.
42. It is estimated that, instead, only about 30 per cent of the surpluses was spent in this way (see Table 1.12) under 'long-term investments', sub-special bilateral arrangements and other investments.
43. *Prospects for the Developing Countries 1978—85* (Washington: World Bank, 1977) p. 96.
44. Ibid, p. 27.
45. Cf. Marilyn Seiber, 'Debt Escalation: Developing Countries in the Euro-currency markets', in L. G. Franko and M. J. Seiber, *Developing Country Debt* (Oxford: Pergamon Press, 1979) p. 44.
46. Bank for International Settlements, *Annual Report 1980*, p. 110. The BIS speaks delicately of a 'lowering of the banks' perception of the risks involved in their international lending business'. For the same point, stated more bluntly, see Cheryl Payer, 'Third World Debt Problems', *Monthly Review*, September 1976, pp. 1—19.
47. World Bank, *Annual Report 1980* (Washington: IBRD, 1980) p. 90.
48. Seiber, 'Debt Escalation', p. 45.

49. *World Development Report 1979*, p. 34.
50. In order of borrowing rank: Brazil, India, Mexico, Indonesia, Iran, Yugoslavia, Pakistan, Korea, Argentina, Chile.
51. *World Development Report 1979*.
52. *Prospects for the Developing Countries 1978–85*, annexe, table 3, p. 112.
53. Ibid, p. 80 (see also table II.4, p. 81).
54. R. Solomon, 'A Quantitative Perspective on the Debt of Developing Countries', in Franko and Seiber, *Developing Country Debt*, p. 31.
55. *World Development Report 1979*, p. 31.
56. This is one of the major policies advocated by, for example, the Brandt Report and the Tinbergen Report (*Reshaping the International Order*). It is also official World Bank policy.
57. E. Mandel, *The Second Slump* (London: New Left Books–Verso, 1980) p. 69. See also Payer, 'Third World Debt Problems'.
58. Payer, 'Third World Debt Problems', p. 11. Here she quotes various bankers who have pleaded for such underwritings. Her critical comment is that this means, in effect, that the taxpayers of the aid-giving countries are being asked to foot the bill to prevent the collapse of their nations' financial institutions ('with the money passing only in theory through the hands of the debtor governments on its way to repay bankloans'). In this context it is most sobering to read the World Bank's *Annual Report, 1980*, p. 67, where it admits that since 1979 the World Bank has decided (for the first time in its history, and – I may add – much against the Bank's own professed preference of lending to the 'poorest of the poor') to go for 'structural adjustment lending' in an effort to help supplement with longer-term finance the relative short-term finance available from the commercial banks.
59. See, for example, the recommendations on this subject presented in the Brandt Report.
60. Cf. the discussion on the negotiations for a New International Economic Order in Chapter 2, especially pp. 84–5.
61. *Prospects for the Developing Countries 1978–85*, p. 100.
62. According to *The Financial Times*, 14 October 1980.
63. Recently the nomenclature *transnational corporation* has gained currency as an alternative term for the *multinational corporation*. The term 'transnational' is favoured in some circles, notably that of international organisations, because it carries the impression that multinational companies truly transcend national boundaries, including that of the home countries. In this book I use the terms interchangeably.
64. The term 'world market factory' is coined by Folker Fröbel,

Jürgen Heinrichs and Otto Kreye, *The New International Division of Labour* (Cambridge University Press, 1980) p. 6.

65. These figures are arrived at by comparing the 'sales' column in *Fortune*'s list of the 500 largest industrial US companies and their list of the 500 largest non-US companies (1978) with the gross national product data per country and region presented in the *World Bank Atlas 1977*.

66. H. Schwamm and D. Germidis, *Codes of Conduct for Multinational Companies: Issues and Positions* (Brussels: ECSIM, 1977) p. 25.

67. On the assumption that individual employees support an average-sized family of three to four persons.

68. A letter from the Director of Information and Public Affairs of the World Bank which was inserted in the *World Bank Development Report 1980*, quoting *The Guardian* without proper reference.

69. UN ECOSOC, *Multinational Companies in World Development* (New York: United Nations, 1973) p. 14. See the footnote to that page for an explanation of how estimates of international production are obtained.

70. UN ECOSOC, *Transnational Corporations in World Development: A Re-examination* (New York: United Nations, 1978) p. 35. See footnote to that page for an explanation of the variations in calculations of 'international production' between the 1973 and the 1978 reports.

71. Ibid, p. 43; but note that most of these intra-firm transactions concern non-manufacturing goods, and that especially the international *oil* trade greatly exaggerates the picture of intra-firm transactions. According to Paul Streeten, intra-firm trade constitutes only 25 per cent of all international trade in *manufacturing*: Paul Streeten, 'Multinationals Revisited', *Finance and Development*, June 1979, p. 40.

72. 'Industrial' includes mining and construction as well as manufacturing activities.

73. These figures are taken from H. Magdoff, 'The US Dollar, Petro-dollars and US Imperialism', *Monthly Review*, January 1979, p. 12. Magdoff appears to suggest here that these figures refer to sales of manufactures. This, however, cannot be the case. For, when we compare his data with those presented in the United Nations ECOSOC Report, *Transnational Corporations in World Development*, it is obvious that what Magdoff is talking about must refer to all US affiliate *industrial* production (manufacturing plus mining and smelting, and construction, but excluding services and banking).

74. *Fortune*, 22 September 1980, p. 114.

75. For the 1960 figure (United Kingdom plus the USA) see M. Barratt Brown, *The Economics of Imperialism* (Harmondsworth: Penguin, 1974) pp. 206, 207. For 1966, see Lester B. Pearson, *Partners in Development* (London: Pall Mall Press, 1970) p. 100. For 1974, see *Transnational Corporations in World Development*, table III,38, p. 242.

76. See H. Magdoff, *The Age of Imperialism* (New York: Monthly Review Press, 1966) pp. 50—1. Magdoff makes the point that with the advent of the jet engine, the gas turbine and nuclear reactors, the USA has become more dependent than before on imports of critical materials. A similar position is taken by Pierre Jalee, *Imperialism in the Seventies* (New York: The Third Press, 1972). Lester Brown, *World Without Borders* (New York: Random House, 1973), estimates that by the end of the century the USA would be dependent on imports for half or more of its supplies of *all* basic industrial raw materials except phosphate, as compared with a similar import dependence only for aluminium, manganese, nickel and tin in 1950, and these four and zinc and chromium in 1970 (quoted in Fishlow *et al.*, *Rich and Poor Nations in the World Economy*, p. 33).

77. W. Arad and U. B. Arad, *Sharing Global Resources* (New York: McGraw-Hill, 1979) p. 42.

78. *Transnational Corporations in World Development: A Re-examination*, p. 56.

79. See also ibid.

80. G. Adams, 'New Trends in International Business', *Acta Oeconomica*, vol. 7, nos 3—4, 1971, pp. 349—67. Adams says that it is something of a 'truism' that competitive exports from less developed countries in manufactured goods are already to a 'significant' extent accounted for by the international companies. And Werner J. Feld, *Multinational Corporations and UN Politics: the Quest for Codes of Conduct* (Oxford: Pergamon Press, 1980), comments that while Brazil, Mexico, India, Malaysia and the tax havens increased their share of foreign investments appreciably in the period 1967—71, that of other less developed countries, including OPEC, declined (cf. p. 10).

81. Fröbel *et al.*, *The New International Division of Labour*, ch. 2. See also Adams, 'New Trends in International Business', who argues that world-wide sourcing is now part and parcel of international business planning and is resulting in a mass exodus of labour-intensive (and production-intensive) industries from the developed to the low-wage developing countries.

82. Fröbel *et al.*, *The New International Division of Labour*, p. 6.

83. Ibid, p. 313.

84. This figure is derived from data presented in *Transnational Corporations in World Development: A Re-examination*, table III,25.
85. Cf. ibid, pp. 35—6, where a comparison is made between present international production statistics and those collected in 1971 by the previous group of experts (*Multinational Corporations in World Development*, 1973). Indeed, it must be said that in relation to total world trade international production has slightly *declined* over the period in question. This is in contrast to an earlier period (1967—71) when it had not only just outgrown international trade but when direct overseas investment stock also grew slightly faster than the GDI of the advanced nations.
86. Helleiner, 'Structural Aspects of Third World Trade: Some Trends and Some Prospects'.
87. For a 'minimal' list of such practices, see Schwamm and Germidis, *Codes of Conduct for Multinational Companies*, pp. 18—19.
88. The 1974 UN programme of action on the establishment of a New International Economic Order (see Chapter 2) includes the desirability of such a code of conduct as one of its main programme points. On the various draft codes, see Dieter Ernst, 'A Code of Conduct for the Transfer of Technology: Establishing New Rules or Codifying the Status Quo?', in K. Sauvant and H. Hasenpflug, *The New International Economic Order* (Boulder, Col.: Westview Press, 1977) pp. 297—314. The need to review and revise the *international patent system* is the subject of UNCTAD Resolution *TAD/RES/88(IV)*, 30 May 1976. For a discussion see Constantine V. Vaitsos, 'The Revision of the International Patent System: Legal Considerations for a Third World Position', *World Development*, vol. 4, no. 2, 1976, pp. 85—102.
89. Cf., for instance, the progress made in this respect by the Andean Pact countries which have already passed novel industrial property legislation. See Commission of the Acuerdo de Cartagena, 'Common Treatment of Foreign Capital, Trademarks, Patents, Licensing Agreements and Royalties in the Andean Common Market', *Journal of Common Market Studies*, vol. 10, 1972, pp. 339—59.
90. See Ernst, 'A Code of Conduct for the Transfer of Technology'. Some empirical evidence of the development of technology-embodied restrictions in response to progressive host government legislation was collected by this author in Nigeria: see Ankie Hoogvelt, 'Indigenization and Technological Dependency', *Development and Change*, vol. 11, 1980, pp. 257—72.
91. C. V. Vaitsos, 'Bargaining and the Distribution of Returns in the Purchase of Technology by Developing Countries', *Bulletin of the Institute of Development Studies*, vol. 3, no. 1, 1970, pp. 16—23.
92. See Hoogvelt, 'Indigenization and Technological Dependency'.

93. Cf. R. Murray, 'Underdevelopment, International Firms and the International Division of Labour', in *Towards a New World Economy*, Papers and Proceedings of the Fifth European Conference of the Society for International Development, The Hague (Rotterdam University Press, 1972) esp. pp. 226–7, which list the monopolistic restrictions that might apply in this area. See also S. Sideri and S. Johns, *Mining for Development in the Third World* (Oxford: Pergamon Press, 1980).
94. *Prospects for the Developing Countries 1978–85*, p. 100.
95. *Transnational Corporations in World Development*, p. 46.
96. Ibid, p. 49.
97. J. D'Arista, 'US Banks Abroad', in United States Congress, House Committee on Banking, Currency and Housing, *FINE: Financial Institutions and the Economy* (Washington, US Government Printing Office, 1976) book II, p. 850, quoted in *Transnational Corporations in the World Economy*, p. 49.

Chapter 2

1. On the history of the non-aligned movement, see P. Willets, *The Non-Aligned Movement: the Origins of a Third World Alliance* (London: Frances Pinter, 1978). More especially in relation to the New International Economic Order, see Odette Jankowitsch and Karl Sauvant, 'The Evolution of the UN-aligned Movement as a Pressure Group for a New International Economic Order', a contribution to the 26th Annual Convention of the International Studies Association, Toronto, February 1976, mimeo, UN Centre on Transnational Enterprises.
2. At that time Raoul Prebisch was the Argentinian-born director of the UN Commission for Latin America. He became the first Secretary-General of the UN Conference on Trade and Development (UNCTAD).
3. R. Prebisch, *Towards a New Trade Policy for Development*, vol. II of *Proceedings of the United Nations Conference on Trade and Development* (Geneva: UNCTAD, 1964). A seminal version of this paper had appeared as an ECLA Document in 1950, and was mainly concerned with Latin America: R. Prebisch, *The Economic Development of Latin America and its Principal Problems* (New York: Economic Commission for Latin America, 1950).
4. For a full discussion of Prebisch's theory and UNCTAD's perspective, see A. S. Friedberg, *The United Nations Conference on Trade*

and Development 1964; the Theory of the Peripheral Economy at the Centre of International Political Discussion (Rotterdam University Press, 1969). Prebisch's thesis was based on the 'deterioration of the terms of trade argument'. Recent years have seen mounting attacks on this supposition: cf. I. M. D. Little, 'Economic Relations with the Third World – Old Myths and New Prospects', *Scottish Journal of Political Economy*, November 1975, pp. 223–5; and J. Spraos, 'The Statistical Debate on the Net Barter Terms of Trade between Primary Commodities and Manufactures', *Economic Journal*, no. 90, March 1980, pp. 107–27.

5. Cf. the collection of papers published by the Economic Commission for Latin America (University of Texas Press, 1969).

6. *Proceedings of the United Nations Conference on Trade and Development.*

7. Third World Forum, 'Intellectual Self-Reliance', opening speech by Mahbub Ul Haq (Director of the Policy Planning and Programme Review Department of the World Bank) at the establishment of Third World Forum in January 1975 at Karachi; printed in *International Development Review*, no. 1, 1975, pp. 8–13. About 100 leading Third World developmentalists attended this conference, including Samir Amin (UNDP) and Gamani Correa (UNCTAD).

8. Cf. Kees den Boer, 'The EEC Generalised System of Preferences: With Special Reference to Latin America', *Development and Change*, vol. VI, no. 4, October 1975, pp. 63–73. Den Boer comes to the conclusion that on the whole no more than 3.9–4.3 per cent of Third World exports to the EEC were given preference under the scheme. Also useful here is the argument developed by Kuhn Pederson in Kirsten Worm *et al.* (eds), *Industrialisation and Development in the Context of Demands for a New International Economic Order* (Copenhagen: Samfunds Videnskare Ugt Forlag, 1978) pp. 41–80. See also G. Helleiner, 'Manufactured Exports from Less Developed Countries and Multinational Firms', *Economic Journal*, March 1973, p. 32, where he suggests that

> the tariffs and trade barriers of the industrial countries are not neutral in their impact upon various types of industrial exports which less developed countries seek to expand. While the UNCTAD sponsored generalised system of preferences and the European Association schemes may partially mitigate the existing structure of industrially effective protection, there is every reason to expect that success with manufactured exports of the 'traditional' final product type – textiles, leather goods, toys, shoes, etc. – will in the future, as in the past, be met with tariff increases, quotas and retaliation.

While expansion of these types of manufactured exports will face 'traditional' barriers to markets, the export of labour-intensive components and processes (or even, in some instances, final product lines) within internationally integrated industries is likely to be 'relatively easy'. Finally, for a balanced assessment see Kathryn Morton and Peter Tulloch, *Trade and Developing Countries* (London: Croom Helm—Overseas Development Institute, 1977) pp. 169—75.

9. *Proceedings of the UN Conference on Trade and Development, 1972, Santiago de Chile* (Geneva: UNCTAD, 1972).

10. The Under-Secretary of the UN Commission for Economic and Social Affairs (ECOSOC), Phillipe de Seynes, in his address to UNCTAD III signalled the phenomenal spread of multinationals since the Second World War, and argued that 'it would be unreasonable to continue to ignore a serious gap in the system of international institutions, namely the lack of any arrangement for the supervision . . . of the activities of multinational corporations'. (It is significant to observe that this important Third World demand was first publicly formulated by a UN official.) Quoted in Orlando Letelier and Michael Moffit, *The International Economic Order, Part II* (Amsterdam: Transnational Institute, 1978) p. 22.

11. UNCTAD was nicknamed 'Under No Circumstances Take a Decision'.

12. The term 'legal instrument' must, however, be treated with caution. The Charter of the United Nations does not confer any legislative powers on the Assembly. Thus neither Resolutions nor Charters are 'legally binding' in any strict technical sense. Such, however, is the interpretation which rests on the conventional view of international law. There is an oppositional view (not surprisingly held by the Third World countries) which does invest the activities of international organisations with some kind of 'legislative authority', and which does therefore see the *Charter of Economic Rights and Duties of States* as an elaboration of the UN Charter. This latter interpretation is realistic in so far as 'customary behaviour' is a source of international law, for resolutions adopted with regularity in international forums are quotable in a legal context, and thus are of potential legal significance. I am grateful to Mr J. Merrills of the Law Faculty, Sheffield University, for pointing out these legal niceties to me. A full discussion within the legal profession on the NIEO and the Charter has appeared in the *Virginia Journal of International Law*, vol. 16, no. 2, 1976. Especially useful are the contributions by D. Bowett and by Gillian White.

13. This interpretation on the convergence between UNCTAD and the non-aligned movement owes much to Karl P. Sauvant's excellent

'Introduction' to K. P. Sauvant and H. Hasenpflug, *The New International Economic Order* (Boulder, Col.: Westview Press, 1979). The interpretation is, however, a fairly common one to make. See also Letelier and Moffit, *The International Economic Order*, and Kirsten Worm's 'Introduction' to Worm *et al.* (eds), *Industrialisation and Development in the Context of Demands for a New International Economic Order.*

14. Cf. Sauvant, 'Introduction', p. 6.
15. *Declaration on the Establishment of a New International Economic Order*, UN Resolution 3201 S–VI, and *Program of Action on the Establishment of a New International Economic Order*, UN Resolution 32–2 S–VI; both are reported in *UN Monthly Chronicle*, vol. XI, no. 5, May 1974, pp. 66ff.
16. *Charter of Economic Rights and Duties of States*, UN Resolution 3281(XXIX), 12 December 1974. The text of the Charter is reprinted in full in R. Meagher, *An International Redistribution of Wealth and Power: a Study of the Charter of Economic Rights and Duties of States* (Oxford: Pergamon Press, 1979). Meagher's study has been an invaluable guide to the present chapter.
17. Sauvant, 'Introduction', p. 10.
18. Meagher, *An International Redistribution of Wealth and Power*, p. 3.
19. As early as 1962, after a protracted debate, the General Assembly of the United Nations had passed a resolution on permanent sovereignty over natural wealth and resources which permitted nationalisation of foreign investments 'on grounds or reasons of public utility, security or national interest'. Nationalisation under this resolution brought with it the duty to pay 'appropriate compensation' in accordance with national rules and 'in accordance with international law'. In case of controversy relating to compensation, 'national jurisdiction of the State taking such measures shall be exhausted'. Preference was stated for 'arbitration or international adjudication on agreement by Sovereign States and other parties concerned'. This resolution received the overwhelming support of both the less developed countries and the developed countries, except for the Soviet Union, Eastern European countries and France. See Meagher, ibid, p. 51.
20. This summary of the integrated community programme (ICP) is taken from H. Hasenpflug, 'Developing Countries in World Trade', in Sauvant and Hasenpflug, *The New International Economic Order*. The ICP has stimulated a vast amount of literature. For general discussion, see UNCTAD, *Problems of Raw Materials and Development*, TD/B/488 (New York: United Nations, 1974); UNCTAD, *An Integrated Programme for Commodities*, Report by

the Secretary General of UNCTAD, TD/B/488 (Geneva: UNCTAD, 1974); J. R. Behrman, *International Commodity Agreements* (Washington: Overseas Development Council, 1977); Geoffrey Goodwin, 'The UNCTAD Common Fund', *The World Today*, vol. XI, 1977, pp. 425–32. As it happens, views from the 'right' and from the 'extreme left' are often both cautious and even negative. Right-wing arguments usually revolve around the undesirability of bureaucratic intervention in the free market, which after all remains, so it is believed, the best allocator of goods and services. It is also argued that such bureaucratic intervention might distract attention from the developing countries' own development responsibility. For a fair representation of such views see the collection of papers edited by J. Bhagwati, *The New International Economic Order: the North–South Debate* (Cambridge: Mass., MIT Press, 1977). For a left-wing, negative, view, see Johan Galtung, 'Poor Countries versus Rich: Poor People versus Rich. Whom Will the NIEO Benefit?', mimeo., Vienna Institute for Development, 1977. His view is that the NIEO (and the commodity programme in particular) will benefit the ruling classes in Third World countries, and will moreover divide the Third World deeply into those countries which can benefit most from increased integration into the world capitalist system (at the expense of their own marginalised masses) and those which cannot. Sympathy for the NIEO demands, and the ICP in particular, comes mainly from progressive liberals in the West (see Chapter 4) who believe that the ICP is the right tool to achieve some form of international redistribution of wealth which will in turn stimulate the capitalist world economy (some of the contributions in Bhagwati, *The New International Economic Order*, reflect this position; cf. Paul Streeten's article). See also R. H. Green and H. W. Singer, 'Toward a Rational and Equitable New International Economic Order', *World Development*, vol. 3, no. 6, June 1975, pp. 427–44; and D. Avromovic, 'Common Fund, Why and of What Kind?', *Journal of World Trade Law*, vol. 12, no. 5, September–October 1978.

21. UNIDO, *Lima Declaration and Plan of Action on Industrial Development and Cooperation*, Resolution adopted at the Second General Conference of UNIDO, Lima, Peru, March 1975. The *Lima Declaration* contains detailed proposals as regards recommended measures for industrialisation of the developing countries within the framework of the NIEO. The 25 per cent target formulated is reckoned by Singer to be attainable by the year 2000: cf. H. Singer, 'Reflections on the Lima (25%) Target', *Conference Proceedings*, Anniversary Conference of the Institute of Social Studies, The Hague, 1977. In this context see also the contribution by W. Bandstecher in William G. Tyler (ed.), *Issues and Prospects*

for the New International Economic Order (Lexington, Mass: Heath & Co., 1977). On the so-called 'adjustment policies' see Helen Hughes, *Prospects for Partnership*, a World Bank seminar report (Baltimore: Johns Hopkins University Press, 1973).

22. For a brief and clear exposition of the IMF and how it works, see a cover story of the new Third World magazine, *South*, no. 2, November 1980, from which the figures presented in this section have been taken. Cheryl Payer, *The Debt Trap* (Harmondsworth: Penguin, 1974) is a good study of how the IMF's conditionality time and again thwarts progressive self-reliance policies of Third World countries.

23. These were the proposals made by the so-called Committee of Twenty at the Meeting of the IMF Interim Committee in Jamaica in 1976. The Committee of Twenty consists of Third World representatives in the IMF and it is not to be confused with the Committee of Ten (advanced countries only), who, because of their collective two-thirds voting majority, hold effective power in the IMF.

24. *International Financial Cooperation and Development*, Report by the UNCTAD Secretariat, TD/188/Supplement 1, 1976.

25. These figures are taken from Jyon Shankar Singh, *A New International Economic Order* (New York: Praeger, 1977).

26. *The Manila Declaration and Plan of Action*, Resolution TAD/RES/ 88(IV) (Geneva: UNCTAD, 1976). See also *Report of the Intergovernmental Group of Experts on a Code of Conduct on Transfer of Technology*, TD/B/C/6/1, submission of the Group of 77. Relevant also is *The Possibility and Feasibility of an International Code of Conduct*, Document TD/B/AC/1/22 (Geneva: UNCTAD, 1974).

27. Cf. *The Manila Declaration and Plan of Action*.

28. *Report on the Conference on Economic Cooperation among Developing Countries*, held in Mexico City, September 1976, Document TD/B/628 (Geneva: UNCTAD, 1976). See also *Elements of a Preferential System of Trade among Developing Countries*, TD/192/Supplement 2, January 1976 (Nairobi: UNCTAD IV, 1976); and *New Directions and New Structures for Trade and Development*, Report of the Secretary-General, TD/183 (Nairobi: UNCTAD IV, 1976).

29. Cf. Article 21 of the *Charter of Economic Rights and Duties of States*.

30. G. Corea, 'UNCTAD and the New International Economic Order', *International Affairs*, vol. 53, no. 2, 1977, pp. 177–87, this on p. 184.

31. Namely, in Mexico City in 1976, Buenos Aires in 1978, and in Vienna in 1979.

32. This contradiction is the major focus of Fishlow's collection of

essays on the NIEO: cf. A. Fishlow *et al.*, *Rich and Poor Nations in the World Economy* (New York: McGraw-Hill, 1978).

33. Ibid, especially p. 24.

34. Cf. Harry Magdoff, 'The Limits of International Reform', *Monthly Review*, vol. 30, no. 1, May 1978, pp. 1—11. Magdoff asks if self-reliant development in the Third World is at all possible if these countries remain enmeshed in the imperialist network and in the basic dependency relationship with the advanced world. It is worth comparing this Marxist critique with that of arch-conservative P. T. Bauer, 'Western Guilt and Third World Poverty', *Commentary*, 59, January 1976, pp. 31—8.

35. Helge Hveem, 'The Politics of the New International Economic Order', *Bulletin of Peace Proposals*, vol. 7, 1976, pp. 3—6, this quote on p. 3.

36. Catherine Gwin, 'The Seventh Special Session', in Sauvant and Hasenpflug, *The New International Economic Order*, p. 110.

37. Meagher, *An International Redistribution of Wealth and Power*, p. 94

38. Gwin, 'The Seventh Special Session', p. 110.

39. This particular topic has probably stimulated more research and academic debate than any other in the NIEO era. I have here quoted the very influential views of the Trilateral Commission, as expressed in one of its *Task Force Reports*, no. 10, p. 66. See Trilateral Commission, *Task Force Reports*, nos 9—14 (New York University Press, 1978). But see also Benson Varon and Keji Tachauchi, 'Developing Countries and Non-Fuel Minerals', *Foreign Affairs*, vol. 52, no. 3, April 1974, pp. 497—510. Varon and Tachauchi see very limited scope for OPEC-type cartelisations by other developing countries, as does Stephen D. Krasner, 'Oil is the Exception', *Foreign Policy*, no. 14. 1972—3. A counter-position has been taken by Fred C. Bergsten, 'The Threat from the Third World', *Foreign Policy*, no. 11, 1971—2, and again in his reply to Krasner in 'The Response to the Third World', *Foreign Policy*, no. 17, 1974—5, pp. 3—34. Michael Tanzer, in his recent book *The Race for Resources* (New York: Monthly Review Press, 1980), sees the prospects for an effective OPEC type of collective action as very limited for almost all minerals except copper (cf. his p. 229).

40. Gwin, 'The Seventh Special Session', p. 111. On this topic see also Theodore Moran, 'Transnational Strategies of Protection and Defense by Multinational Corporations: Spreading the Risk and Raising the Cost for Nationalization in Natural Resources', *International Organization*, vol. 27, 1973, pp. 273—88. Moran suggests that in the absence of military options to counter risks of national-

isation, MNCs have taken to lining up 'transnational alliances' to defend their positions.

41. Gwin, 'The Seventh Special Session', p. 111.

42. Cf. Jeff Frieden, 'The Trilateral Commission: Economics and Politics in the 1970s', *Monthly Review*, vol. 29, no. 7, December 1977, pp. 1—18.

43. Ibid, p. 11.

44. Trilateral Commission, *Task Force Reports*, vols I and II, final chapter entitled 'On the Trilateral Process'. See also *Task Force Report*, no. 12, which deals with the problem of international consultations.

45. Report by Congressional Advisors to the Seventh Special Session of the UN Committee on International Relations, US House of Representatives and Committee on Foreign Relations, US Senate, 13 October 1975. The twenty-seven-page speech entitled 'Global Consensus and Economic Development' is included in the appendix of the Report.

46. Quoted in Meagher, *An International Redistribution of Wealth and Power*, p. 96.

47. Gwin, 'The Seventh Special Session', p. 111.

48. Roger Hansen, 'The Political Economy of North—South Relations: How Much Change?', *International Organizations*, Autumn 1975, quoted in Letelier and Moffitt, *The International Economic Order*, p. 53. See also Bergsten, 'Response to the Third World', p. 10, who speaks of the world's 'new middle class' in this context.

49. Trilateral Commission, *Task Force Reports*, vol. II, p. 113. Note also the caption on p. 112: 'Integration of newcomers and drop-outs'.

50. Ibid, p. 113.

51. Meagher, *An International Redistribution of Wealth and Power*, p. 103.

52. Ibid, p. 99.

53. *Development Forum*, September 1980, p. 13.

54. The Trilateral Commission has suggested that OPEC should participate together with the trilateral countries in a special fund of $3 billion to aid the countries of the 'Fourth' World: *Task Force Reports*, vol. I, p. 64. More recently there has been strong pressure from the IMF on the capital-surplus oil-exporting countries to recycle their petro-dollars through the IMF so that the IMF may better assist the balance-of-payments problems of the Third World oil importers (as well as those of the developed countries).

55. This is the major theme of both the Tinbergen (*Reshaping the International Order*, 1976) and the Brandt (*North—South: a*

Programme for Survival, 1980) Reports. It has also been emphasised in the World Bank's trend-setting volume *Redistribution with Growth* (Oxford University Press, 1974) edited by the World Bank's Vice-President, Hollis Chenery.

56. Cf., in particular, the Brandt Report, p. 128.

57. Not much is known about the actual process of social interaction and opinion-making that goes on inside these international organisa- . tions. It is indeed a much neglected area of social study. However, there is one interesting study which examines the process of opinion formation inside UNCTAD's Secretariat: Robert L. Rothstein, *Global Bargaining* (Princeton University Press, 1979). See also Thomas George Weiss, *International Bureaucracy: an Analysis of the Operation of Functional and Global International Secretariats* (Lexington, Mass.: Lexington Books, 1975).

58. The most influential and internationally reputable of these are: Samir Amin, who is a prolific Marxist writer, and Director of UNDP in Dakar; Gamani Corea, Secretary-General of UNCTAD; and Mahbub Ul Haq, who holds a key position in the World Bank and has written various books and articles on economic development from a progressive liberal perspective. Further, on the overlap of membership of radical Third World writers and the permanent staff of international organisations, see R. W. Cox, 'On Ideologies and the NIEO', *International Organization*, vol. 33, no. 2, Spring 1979, pp. 257–302, esp. p. 262.

59. Trilateral Commission, *Task Force Reports*, vol. I, p. 67. This sentiment is also echoed by Kurt Waldheim, Secretary-General of the United Nations, in his Foreword to the Tinbergen Report (*Reshaping the International Order*):

> Moreover the dependence of the developing world on the developed world is changing — indeed in certain cases has been reversed. Many developed nations are also finding themselves in serious economic difficulties. The international system of economic and trade relations which was devised thirty years ago is now manifestly inadequate for the needs of the world community as a whole. The charge against that order in the past was that it worked well for the affluent nations, and against the poor. It cannot now even be said that it works well for the affluent. This is an additional incentive for evolving a new economic order.

60. For the successfully industrialising Third World countries, exports of manufactures grew by 14 per cent between 1965 and 1972; and

they increased their share of total trade in manufactures by 50 per cent in this period. Cf. A Singh, 'The Basic Needs Approach to Development versus the New International Economic Order: the Significance of Third World Industrialisation', *World Development*, vol. 7, 1979, pp. 585–606, esp. p. 587. In this same context it is worth noting that while between 1954 and 1964 imports into developing countries of *capital goods* from the advanced countries had risen faster than any other imports, namely by an average rate of 9 per cent, this growth of capital imports had begun to decline after 1965, possibly a sign that the benefits for the advanced world of Third World industrialisation had come to an end: cf. table 9 in Paul Bairoch, 'Trends in 1960–67 and Short-term Perspectives of Third World Economy', in Colin Legum (ed.), *The First UN Development Decade and the Lessons for the 1970s* (New York: Praeger, 1970) ch. 2.

61. The growing protectionism which started in the 1970s has been a cause of major concern for the 'internationalists' and the 'global Keynesians'; cf. President McNamara's *Address to UNCTAD* in Manila, the Philippines, in 1979, where he warns against, and quotes examples of, 'the New Protectionism' (cf. pp. 7, 8).

62. J. McHale and M. C. McHale, *Basic Human Needs: a Framework for Action* (New Jersey: Transaction Books) esp. Introduction.

63. The leading text was written by a team from the World Bank and edited by its Vice-President: Chenery *et al.*, *Redistribution with Growth*.

64. The ILO World Employment Programme (WEP) was launched in 1969 as the ILO's main contribution to the Second UN Development Decade. It reported to the World Employment Conference in 1976. It introduced the 'trickle-up' argument, linking it to the basic needs strategy. For an elaboration of this argument, see *Employment, Growth and Basic Needs: a One-World Problem*, Report of the Director-General prepared for the Tripartite World Conference on Employment, Income Distribution and Social Progress, and the International Division of Labour (Geneva: ILO, 1976). A great influence on this Report and its vision had been, in turn, one of the 'mission reports' commissioned by the ILO in preparation for the conference, namely *Employment, Incomes and Equality: a Strategy for Increasing Productive Employment in Kenya* (Geneva: ILO, 1972). One of the main contributors to this mission report was Hans Singer, whose *Technology and Basic Needs* (Geneva: ILO, 1977) goes through the same argument again.

65. N. Hicks and P. Streeten, 'Indicators of Development: the Search for a Basic Needs Yardstick', *World Development*, vol. 7, 1979, pp. 567–80 (quote on p. 568).

66. Paul Streeten and S. J. Burki, 'Basic Needs: Some Issues', *World Development*, vol. 6, 1978, pp. 411–21 (quote on p. 412).

67. The seven characteristics listed in the text are largely culled from Dharam Gai, 'What the Basic Needs Approach to Development is All About', paper presented at the Kenya National Seminar on Employment and Basic Needs, May 1977. For a discussion of the pros and cons of basic needs strategies in relation to economic development, see R. H. Green, 'Basic Human Needs: Concept or Slogan, Synthesis or Smoke-Screen?, *IDS Bulletin*, June 1978; and Dharam Gai, 'Basic Needs and its Critics', *IDS Bulletin*, June 1978. Furthermore, the IMF/World Bank monthly entitled *Finance and Development* has produced numerous articles on basic needs: cf. the issues of September 1979, December 1979, March 1980 and June 1980. This serves as an indication of these institutions' great interest in this particular development strategy. The most prolific World Bank scribe on the basic needs approach is Paul Streeten, who has written many articles in *World Development* and other journals on the subject. He has also written a book: Paul Streeten, *Basic Needs* (Washington: IBRD, 1977).

68. Amilcar O. Herrera *et al.*, *Catastrophe or New Society? A Latin American World Model*, prepared by a group of scholars of the Bariloche Foundation, International Development Research Centre, Ottawa, 1975. Indeed, two more statements from radical Third Worldists informed the basic needs ideology: (1) The *Declaration of Cocoyoc* (1974) was a statement issued by a group of social scientists, natural scientists and economists at the end of a seminar organised under the joint auspices of UNCTAD and UNEP on 'Patterns of Resource Use, Environment and Development Strategies'; (2) *What Now – Another Development* (1975) was prepared by a group of individuals on the initiative of the Dag Hammarskjöld Foundation on the occasion of the Seventh Special Session of the UN General Assembly.

69. Enough has been said already about the World Bank's intimate association with the basic needs ideology. At a high-level meeting in October 1977 the member countries of the OECD's Development Assistance Committee (DAC countries for short) affirmed *their* determination 'to direct, in co-operation with the developing countries, progressively larger efforts to programmes meeting basic human needs': cf. *Development Co-operation 1978 Review* (Paris: OECD, 1978).

70. Trilateral Commission, *Task Force Reports*, vol. I, p. 70.

71. *Development Co-operation 1979 Review* (Paris: OECD, 1979) p. 51. The developing world's objections to basic needs occasioned Mahbub Ul Haq, senior official from the World Bank and Third

Worldist himself, to write a thoughtful article to lay such objections to rest. Mahbub Ul Haq, 'An International Perspective on Basic Needs', *Finance and Development*, September 1980.

72. 'LDC Report: World Bank advocates Socialism', *International Currency Review*, vol. 11, no. 4, 1979, pp. 15–24.

73. Veronika Bennholdt-Thomsen, 'Investment in the Poor, a Critical Analysis of the New World Bank Policy', Bieleveld, Department of Sociology, unpublished manuscript, 1979. Her interpretation of the concept of 'marginalisation' as both a consequence of and functional to capitalism goes back to Quijano's original definition of the concept: cf. A. Quijano, 'Pole marginal de l'économie et main d'oevre marginalisée', in A. Abdel-Malek (ed.), *Sociologie de l'impérialisme* (Paris: Anthropos, 1971).

74. These data are from *South Magazine*, no. 1, October 1980, p. 41, where Frances Moorelappe, Joseph Collins and David Kinley, *Aid as Obstacle* (New York: Institute for Food and Development Policy, 1980) is quoted.

75. Cf. A. v. d. Laar, 'The World Bank and the Poor', thesis (Amsterdam: Vrije Universiteit, 1979) pp. 130–1. This writer, too, comes to the conclusion that 'a major concentration of effort and funds on the poorer countries would seem to call for a more drastic curtailment of countries that are eligible for bank lending in the future' (p. 127).

76. *Development Co-operation 1979 Review* (Paris: OECD, 1979) p. 41.

Chapter 3

1. Cf. Sidney Pollard, *The Idea of Progress* (New York: Basic Books, 1968) pp. ix–x.

2. Cf. T. B. Bottomore, *Sociology: a Guide to Problems and Literature* (London: Allen & Unwin, 1962) p. 48.

3. H. Morgan, *Ancient Society*, quoted by E. Service in his contribution on 'Evolution' in *International Encyclopedia of the Social Sciences* (New York: Macmillan, 1968) p. 223.

4. The present chapter is largely an abbreviated version of Part One of my previous book *The Sociology of Developing Societies* (London: Macmillan, 1976). The various steps in the argument are elaborated in much greater depth and all the necessary referencing is to be found there (see ch. 3).

5. S. N. Eisenstadt, 'Social Differentiation, Integration and Evolution', *American Sociological Review*, June 1954, p. 376.

6. T. Parsons, 'Evolutionary Universals', *American Sociological Review*, June 1964, p. 341.

7. T. Parsons, *The Social System* (Glencoe, Ill.: Free Press, 1951) p. 167.

8. Max Weber, quoted in D. Beetham, *Max Weber and the Theory of Modern Politics* (London: Allen & Unwin, 1974) p. 68.

9. For a thorough review of the economic development and social change literature, see Hoogvelt, *The Sociology of Developing Societies*, ch. 3. During the 1950s, the economic development and social change perspective was sufficiently dominant to justify the founding of a special journal devoted to it: *Economic Development and Cultural Change* (Harvard University Press). This journal continues to be published, although there has been a notable shift away from theoretical 'modernisation' articles and towards empiricist contributions, dominantly in the field of population and economic development, migration and the reporting of community projects.

10. Parsons, *The Social System*, p. 177.

11. A. Inkeles, *Becoming Modern: Individual Change in Six Developing Countries* (London: Heinemann, 1974).

12. D. McClelland and D. G. Winter, 'Motivating Economic Achievement' in R. D. Ward (ed.), *The Challenge of Development* (Chicago: Aldine, 1967). The theoretical basis for this bizarre attempt at social engineering can be found in D. McClelland, *The Achieving Society* (New York: Van Nostrand, 1961).

13. N. J. Smelser, 'Towards a Theory of Modernization' in A. Etzioni and E. Etzioni (eds), *Social Change* (New York: Basic Books, 1964).

14. Hoogvelt, *The Sociology of Developing Societies*, ch. 3.

15. Cf. H. R. Barringer, G. L. Blanksten and Raymond W. Mack (eds), *Social Change in Developing Areas* (Cambridge, Mass.: Schenkman, 1965), for an assessment of the influence of evolutionism in the literature of development and modernisation.

16. For internationally accepted 'standard' compilations of such indicators, see, for example, *Compilation of Indicators of Development* (Geneva: UNRISD, 1969); *Contents and Measurement of Socio-Economic Development*, a staff study of the United Nations Research Institute for Social Development (New York: Praeger, 1972) pp. 45–6; N. Ginsberg, *Atlas of Economic Development* (Chicago University Press, 1961); A. S. Banks and R. B. Texter, *A Cross-Polity Survey* (MIT Press, 1963); B. M. Russett *et al.*, *World Handbook of Political and Social Indicators* (Yale University Press, 1964); C. L. Taylor and M. Hudson, *World Handbook of Political and Social Indicators*, 2nd edn (Yale University Press, 1972).

17. Ivan Illich, 'Outwitting the "Developed" Countries', in H. Bernstein

(ed.), *Underdevelopment and Development* (Harmondsworth: Penguin, 1974) pp. 357–68.

18. Talcott Parsons, *The Evolution of Societies*, edited and with an introduction by Jackson Toby (Englewood Cliffs, N.J.: Prentice-Hall, 1977) p. 229. Apart from the introduction by Toby and his editorial work, this volume is mostly a reprint of Parsons's two small 1967 volumes: *The Evolution of Societies* and *The System of Modern Societies*. It does, however, also contain an additional chapter, 'Continuing Evolution'.

19. H. Kahn, *World Economic Development, 1979 and Beyond* (Boulder, Col.: Westview Press, 1979).

Chapter 4

1. This is as Wallerstein sums it up in a title of one of his essays, 'Modernization, *Requiescat in Pace*', in I. Wallerstein, *The Capitalist World Economy* (Cambridge University Press, 1979). This is not to say that the modernisation perspective is entirely dead. Some of the old-timers continue to whistle the same tune, even in the 1970s. There is the new edition of Talcott Parsons's *The Evolution of Societies* (Englewood Cliffs, N. J.: Prentice-Hall, 1977); Wilbert Moore's article 'Modernization and Rationalization, Processes and Restraints', *Economic Development and Cultural Change*, vol. 25, supplement, 1977; S. N. Eisenstadt, *Tradition, Change and Modernity* (New York: Wiley, 1973); and Marion Levy, *Modernization, Latecomers and Survivors* (New York: Basic Books, 1973). However, I would yet maintain that as a theory it has lost much of its vigour, its capacity to innovate and come forward with new concepts and/or ideas, and that, above all, it has been driven back from its position as the dominant intellectual paradigm by both the neo-Marxist dependency theories, and the bourgeois world development writers.

2. For the most comprehensive collection of essays on the methodology of world futures theories, see J. I. B. Fowles (ed.), *Handbook of Future Research* (Westport, Conn.: Greenwood Press, 1978).

3. T. Parsons, 'Social Systems', Part II of 'Systems Analysis' in *International Encyclopedia of the Social Sciences* (New York: Macmillan, 1968) p. 458.

4. Cf. Anatol Rapaport, 'General Systems Theory', Part I of 'Systems Analysis' in *International Encyclopedia of the Social Sciences*, p. 457.

5. This description of the sequence of methodological steps is indebted

to Roy Amara, 'Probing the Future', in Fowles (ed.), *Handbook of Future Research*.

6. An example here is Amilcar O. Herrera *et al.*, *Catastrophe or New Society?* (Ottawa: International Development Research Centre, 1976).

7. T. Parsons, *Societies* (Englewood Cliffs, N. J.: Prentice-Hall, 1966) p. 111, where he argues the case for structural analysis to take precedence over the analysis of process and change. In presenting his 'systems' of different societies he speaks of 'paradigms' throughout the book.

8. This section is in particular indebted to the excellent review of world futures theories by Sam Cole, 'The Global Futures Debate, 1965–1976', in Christopher Freeman and Marie Jahoda (eds), *World Futures: The Great Debate* (London: Martin Robertson, 1978) pp. 9–49.

9. H. Kahn and A. J. Wiener, *The Year 2000* (London: Macmillan, 1967) p. 116, quoted in Cole, 'The Global Futures Debate', p. 20.

10. D. Meadows *et al.*, *The Limits to Growth* (New York: Universe Books, 1972; and London: Pan Books, 1974).

11. See, for instance, William D. Nordhauss, 'World Dynamics, Measurement without Data', *Economic Journal*, vol. 83, 1973, pp. 1156–83. For a useful collection of *pro* and *contra* arguments, see A. Weintraub, E. Schwartz and J. R. Aronson, *The Economic Growth Controversy* (New York: International Arts & Sciences Press, 1973).

12. For a useful and critical summary of the Meadows argument, which has been closely followed here, see H. M. Enzensberger, 'A Critique of Political Ecology', *New Left Review*, vol. 84, 1974, pp. 3–32.

13. Jay Forrester, *World Dynamics* (Cambridge, Mass.: Wright–Allen, 1971).

14. Meadows *et al.*, *The Limits to Growth*, ch. 3.

15. Enzensberger, 'A Critique of Political Ecology'.

16. H. Kahn *et al.*, *World Economic Development, 1979 and Beyond* (Boulder, Col.: Westview Press, 1979) p. 54.

17. Ibid, p. 61.

18. Ibid, p. 62.

19. W. W. Rostow, *Getting from Here to There* (London: Macmillan, 1978).

20. Ibid. This is precisely the title of his book.

21. Ibid, p. 52.

22. Ibid, p. 241.

23. Ibid, p. 237.

24. Ibid, p. 243.

25. E. Schumacher, *Small is Beautiful* (London: Sphere, 1974).
26. J. Tinbergen and A. Dolman (eds), *Reshaping the International Order* (New York: Dutton, 1976).
27. R. L. Heilbroner, *Business Civilisation in Decline* (London: Boyars, 1976).
28. The Ecologist, *A Blueprint for Survival* (Harmondsworth: Penguin, 1972).
29. Barbara Ward and R. Dubois, *Only One Earth* (London: Deutsch, 1972).
30. Cf. Cole, 'The Global Futures Debate', p. 31.
31. D. Gabor, U. Colombo *et al.*, *Beyond the Age of Waste* (Oxford: Pergamon, 1978). This is a fourth report of the Club of Rome. It is written by what one might call 'technological optimists' who stress that the technical problems associated with the physical limits to growth are far less intractable than the social-psychological, political and economic problems. They also make the point that the population factor is much less critical than it was thought to be at the time of the first report to the Club of Rome (*The Limits to Growth*).
32. M. Mesarovic and E. Pestel, *Mankind at the Turning Point* (New York: New American Library, 1976).
33. Ibid, p. 18.
34. Ibid, p. 31.
35. Tinbergen and Dolman, *Reshaping the International Order*.
36. Ibid, p. 16.
37. Ibid, p. 26.
38. Ibid, pp. 82–4.
39. W. W. Leontief, *The Future of the World Economy* (New York: United Nations, 1976).
40. Y. Kaya and Y. Susuki, 'Global Constraints and a New Vision for Development', *Technological Forecasting and Social Change*, vol. 6, nos 3–4, 1974.
41. *North–South: a Programme for Survival*, the Report of the Independent Commission on International Development Issues under the Chairmanship of Willy Brandt (London: Pan Books, 1980).
42. OECD, *Interfutures: Facing the Future* (Paris: OECD, 1979).
43. Brandt Report, p. 21.
44. Ibid, p. 239.
45. Ibid, p. 10.
46. Ibid, p. 230.
47. Ibid, p. 128.
48. Ibid, p. 42.
49. A. Herrera *et al.*, *Catastrophe or New Society?* (Ottawa: Inter-

national Development Research Centre, 1976). This work was carried out by the Bariloche Foundation, Argentina, under the auspices of the Club of Rome.

50. Ibid, p. 26.
51. Ervin Laszlo, *The Inner Limits of Mankind: Heretical Reflections on Today's Values, Culture, and Politics*, with a commentary by A. Peccei (Oxford: Pergamon, 1978). See also E. Laszlo and J. Bierman, *Goals in a Global Community*, the original background papers for *Goals for Mankind*, a report to the Club of Rome (Oxford: Pergamon, 1977) 2 vols.
52. World Order Models Project's series 'Preferred Worlds for the 1990s' (New York Institute for World Order) Titles include Falk, *A Study of Future Worlds*; Galtung, *The True Worlds*; Rajni, *Footsteps into the Future: Diagnosis of the Present World and a Design for an Alternative*; Godoy Lagos, *Revolution of Being: A Latin American View of the Future*; Mazrui, *A World Federation of Cultures: An African Perspective*; Mendlovitz (ed.), *On the Creation of a Just World Order: Preferred Worlds for the 1990s*.
53. Falk *et al.*, *A Study of Future Worlds*.

Chapter 5

1. V. Pavlov Vlyanovsky, *Asian Dilemma: A Soviet View and Myrdal's Concept* (Moscow: Progress Publishers, 1973) p. 156.
2. Immanuel Wallerstein, *The Capitalist World Economy* (Cambridge University Press, 1979) p. 52.
3. See especially David Booth, 'André Gunder Frank: An Introduction and Appreciation', and Phillip J. O'Brien, 'A Critique of Latin American Theories of Dependency', both in I. Oxaal *et al.*, *Beyond the Sociology of Development* (London: Routledge & Kegan Paul, 1976).
4. John Taylor, *From Modernisation to Modes of Production* (London: Macmillan, 1979) p. 101.
5. L. Althusser and E. Balibar, *Reading 'Capital'* (London: New Left Books, 1970). Balibar's section is especially relevant to us. For the link between the new orthodoxy and the dependency theorists, see John Clammer, 'Economic Anthropology and the Sociology of Development: Liberal Anthropology and its French Critics', in Oxaal *et al.*, *Beyond the Sociology of Development*.
6. Karl Marx, *Pre-capitalist Economic Formations*, edited and introduced by E. Hobsbawm (London: Lawrence & Wishart, 1964) pp. 19–20.
7. This section is particularly indebted to three works; Hobsbawm's

edition of Marx and Engels, *Pre-capitalist Economic Formations*; Barry Hindess and Paul Q. Hirst, *Pre-capitalist Modes of Production* (London: Routledge & Kegan Paul, 1975); and Umberto Melotti, *Marx and the Third World* (London: Macmillan, 1977).

8. This, for instance, is the comment made by Peter L. Berger, *Pyramids of Sacrifice* (Harmondsworth: Penguin, 1976) p. 25.

9. For this view of capitalism, see Wallerstein, *The Capitalist World Economy*; and A. Frank, *Capitalism and Underdevelopment in Latin America* (New York: Monthly Review Press, 1969).

10. This is the position taken by Maurice Dobb in *Studies in the Development of Capitalism* (London: Routledge, 1946); and more recently by E. Laclau, 'Feudalism and Capitalism in Latin America', *New Left Review*, May 1971.

11. This, it would appear, is the orthodox position taken by Soviet writers.

12. Cf. D. K. Fieldhouse, *The Theory of Capitalist Imperialism* (London: Longman, 1967) Introduction.

13. See, for example, J. A. Schumpeter, 'The Sociology of Imperialism', in *Imperialism and Social Classes: Two Essays* (New York: Meridian Books, 1958).

14. V. I. Lenin, *Imperialism, the Highest Stage of Capitalism* (London: Lawrence & Wishart, 1916); and J. A. Hobson, *Imperialism: A Study* (London: Allen & Unwin, 1902).

15. Rosa Luxemburg, *The Accumulation of Capital* (New York: Monthly Review Press, 1968).

16. Of all writers on dependency and the dependency debate, Gabriel Palma most clearly places the debate within the Marxist tradition of writings on imperialism: Gabriel Palma, 'Dependency: A Formal Theory of Underdevelopment or a Methodology for the Analysis of Concrete Situations of Underdevelopment?', *World Development*, vol. 6, 1978, pp. 881–924.

17. See, for instance, Colin Leys, 'Underdevelopment and Development: Critical Notes', *Journal of Contemporary Asia*, vol. 7, no. 1, 1977, pp. 82–115; Alejandro Portes, 'On the Sociology of National Development: Theories and Issues', *American Journal of Sociology*, vol. 82, no. 1, 1976–7, pp. 55–63; Adrian Foster Carter, 'From Rostow to Gunder Frank: Conflicting Paradigms in the Analysis of Underdevelopment', *World Development*, vol. 4, no. 3, 1976; and J. Samuel Valenzuela and Arturo Valenzuela, 'Modernization and Dependence: Alternative Perspectives in the Study of Latin American Underdevelopment', in J. Villamil (ed.), *Transnational Corporations and Transnational Culture* (Brighton: Harvester Press, 1979).

18. This was the central point made by André Gunder Frank in his

original formulation of dependency in *The Sociology of Development and the Underdevelopment of Sociology* (London: Pluto Press, 1967).

19. Paul Baran, *The Political Economy of Growth* (New York: Monthly Review Press, 1967). (Originally published in Spanish in 1957).

20. A. G. Frank, *Capitalism and Underdevelopment in Latin America* (New York: Monthly Review Press, 1967).

21. James A. Caporoso, 'Dependence and Dependency in the Global System', *International Organization*, vol. 32, no. 1, January 1978, p. 2.

22. Probably the best review and methodological critique of the Baran–Frank dependency theory is Palma, 'Dependency'. Useful criticisms of dependency theory from the point of view of the 'empirical' usability of the concept can be found in Christopher Case-Dunn, 'The Effects of International Economic Dependence on Development and Inequality: a Cross-National Study', *American Sociological Review*, December 1975; and the contribution by P. J. McGowan and D. L. Smith, 'Economic Dependency in Black Africa', *International Organization*, vol. 32, no. 1, 1978, pp. 179–235. This whole issue of *International Organization* was devoted to a critical assessment of 'Dependence and Dependency in the Global System'.

23. Frank, *Capitalism and Underdevelopment in Latin America*, Introduction.

24. Cf. Laclau, 'Feudalism and Capitalism in Latin America'.

25. Booth, 'André Gunder Frank', pp. 68–9.

26. I am referring here to R. Prebisch's seminal paper, *The Economic Development of Latin America and its Principal Problems* (New York: Economic Commission for Latin America, 1950).

27. For good summaries of the ECLA–Prebisch–Frank connection, see Palma, 'Dependency', and O'Brien, 'A Critique of Latin American Theories of Dependency'.

28. A. G. Frank, *Lumpenbourgeoisie, Lumpendevelopment* (New York: Monthly Review Press, 1972).

29. Ibid, p. 109.

30. Ibid, p. 94.

31. Leys, 'Underdevelopment and Development: Critical Notes', p. 95.

32. Frank, *Lumpenbourgeoisie, Lumpendevelopment*, p. 4.

33. Ibid, Introduction.

34. Leys, 'Underdevelopment and Development: Critical Notes' p. 95.

35. Ibid, pp. 99–100.

Chapter 6

1. G. Palma, 'Dependency: a Formal Theory of Underdevelopment', *World Development*, vol. 6, 1978, p. 903.

2. See, for instance, the critique of Frank made by John Taylor, *From Modernisation to Modes of Production* (London: Macmillan, 1979) pp. 86ff.

3. F. H. Cardoso and E. Faletto, *Dependency and Development in Latin America* (Berkeley: University of California Press, 1979) Preface to the American edition, p. xxiv.

4. E. Laclau, *Politics and Ideology in Marxist Theory* (London: Verso, 1979).

5. E. Laclau, 'Feudalism and Capitalism in Latin America', *New Left Review*, no. 67, 1971, reprinted in Laclau, *Politics and Ideology in Marxist Theory*.

6. Notably Clause Meillassoux, Pierre Phillippe Rey, Georges Dupré and Emmanuel Terray.

7. Laclau, *Politics and Ideology in Marxist Theory*, p. 22.

8. Cf. David Booth, 'André Gunder Frank: an Introduction and Appreciation', in I. Oxaal *et al.*, *Beyond the Sociology of Development* (London: Routledge & Kegan Paul, 1976); Palma, 'Dependency'; and Laclau, *Politics and Ideology in Marxist Theory*.

9. Laclau, *Politics and Ideology in Marxist Theory*, p. 31.

10. E. Feder, *The Rape of the Peasantry* (Harmondsworth: Penguin, 1974) p. 128.

11. Laclau, *Politics and Ideology in Marxist Theory*, p. 42.

12. Feder, *The Rape of the Peasantry*.

13. Claude Meillassoux, 'Development or Exploitation: Is the Sahel Famine Good Business?', *Review of African Political Economy*, vol. 1, no. 1, 1974, pp. 27—33; and 'From Reproduction to Production', *Economy and Society*, vol. 1, no. 1, 1972.

14. Meillassoux, 'From Reproduction to Production', p. 102.

15. Quoted in S. Amin, 'The Class Structure of the Contemporary Imperialist System', *Monthly Review*, vol. 31, January 1980, p. 23.

16. Laclau, *Politics and Ideology in Marxist Theory*, p. 42.

17. Ibid, p. 43.

18. G. Massiah, 'Multinational Corporations and a Strategy for National Dependence', in Carl Widstrand and Samir Amin (eds), *Multinational Firms in Africa* (Uppsala: Nordiska Afrika Institutet, 1975) pp. 386—425.

19. F. Cardoso and E. Faletto, *Dependency and Development in Latin America* (Berkeley: University of California Press, 1979). (First published in Spanish in 1967).

20. Palma, 'Dependency', p. 910, summarises Cardoso and Faletto's position in this manner.

21. Cardoso and Faletto, *Dependency and Underdevelopment in Latin America*, Preface to the American edition, p. xxiv.

22. Ibid. This emphasis on the increasingly dominant role of the state in production is also the key theme of James Petras's theory of

dependency: *Critical Perspectives on Imperialism and Social Class in the Third World* (New York: Monthly Review Press, 1979).

23. Cardoso and Faletto, *Dependency and Underdevelopment in Latin America*, Postscript, p. 213.
24. F. Cardoso, 'The Consumption of Dependency Theory', *Latin American Research Review*, vol. 12, 1977, p. 20.
25. Cardoso and Faletto, *Dependency and Underdevelopment in Latin America*, Postscript, p. 213.
26. Ibid, p. 201.
27. Cf. Bill Warren, 'Imperialism and Capitalist Industrialisation', *New Left Review*, no. 81, 1973.
28. Bill Warren, *Imperialism, Pioneer of Capitalism* (London: New Left Books, 1980) ch. 7.
29. Ibid, p. 252.
30. Ibid, pp. 170ff.
31. Ibid, pp. 5–6.
32. Osvaldo Sunkel, 'Transnational Capitalism and National Disintegration', *Social and Economic Studies*, vol. 22, no. 1, 1973, pp. 132–76.
33. Cf. the summary of Wallerstein's ideas in W. Goldfrank (ed.), *The World System of Capitalism, Past and Present* (London: Sage, 1979) p. 73.
34. I. Wallerstein, *The Capitalist World Economy* (Cambridge University Press, 1980) p. 5.
35. Ibid, p. 15.
36. R. Brenner, 'The Origins of Capitalist Development: A Critique of Neo-Smithian Marxism', *New Left Review*, no. 104, July–August 1977, p. 61.
37. A. Emmanuel, *Unequal Exchange* (New York: Monthly Review Press, 1972).
38. Wallerstein, *The Capitalist World Economy*, p. 19.
39. Ibid, p. 68 (Wallerstein here quotes Galtung).
40. W. A. Selcher, *Brazil's Multilateral Relations between First and Third World* (Boulder, Col.: Westview Press, 1977).
41. Wallerstein, *The Capitalist World Economy*, p. 70.
42. Ibid, p. 82.
43. Ibid, pp. 76–7.
44. Ibid, p. 83.
45. Ibid, p. 64.
46. Ibid.
47. E. Mandel, *Late Capitalism* (London: New Left Books, 1976) p. 48.
48. Ibid, p. 374.
49. Ibid, p. 316.
50. Ibid, p. 374.

51. Ibid, pp. 375—6.
52. Ibid, p. 376.
53. S. Amin, *Class and Nation, Historically and in the Current Crisis* (London: Heinemann, 1980) p. 131.
54. Ibid, p. 189.
55. Ibid, p. 194.
56. Ibid, pp. 194—5.
57. S. Amin, *Unequal Development* (New York: Monthly Review Press, 1976) p. 73.
58. Ibid, p. 74.
59. Ibid, p. 192. See also S. Amin, 'Accumulation on a World Scale', *Review of African Political Economy*, vol. 1, no. 1, 1974, p. 1.
60. Amin, *Unequal Development*, p. 144.
61. Ibid, ch. 4.
62. Amin, 'Accumulation on a World Scale', p. 3.
63. This periodisation stems from S. Amin, 'Towards a New Structural Crisis of the Capitalist System', conference paper submitted to Third World Forum (Karachi, Pakistan, 5—10 January 1975).
64. Amin, *Unequal Development*, pp. 381—2.
65. Amin, 'The Class Structure of the Contemporary Imperialist System', p. 15.
66. Amin, 'Towards a New Structural Crisis of the Capitalist System', p. 13.
67. S. Amin, *The Law of Value and Historical Materialism* (New York: Monthly Review Press, 1978) pp. 73ff.
68. See, for instance, E. Mandel, *Long Waves of Capitalist Development* (Cambridge University Press, 1980).
69. Amin, *Class and Nation*, pp. 136—7.
70. Amin, 'The Class Structure of the Contemporary Imperialist System', p. 10.
71. Amin, 'Towards a New Structural Crisis of the Capitalist System'.
72. Amin, *Class and Nation*, p. 143.
73. Amin, *The Law of Value and Historical Materialism*, p. 78.
74. Amin, *Class and Nation*, p. 175.
75. Ibid, p. 175.
76. Ibid, p. 188.

Conclusions

1. Yann Fitt, A. Faire and J.-P. Vigier, *The World Economic Crisis* (London: Zed Press, 1979), argue that the 1973 oil price increases were a US-inspired plot to help reassert US hegemony after the decline of the dollar in 1970. They point out that, after all, the EEC

countries and Japan were much more vulnerable to oil price increases, as their economies are more heavily dependent on imported oil.

2. This is the main criticism of Amin made by Sheila Smith in a recent contribution to the *Journal of Development Studies*: Sheila Smith, 'The Ideas of Samir Amin: Theory or Tautology?', *Journal of Development Studies*, vol. 17, no. 1, October 1980, pp. 5—21.

Name Index

Abdel-Malek, A.   235
Adams, G.   222
Ahluwalia, M.   43, 218
Algiers Conference   79
Althusser, L.   152, 174, 240
Amara, R.   238
Amin, S.   198–208 *passim*,
    225, 232, 243, 245
Anell, L.   217
Arad, U. B.   61, 222
Arad, W.   61, 222
Aronson, J. R.   238
Avromovic, D.   228

Bairoch, P.   233
Balibar, E.   152, 240
Bandstecher, W.   229
Bandung Conference   74
Bank for International
    Settlements (BIS)   49, 50,
    58, 219
Banks, A. S.   236
Baran, P.   165ff, 242
Bariloche Foundation   144, 240
Barratt Brown, M.   221–2
Barringer, H. R.   236
Bauer, P. T.   230
Beetham, D.   236
Behrman, J.   228
Belgrade Conference   75
Bennholdt-Thomsen, V.   235
Berger, P. L.   241
Bergsten, F. C.   230
Bernstein, H.   236
Bhagwati, J.   228
Bierman, J.   240
Blanksten, G. L.   236
Boer, K. den   225
Booth, D.   240

Bottomore, T. B.   235
Boumedienne, President   80
Bouteflika, A.   80
Bowett, D.   226
Brandt Commission   29, 142,
    203, 209, 219, 220, 232,
    239
Brenner, R.   244
Bretton Woods Agreement   83
Brezinski, Z.   90
Brown, L.   222
Bukharin, N.   164
Burk, S. J.   234

Cairo Conference   75
Caporoso, J. A.   242
Cardoso, F. H.   185ff, 243, 244
Carter, President   90
Case-Dunn, C.   242
Chenery, H.   43, 217, 218, 232,
    233
Clammer, J.   240
Club of Rome   130–48 *passim*,
    239–40
Cohen, B. I.   64
Cole, S.   238, 239
Collins, J.   235
Colombo, U.   239
Commission of the Acuerdo de
    Cartagena   223
Committee of Ten   229
Committee of Twenty   229
Commission on International
    Economic Co-operation
    (CIEC)   93
Corea, G.   225, 229, 232
Cox, R. W.   232

D'Arista   224

Development Assistance
    Committee (DAC)   100,
    102, 234
Dobb, M.   241
Dolman, A.   239
Drenowski, J.   215
Dubois, R.   239
Dupré, G.   243
Durkheim, E.   107

Echeverria, L.   78
Ecologist, The   137
Economic Commission for Latin
    America (ECLA)   75, 167,
    175
Enzensberger, H. M.   133, 238
Eisenstadt, S. N.   235, 237
Eleventh Special Session of the
    UN General Assembly   94
Emmanuel, A.   192, 193, 200,
    244
Engels, F.   154
Ernst, D.   223
Etzioni, A.   236
Etzioni, E.   236

Faire, A.   245
Faletto, E.   185, 243, 244
Falk, R.   148
Feder, E.   176, 243
Feld, W.   222
Fieldhouse, D. K.   241
Fishlow, A.   217, 218, 222, 230
Fitt, Y.   245
Forrester, J.   132, 238
Foster Carter, A.   241
Fowles, J. I. B.   237
Frank, A. G.   165–75 *passim*,
    190, 195, 240, 242
Franko, L. G.   219
Freeman, C.   238
Friedberg, A. S.   224
Frieden, J.   231
Fröbel, F.   65, 220, 222

Gabor, D.   239
Gai, D.   234
Galtung, J.   148, 192, 228, 240

General Agreement on Tariffs and
    Trade (GATT)   31–2, 216
Germidis, D.   221, 223
Gilbert, M.   215
Ginsberg, N.   236
Goldfrank, W.   244
Goodwin, G.   228
Green, R. H.   228, 234
Group of Ten   78
    see also Committee of Ten
Group of 77   76, 78, 79, 85, 92,
    96
Griffin, K.   217
Gwin, C.   230, 231

Hammarskjöld Foundation   234
Hansen, R.   93, 231
Hasenpflug, H.   223, 224, 227,
    230
Heilbroner, R.   137, 239
Heinrichs, J.   221
Helleiner, G. K.   64, 216, 225
Hellinger, D. A.   217
Hellinger, S.   217
Herrera, A. O.   144, 145, 234,
    238, 239
Heston, A. W.   215
Hicks, N.   233
Hilferding, F.   164
Hindess, B.   241
Hirst, P. Q.   241
Hobsbawm, E.   152, 240
Hobson, J. A.   163, 164, 241
Hoogvelt, A. M. M.   223, 224,
    236
Hopkins, M.   216
Hudson, M.   236
Hveem, H.   230

Illich, I.   236
Inkeles, A.   236
Institute for World Order   148
International Bank for Recon-
    struction and Development
    (IBRD)   *see* World Bank
International Fund for Agricul-
    tural Development   84

International Labour Office 7, 97, 100, 233
International Monetary Fund 7, 83–4, Chapter 2 *passim*

Jahoda, M. 238
Jalee, P. 222
Jankowitsch, O. 224
Johns, S. 224

Kahn, H. 119, 129, 133–4, 142, 188, 209, 237, 238
Kaya, Y. 142, 239
Khan, A. R. 217
Kinley, D. 235
Kissinger, H. 88, 89, 90
Krasner, S. D. 230
Kravis, I. 215, 219
Kreye, O. 221

Laar, A. v. d. 218, 235
Laclau, E. 174, 200, 240, 243
Laszlo, E. 147, 240
Legum, C. 233
Lenin, V. I. 142, 163–4, 241
Leontief, W. 142, 239
Letelier, O. 217, 226, 227, 231
Levy, M. 237
Leys, C. 170, 241, 242
Lima Target 82, 228
Little, I. M. D. 225
Lusaka Conference 75, 79
Luxemburg, R. 164, 241

McClelland, D. 236
McGowan, P. J. 242
McHale, J. 233
McHale, M. C. 233
Mack, R. W. 236
McNamara, R. 233
Magdoff, H. 221, 222, 230
Maine, H. 107
Mandel, E. 196, 220, 224, 245
Manila Declaration 229
Marx, K. 149–58 *passim*, 240
Massiah, G. 183, 243
Mazrui, A. 148, 240
Meadows, D. 238

Meagher, R. 227, 230, 231
Melotti, U. 241
Mendlowitz, S. 240
Mesarovic, M. 123, 138, 139, 209, 239
Meillassoux, C. 179, 180, 200, 243
Merrills, J. 226
Moffit, M. 217, 226, 227, 231
Moore, W. 237
Moorelappe, F. 235
Moran, T. 230
Morgan, H. 108, 235
Morton, K. 226
Murray, R. 224

Nordhauss, W. D. 238
Nygaren, B. 217

O'Brien, P. J. 240, 242
Official Development Assistance (ODA) 102
Organisation for Economic Co-operation and Development (OECD) Chapters 1 and 2 *passim*, 219, 239
Organisation of Petroleum Exporting Countries (OPEC) Chapters 1 and 2 *passim*, 231
Oxaal, I. 240

Palma, G. 241, 242, 243
Payer, C. 219, 220, 229
Parsons, T. 109–23 *passim*, 155, 156, 157, 236, 237, 238
Pearson, L. B. 216, 222
Peccei, A. 240
Pederson, K. 225
Pestel, E. 123, 138, 139, 209, 239
Petras, J. 243
Pollard, S. 235
Portes, A. 241
Prebisch, R. 75, 167, 224, 242

Quijano, A. 235

Rapaport, A. 237

Redker, R. J.   62
Rey, P. P.   180, 243
Ricardo, D.   161, 163, 177
Rockefeller, D.   90
Rostow, W. W.   136, 137, 142, 188, 209
Rothstein, R. L.   232
Russett, B. M.   236

Santos, Th. dos   218
Sauvant, K.   223, 224, 226, 227, 230
Schumacher, E.   137, 239
Schumpeter, J. A.   241
Schwamm, H.   221, 223
Schwartz, E.   238
Scott, W.   215
Seiber, M.   219
Selcher, W. A.   193, 244
Service, E.   235
Seventh Special Session of the UN General Assembly   91, 230, 231
Seynes, P. de   226
Sheenan, G.   216
Sideri, S.   224
Singer, H. W.   228, 233
Singh, A.   233
Singh, J. S.   229
Sixth Special Session of the UN General Assembly   79, 80, 87
Smelser, N. J.   236
Smith, D. L.   242
Smith, S.   246
Solomon, R.   220
Special Drawing Rights   83, 84
Spencer, H.   107
Spraos, J.   225
Stalin, J.   149
Streeten, P.   221, 228, 233, 234
Summers, R.   215
Sunkel, O.   189, 244
Susuki, Y.   239
Syrguin, M.   217

Tachauchi, K.   230
Tanzer, M.   230

Taylor, C. L.   236
Taylor, J.   240, 243
Terray, E.   243
Texter, R. B.   236
Tharakan, P. K. M.   64
Third World Forum   225, 245
Tinbergen, J.   123, 139, 140, 203, 218, 220, 231, 232, 239
Toby, J.   237
Tönnies, F.   107
Trilateral Commission   90, 91, 96, 100, 230, 231, 232, 234
Tulloch, P.   226
Tyler, W. G.   229

Ul Haq, M.   225, 232, 234, 235
United Nations (UN)   2, 7, 15
United Nations Committee for Development Planning (UNDP)   216
United Nations Conference on Trade and Development (UNCTAD)   Chapter 2 *passim*, 167
United Nations Economic and Social Committee (ECOSOC)   7, 221
United Nations Employment Programme (UNEP)   234
United Nations Industrial Development Organisation (UNIDO)   228

Vaitsos, C. V.   70, 223
Valenzuela, A.   241
Valenzuela, J. S.   241
Varon, B.   230
Vigier, J.-P.   245
Villamil, J.   241
Vlyanovsky, V. P.   240

Waldheim, K.   232
Wallerstein, I.   150, 191–7 *passim*, 237, 240, 241, 244
Ward, B.   137, 239
Ward, R. D.   236
Warren, B.   188, 244

Weber, M.   109, 236
Weintraub, A.   238
Weiss, T. G.   232
Widstrand, C.   243
Wiener, A. J.   129, 238
White, G.   226

White, L.   109
Willets, P.   224
Winter, D. G.   236
World Bank   2, 7, Chapters 1
    and 2 *passim*
Worm, K.   225

Subject Index

abolitionist movement   148
accumulation on a world scale
   192
   defined   180
aid   *see* transfer of resources
American hegemony, decline of
   137, 187
anti-colonialism   74
anti-growth theories   129ff
apartheid   180
'Apollovision'   148
arms race   141
   arms trade   143
autarchy   143—45
authoritarian regimes in the
   Third World
   imperial alliance of   *see*
      under imperialism
   their role in world capita-
      lism   178, 206—7, 210
   see also state in the Third
      World

basic needs   8, 141
   critique of   100—2
   defined   99, 145
   development strategy   98ff
   and employment pro-
      grammes   97—8
Brazil, economic miracle   40
buffer stocks   77
bureaucracy   115

capitalism   158—62
   capitalist mode of produc-
      tion, laws of motion of
      161—2, 172, 182—3,
197, 199, 204
capitalist world economy
   34, 77, 101, 165, 189
defined   159, 196—7
dependent capitalist
   development in Latin
   America   185ff, 212
and imperialism   162,
   188—9
international capitalism
   117, 210
mature capitalism   159
peripheral *vs* autocentric
   capitalism   199ff
centre—periphery   167
core—periphery   190—4
*Charter of Economic Rights
   and Duties of States*   5,
   7, 9, 79—80
China, People's Republic of
   economy   16
   measurement of GNP   16—
     17
citizenship, legal concept of
   115
class
   alliance   146 (*see also*
     under imperialism)
   class reductionism   174,
     180, 185ff
   class relations   154, 162
   class struggle (in Third
     World   185; in world
     capitalism   173)
   conflict   146, 157—8, 162,
     170

codes of conduct 68
for transfer of technology
85 (*see also* multi-
national corporations)
colonialism 179, 183
defined 163–4
commodity exchange 154,
159–60, 175, 180
comparative advantage 140
theory 75, 163
compensatory finance 91
comprador 166
computer, role in system
analysis 125, 132, 133,
147
cross-border arrangements 66–8
see also multinational
corporations

debt of Third World 51–5
debt explosion 53, 214
debt relief 84 (*see also*
transfer of resources)
democracy
as stage of evolution
115–16, 118
substantive *vs* restrictive
187
dependency 141, 165ff
defined 166
dependista writers 184ff,
190, 195–6
dependency theory 120–1
(earlier versions of
dependency theory
166–70; criticised
169–70, 188; role in
international organisa-
tions 170; voluntary *vs*
mechanistic versions
185; contemporary
versions of dependency
theory 185ff)
dependent capitalist
development in Latin
America 185–7 (*see
also under* capitalism)
historical stages of depend-

ency in Latin America
186–7
present prospects of
dependency 187
technological dependency 169
and underdevelopment 166ff
developing countries
category of 1, 22
as markets for industrial
countries' exports 31 (*see
also* Third World)
Soviet view of 149–50
development assistance 118
see also transfer of resources
development indicators 15, 16, 118
development theories
contrasting perspectives 1, 9,
105, 208–9
origins 105ff
dialectical materialism 146
direct overseas investment *see*
foreign direct investment
disarticulation (disintegration)
of domestic economy 65–6,
202
national disintegration *vs*
transnational integration
189–90

ecology
debate 130–8
ecological balance/imbalance
122–30
economic reductionism 174, 180
economic surplus 151, 168,
171–2, 175
embourgeoisement, of countries
in the international
hierarchy 89
ethnocentrism 120
euro-centricity (of development
models) 155
euro-dollar market 50–1
evolution
difference between bourgeois
and Marxist theories 156–
7 (*see also* neo-evolutionary
theory)

evolution *(contd)*
   stages of evolution (Marxist
      conceptions   149ff; early
      bourgeois conceptions
      106ff; neo-Marxist concep-
      tions   152ff; late
      bourgeois conceptions
      112)
   theories of evolution (early
      bourgeois versions   106–9;
      new bourgeois models
      110–13; Marxist theories
      154–8)
evolutionary universals   110
   interpretation in historical
      materialism   156
exploitation   156, 158
   imperialist   175
   productionist *vs* circulationist
      conceptions   172, 174ff,
      191, 199
   reproduced through time   151,
      172, 181–3
   super-   178, 201
   through unequal exchange
      151, 180
exponential growth   132–3
   vs organic growth   123, 139
export-processing zone   65–6
exports, of manufactures from
      Third World countries   24,
      26–9, 97
   see also industrialisation,
      middle-income countries,
      multinational corporations,
      newly industrialising coun-
      tries
extrapolation   124, 130
extraversion   201

feedback loops, in systems   132
feudalism, in Latin America 176–7
   see also mode of production
financial transfers   *see* transfer of
      resources
First United Nations Develop-
      ment Decade   22, 25

forces of production   153–4,
      157
foreign direct investment,
   by banking sector   72
   in developing countries   51–
      2, 60ff, 168–9
   as development agent   185ff
   see also multinational corpora-
      tions, transfer of resources
Fourth World   2, 102, 207, 214
   in international hierarchy   39
franchise agreements   166–7
free enterprise   118
free market *vs* centrally planned
      economies   16
   their trade with Third World
      29
free producing zones   65–6

generalised system of preferences
      (GSPs)   77, 83
global growth
   critique of global limits   134
   from global limits to inter-
      national redistribution
      138–9
   limits to   119, 121–2, 129,
      130–2
global modelling   130
global planning   148
global social democracy   76, 100,
      101
   evolution to   196
globalism   8, 122
   see also global growth,
      international Keynesianism
go-between nations   192–3
Green Revolution   133
Gross National Product *per
      capita*
   discussed   34–5, 40
   downward bias of   44
   as measure of economic
      performance   15
growth rate, as measure of
      economic performance
      15

hacienda 176
historical materialism 146, 157, 199, 211
humanitarianism 120

imperialism
  anti-imperialist struggles 170
  classical liberal and classical Marxist theories 162—4
  classical Marxist *vs* modern Marxist theories 161, 181—3
  defined 164
  diachronic theory of 174, 181—3
  imperial alliances in Third World 168, 178, 183—4, 186—7, 195, 202, 213—14 (*see also under* class)
  inter-imperialist rivalries 187—9
  progressive nature of imperialism 188—9
  Third Worldist theory of imperialism 198ff
import dependence, of advanced countries on Third World exports 60—1, 80, 97, 139
import substitution 31, 168—9, 202
income distribution
  between nations 36—40, 140, 189—90
  and development 40—1, 43, 135
  globally, between rich and poor people 45
  internal, in developing countries 95, 141, 168—9
individualisation 107, 111, 155
industrial (re-) adjustment policies 143
  and international trade 58

industrial parks 65—6
industrial relocation 65—6, 139, 142, 143
industrial reserve army 101—2
industrialisation
  as development strategy 118, 167—8
  labour absorption of Third World industry 97, 169
  in middle-income countries 24, 26
  self-reliant 97
  as stage of social evolution 113
  in Third World 26, 65—6, 97, 132—3, 166—9, 197
  Third World demands for 82
  world industrialisation 122, 130
  see also international production, middle-income countries, multinational corporations, newly industrialising countries
inequality
  domestic inequality and economic growth in Third World 40—1, 183, 188 (*see also* income distribution)
  trade-generated international inequality 75, 167
integration, transnational 189—90
integrated commodity programme 82
interdependence, global 122—3
international credit
  international capital/financial markets 51—5, 210—11
  see also debt, petro-dollars, transfer of resources
international economic reform 76, 121, 128—9, 133, 138, 145
  see also international Keynesianism

international Keynesianism   90,
    96—7, 137ff, 210—11
international monetary order   77
    reorganisation of   83—4
international organisations
    co-optation of dependency
        perspective   165, 170
    as global authorities   137,
        142
    perspectives on world develop-
        ment   76, 96—7
    role of radical Third Worldists
        in 170
    statistical recordings of world
        economy   16
international patent system, reform
    of   85
international production   3, 57,
    171, 214
    and control over production
        67ff
    defined   58
    developments in   66—7, 189
    and economic differentiation of
        Third World   3, 64—5
    and international credit   3,
        71—2, 210 (*see also*
        multinational corporations)
    vs international trade   58—9
international stratification
    hierarchy of nations   2, 15
    historical comparison of
        36—40
    and international production
        57
international trade
    proposed reforms   82—3, 142
    orthodox theory of   75 (*see
        also* comparative advantage)
    see also international
        production, New
        International Economic
        Order
intra-firm trade   59, 67, 70
Islamic Revolution in Iran   155

joint ventures   66

Keynesianism, view of world
    economy   7
    see also international
        Keynesianism
Kuznets curve   41

labour theory of value   161
    surplus value of labour   153—4
least developed countries
    category   22
    defined   22—3
    as recipients of official aid   100—2
licensing agreements   66—7
low-income countries   17, 23
    causes of poverty in   17, 22
lumpenbourgeoisie   170
lumpendevelopment   170

management agreements   66—7
marginalisation   40, 101, 185—6,
    88, 202
market economies, *vs* centrally
    planned economies   16
market-place *vs* market principle
    160
metaphysical dualism   115
metropolis–satellite
    contradiction   166—7
middle-income countries   24, 39,
    47—8, 51, 58, 135
migration, internal   180
mineral exporting countries   31
    as recipients of foreign direct
        investment   62
model
    global model-building   130
    methodology of model-building
        124
mode of production
    articulation of   151, 164,
        174—83
    capitalist mode of production
        see under capitalism
    and class struggle   158
    defined   152
    historical modes   152ff
    in theory of imperialism   200ff

modern societies, structural and
  cultural properties of   110
modernisation theories   116—19,
  156, 165
  vs dependency theory   120,
    150
  and development assistance
    118, 149
  origin   116
  recent departures   119, 120ff
most needy countries (MNCs)   2
most seriously affected nations
  (MSANs)   2, 23, 84
multinational corporations
  codes of conduct for   68,
    185, 141
  defined   57
  and exports of manufactures
    from Third World   64—5,
    77, 203
  first calls for global super-
    vision of   78
  integrating forces of   189—
    190
  and nationalisation policies
    66, 188
  profit strategies and alliances in
    Third World   183—4, 195
    (*see also under* imperialism)
  size   57—8
  and transfers of payments
    69—70
  see also international
    production

national bourgeoisie   *see under*
  Third World, *and*
  lumpenbourgeoisie
national liberation
  and multinational corporations
    68, 188
  struggles   202, 204
  vs world class struggles   17
national sovereignty   141
need for achievement   117
neo-evolutionary theory
  critique   111—12

essential characteristics
  109—10
as programme for
  modernisation   116
and world systems theory
  123
see also evolution
neo-Malthusianism   132
new international division of
  labour   140, 206
New International Economic
  Order (NIEO)   5, 23, 55,
  74ff, 138, 140
  as anti-imperialist struggle
    204—6, 210
  contents   80—7
  critique of   86—7
  developed world's response to
    87ff
  progress towards   94—5
  UN declaration of establishment
    of   74, 79
  see also international economic
    reform, international
    Keynesianism
newly industrialising countries
  (NICs)   1, 24—6
  defined   25
  as recipients of foreign direct
    investment   62
  upward mobility of   39, 135
  see also international
    production, new
    international division of
    labour, middle-income
    countries, multinational
    corporations
non-aligned movement   74, 78—9
  conferences   74, 75, 79
North—South dialogue   6, 74, 92,
  205
  origin   92
  role of Soviet Union and
    Eastern Europe in   92—4
nuclear family   118, 132

oil-exporting countries   31

oil-exporting countries (*contd*)
  aid to other developing
    countries 95
  capital-surplus oil exporters
    23–4, 55, 80
  oil price increases 23, 46–7,
    121, 138–9 (as anti-
    imperialist struggle 140,
    206–7, 210–11; financial
    consequences for advanced
    countries 46; and for
    developing countries 23,
    47; adjustment responses to
    47)
  OPEC 2
  OPEC-type cartelisation in other
    minerals 89
  solidarity with the rest of Third
    World 80, 88
  upward mobility of 39
  see also petro-dollars

patents, revision of Paris
    convention of international
    patent rights 85
pattern variables 117
peripheral capitalism 201ff
  vs autocentric capitalism 199ff
petro-dollars 2, 50
  current-account surpluses of
    OPEC countries 46–7
  recycling of 2, 51, 54, 210–
    11
pollution 122, 131, 138
population, world growth of
    122–3, 130–1, 132, 138
poverty 41–5
  absolute poverty, defined 41
  absolute poverty *vs* relative
    poverty 41–2, 98
  as focus of development
    assistance 98
  poverty strategies of World
    Bank 97
pre-capitalist formations *see*
    mode of production
price stabilisation measures of
    Third World export
    commodities 77

primitive, *vs* 'modern' category
    107–9
  see also evolution
production-sharing agreements
    66–7
profit
  in intra-company trade 70
  maximisation 113, 117, 161,
    174
  multinational corporations'
    profit strategies 183–4
  rate of profit, tendency to fall
    162, 163–4, 181, 200
*Program of Action on the
    Establishment of a New
    International Economic
    Order* 79–81
progress
  bourgeois conception of
    progress 109
  idea of progress 105
  Marxist conception of progress
    154–6
proletarianisation 179
property relations 154, 157
protectionism 97, 143
Protestant Reformation 115

rapid deployment force 209
rationality 115
  bureaucratic 115
  economic 113, 117
redistribution *see* international
    economic reform,
    international Keynesianism
relations of production 154, 157
reproduction
  expanded reproduction 161
  of labour 153, 178
research and development (R &
    D) expenditure 136–7
resource depletion 122–3,
    130–1, 132–3, 138, 203
  see also global growth
revolutionary change 146, 157, 171
revolutionary *praxis* 158, 184

scenario, futurist scenarios
  defined 124–5

scientific method   106
Second United Nations Develop-
    ment Decade   1, 45, 56–7,
    118
  international development
    strategy of   22
secularisation   118
self-reliance
  collective self-reliance   86,
    141
  of Third World countries   99,
    141, 143–4, 148, 195
semi-periphery   192–4, 196
service contracts   66–7
simulation   124
social change
  general laws of   106, 107, 146
  Marxist theory of   128, 146
  voluntarist theory of   127,
    147, 156
social democracy   *see* global
    social democracy
social differentiation   109–110
social evolution   *see* evolution
socialism   172, 185
  socialist revolution   164
  socialist transition   187, 189,
    196, 198ff
socially necessary labour-time
    177–8
'spaceship' metaphor   122, 133,
    148
Special Drawing Rights (SDRs)
    83–4
state in the Third World
  role in production   186
  role in international
    production   186   (*see
    also under* imperialism)
structural compatibility   113, 116,
    158
sub-contracting   66
subsistence sector, role of in
    capitalist exploitation
    179
  see also under mode of
    production
sub-imperialism   203, 207, 212
supra-national state   137

surplus appropriation   153, 159,
    160–1, 166
  different modes of   154ff,
    175, 191
  by parent companies from
    subsidiaries   69–70
surplus labour   153, 180
  see also surplus value
surplus value   160–1, 182–3,
    194
systems theory   122
  applied to world futures
    research   125–7
  critique   125–7
  methodology   123–6
  systems analysis   123ff

target wage   179
technology
  alternative technology   69
  regulating transfer of
    technology to developing
    countries   85 (*see also*
    codes of conduct)
  special technology treatment
    85
  technological dependency
    69, 169, 202–3
  technological optimism   129
  technological overspecification
    70
  technology-embodied
    restrictions   69
  Western technology as agent
    of development   118
terms of trade, deterioration of
    121, 167
Third World   16, 26, 60
  demands for New International
    Economic Order   80, 173,
    198, 203
  economic co-operation amongst
    Third World countries   86
  economic differentiation of
    Third World   1, 3, 22,
    33–4, 171, 183–4
  origin of term   74
  as part of world system
    122–3

Third World (*contd*)
  perspective on world economy
    76, 99, 138, 144–5
  political defiance of   123
  radical Third World writers,
    role of in international
    organisations   96, 121
  solidarity   5, 73ff, 173
  Third World bourgeoisie   190,
    203, 206 (*see also* lumpen-
    bourgeoisie, national
    bourgeoisie, state in the
    Third World)
  see also developing countries,
    New International Economic
    Order
trade unions
  in Europe   177
  Third World trade unions
    compared   178
transfer of resources from rich to
    poor countries   45–6, 52
  official aid   54–5, 100, 102
  private lending to Third World
    52–3, 143
  suggested reforms   84–5, 142
  see also debt, development
    assistance, foreign direct
    investment, international
    monetary order

unequal exchange   167, 175–6,
    192–3, 201–2
unemployment, in Third World
    97, 168
  see also marginalisation

urbanisation   118

voluntarism   115
  vs determinism   204, 211
  in Marxism   199
  see also social change
voluntary association   118

wages
  cash wages, role of cash wage in
    subsistence sector   179
  differences of wage levels in
    advanced and in Third World
    countries   178–9, 193,
    200–1
widening gap   121, 130, 133–4,
    203
  debate   34ff, 121
  relative *vs* absolute gap   35
world community   137, 139,
    142
world economic recession   121
world (market) factory   57,
    65–6
world futures debate   123ff
world inflation   121
world system
  organic growth of   123
  world capitalist system, defined
    191, 196–7 (Third Worldist
    perspective of   198)
  world system perspective   123,
    141–2, 165, 173, 180, 191